Ec
Scholas
A Contemp

MW01284941

editiones scholasticae
Volume 39

Edward Feser

Scholastic Metaphysics

A Contemporary Introduction

editiones scholasticae

Bibliographic information published by Deutsche Nationalbibliothek
The Deutsche Nationalbibliothek lists this publication in the Deutsche Nationalbibliographie;
detailed bibliographic data is available in the Internet at http://dnb.ddb.de

Distribution:

North and South America by
Transaction Books
Rutgers University
Piscataway, NJ 08854-8042
trans@transactionpub.com

United Kingdom, Ireland, Iceland, Turkey, Malta, Portugal by
Gazelle Books Services Limited
White Cross Mills
Hightown
LANCASTER, LA1 4XS
sales@gazellebooks.co.uk

©2014 editiones scholasticae
Postfach 15 41, D-63133 Heusenstamm
www.editiones-scholasticae.de

ISBN 978-3-86838-544-1

2014

Printed on acid-free paper

Printed in Germany
by CPI buchbücher.de

Table of Contents

Acknowledgements

I want to thank Rafael Hüntelmann for his kind invitation to write this book, as well as for his other acts of kindness and his patience in waiting for delivery of the book. I thank my beloved wife and children -- Rachel, Benedict, Gemma, Kilian, Helena, John, and Gwendolyn -- for their patience and self-sacrifice in tolerating the many hours I put into writing this book. And I thank my dear friend David Oderberg, to whom this book is dedicated, for his work, for our many hours of conversation about philosophy and much else, and for our friendship itself. If this book leads the reader to study David's work, I will have done well.

0. Prolegomenon

0.1 Aim of the book

The title of this book, *Scholastic Metaphysics: A Contemporary Introduction*, was chosen quite deliberately, and each word merits a brief comment. *Scholasticism* is, of course, that tradition of thought whose most illustrious representative is Thomas Aquinas (c. 1225-1274) and whose other luminaries include John Duns Scotus (c. 1266-1308), William of Ockham (c. 1287-1347), Thomas de Vio Cajetan (1469-1539), and Francisco Suárez (1548-1617), to name only some of the most famous. By no means only a medieval phenomenon, the Scholastic tradition was carried forward in the twentieth century by Neo-Scholastics like Désiré-Joseph Mercier (1851-1926) and Reginald Garrigou-Lagrange (1877-1964), and Neo-Thomists such as Jacques Maritain (1882-1973) and Etienne Gilson (1884-1978). In contemporary analytic philosophy it finds sympathizers among writers sometimes identified as "analytical Thomists" (Haldane 2002b; Paterson and Pugh 2006).

The philosophical core of the mainstream of the Scholastic tradition is Aristotelian, with key insights drawn from the Neoplatonic tradition but suitably Aristotelianized. This book has been written in that vein. More specifically, its point of view is Thomist, but Scotist, Suarezian, and Ockhamist positions on matters of dispute among Scholastics are discussed as well.

It is Scholastic *metaphysics* that is the subject of the book, not Scholastic theology (whether dogmatic theology or natural theology), nor Scholastic views on epistemology, logic, ethics, philosophical psychology, or even philosophy of nature *per se*. Occasionally I have reason to touch upon issues in some of these other fields, and those familiar with Scholastic thought will know how the topics treated here are relevant to them. But this is a book about "the science of the absolutely first principles of being" (Wuellner 1956a, p. 76), about fundamental issues in ontology -- causation, substance, essence, modality, identity, persistence, teleology, and the like. In other writings I have provided substantive treatments of topics in natural theology (Feser 2009, Chapter 3; 2011a; 2013b; 2013f), philosophy of mind (Feser 2006; 2009, Chapter 4; 2011b; 2013a), ethics (Feser 2009, Chapter 5; 2010b; 2013e; 2013g), and philosophy of nature (Feser 2010; 2012; 2013d). Readers interested in those topics are directed to those writings. Readers interested in a deeper analysis of the metaphysical underpinnings of arguments presented in those works will want to read on in this one.

The Aristotelian theory of actuality and potentiality provides the organizing theme, and the book aims both to defend that theory and to show how the rest of the key elements of Scholastic metaphysics -- efficient and final causality, substantial form and prime matter, substance and accident, essence and existence, and so on -- follow from it. A more detailed list of precisely which topics will be treated and in what order of presentation can be found in the table of contents.

The book is *an* introduction to Scholastic metaphysics. There are others. For those who want to pursue these matters beyond the treatment I offer here, I recommend seeking out those unjustly long-neglected twentieth-century manuals of Scholastic philosophy once so familiar to anyone seeking to learn the subject -- works by Bittle, Coffey, De Raeymaeker, De Wulf, Gardeil, Garrigou-Lagrange, Harper, Hart, Klubertanz, Koren, McCormick, Mercier, Phillips, Renard, Rickaby, Smith and Kendzierski, Van Steenberghen, Wuellner, and others, which are now and again cited in the pages to follow. It has become something of a cliché, rather thoughtlessly repeated by well-meaning people of a certain generation, that to learn Thomism one ought to read Thomas himself and ignore the Thomist commentators and manualists who built on his work. I couldn't disagree more. No great philosopher, no matter how brilliant and systematic, ever uncovers all the implications of his position, foresees every possible objection, or imagines what rival systems might come into being centuries in the future. His work is never finished, and if it is worth finishing, others will come along to do the job. Since their work is, naturally, never finished either, a tradition of thought develops, committed to working out the implications of the founder's system, applying it to new circumstances and challenges, and so forth. Thus Plato had Plotinus, Aristotle had Aquinas, and Aquinas had Cajetan – to name just three famous representatives of Platonism, Aristotelianism, and Thomism, respectively. And thus you cannot fully understand Plato unless you understand Platonism, you cannot fully understand Aristotle unless you understand Aristotelianism, and you cannot fully understand Thomas unless you understand Thomism. True, writers in the traditions in question often disagree with one another and sometimes simply get things wrong. But that is all the more reason to study them if one wants to understand the founders of these traditions; for the tensions and unanswered questions in a tradition reflect the richness of the system of thought originated by its founder.

In that sense the works of the Scholastic commentators and manualists of the past remain *contemporary*. But of course, they are very far from contemporary in another sense. You will not find in them treatments of ideas, arguments, and problems that are currently the focus of attention in philosophy. You will in this book, which interacts heavily with the literature in contemporary analytic metaphysics, so as to facilitate the analytic reader's understanding of Scholastic ideas and the Scholastic reader's understanding of contemporary analytic philosophy. The analytic tradition has always put great emphasis on conceptual precision, rigorous argumentation, and clarity of expression. In at least this respect the best analytic philosophers resemble no one so much as the greatest Scholastics. They increasingly resemble them in other respects as well, for not only has metaphysics in general seen a powerful revival in analytic philosophy, but interest in specifically Aristotelian metaphysical ideas has (as we shall see) been steadily increasing (Novák, Novotný, Sousedik, and Svoboda 2012; Tahko 2012; Feser 2013c; Groff and Greco 2013; Novotný and Novák 2013). If the Scholastic is going to find serious interlocutors within contemporary philosophy, he is most likely to find them within the ranks of analytic philosophers; and if there is any great tradition of the past the contemporary analytic philosopher ought to take seriously, it is the Scholastic tradition.

This book is an *introduction*. To be sure, some issues are treated in significant depth. For that reason, however, I have not tried to be comprehensive, and some matters are not treated at all. (For example, I have nothing to say here about the metaphysics of value and the related doctrine of the transcendentals. I have treated these issues elsewhere, however, in Feser 2013e.) I have also largely avoided pursuing issues the treatment of which would require too great an excursus beyond general metaphysics. For example, while I have a lot to say about substance, and address at length objections to the effect that modern science has somehow cast doubt on the Aristotelian notion of substantial form, I do not say *everything* that could be said about how the Scholastic would interpret the results of modern chemistry and biology. The reason is that doing so would take us beyond general metaphysics and into the philosophy of chemistry, the philosophy of biology, and the philosophy of nature more generally. Since this is a book on general metaphysics rather than on those subjects -- and since I intend in any case to follow up this book with a book on the philosophy of nature -- I have restricted myself to points sufficient to show that modern science in no way casts doubt on the reality of substantial form and related notions, however these end up getting applied in various specific contexts.

Readers who, after finishing this book, want to pursue some of the issues treated in greater depth, are urged to consult the many books and articles I refer to through the course of the chapters to follow. Especially recommended is David Oderberg's brilliant book *Real Essentialism* (2007), which, like mine, brings Scholastic and analytic metaphysics into conversation. I see my own book and Oderberg's as somewhat complementary. Some issues, such as those concerning efficient and final causality, are treated at much greater length in this book than they are in Oderberg's. Other issues, such as the approach the Scholastic takes toward the metaphysics of biological phenomena, are treated at much greater length by Oderberg. Where the two books treat the same issues the approach is somewhat different. I am, in any event, satisfied if I have at least complemented Oderberg's book. I have certainly not surpassed it.

0.2 Against scientism

Of course, not every contemporary analytic philosopher welcomes the revival of old-fashioned metaphysics. There are those who decry it in the name of the scientistic or naturalist position that science alone plausibly gives us objective knowledge, and that any metaphysics worthy of consideration can only be that which is implicit in science (Ladyman, Ross, Spurrett and Collier 2007; Rosenberg 2011). Yet, the glib self-confidence of its advocates notwithstanding, there are in fact no good arguments whatsoever for scientism, and decisive arguments against it.

We will in the course of the chapters to follow have reason to consider various specific scientism-based objections to traditional metaphysical theses and to see why the objections fail. For the moment, though, it is worthwhile noting four general problems with scientism. First, scientism is self-defeating, and can avoid being self-defeating only at the cost of becoming trivial and uninteresting. Second, the scientific method cannot even in principle provide us with a complete description of reality. Third, the "laws of nature" in terms of which science explains phenomena cannot in principle provide us with a complete explanation of reality. Fourth, what is probably the main argument in favor of scientism -- the argument from the predictive and technological successes of modern physics and the other sciences -- has no force. Let us examine each of these points in order.

0.2.1 A dilemma for scientism

First, as I have said, scientism faces a dilemma: It is either self-refuting or trivial. Take the first horn of this dilemma. The claim that "the methods of science are the only reliable ways to secure knowledge of anything" (Rosenberg 2011, p. 6) is not itself a scientific claim, not something that can be established using scientific methods. Indeed, that science is even *a* rational form of inquiry (let alone *the only* rational form of inquiry) is not something that can be established scientifically. For scientific inquiry rests on a number of philosophical assumptions: the assumption that there is an objective world external to the minds of scientists; the assumption that this world is governed by regularities of the sort that might be captured in scientific laws; the assumption that the human intellect and perceptual apparatus can uncover and accurately describe these regularities; and so forth. Since scientific method *presupposes* these things, it cannot attempt to *justify* them without arguing in a circle. To break out of this circle requires "getting outside" of science altogether and discovering from that extra-scientific vantage point that science conveys an accurate picture of reality – and, if scientism is to be justified, that *only* science does so. But then the very existence of that extra-scientific vantage point would falsify the claim that science *alone* gives us a rational means of investigating objective reality.

The rational investigation of the philosophical presuppositions of science has, naturally, traditionally been regarded as the province of philosophy. Nor is it these presuppositions alone that philosophy examines. There is also the question of how to interpret what science tells us about the world. For example, is the world fundamentally comprised of substances or events? What is it to be a "cause"? What is the nature of the universals referred to in scientific laws – concepts like *quark*, *electron*, *atom*, and so on? Do they exist over and above the particular things that instantiate them? Do scientific theories really give us a description of objective reality in the first place or are they just useful tools for predicting the course of experience? Scientific findings can shed light on such metaphysical questions, but can never fully answer them. Yet if science depends upon philosophy both to justify its presuppositions and to interpret its results, the falsity of scientism is doubly assured. As John Kekes concludes: "Hence philosophy, and not science, is a stronger candidate for being the very paradigm of rationality" (1980, p. 158).

Here we come to the second horn of the dilemma facing scientism. Its advocate may now insist: If philosophy has this status, it must really be a part of science, since (he continues to maintain, digging in his heels) all rational inquiry is scientific inquiry. The trouble now is that scientism becomes completely trivial, arbitrarily redefining "science" so that it includes anything that could be put forward as evidence against scientism. Worse, this move makes scientism consistent with views that are supposed to be *incompatible* with it.

For example, Aristotle argued that the very possibility of a world of changing things requires the existence of a divine Unmoved Mover which continuously keeps the world going. Aquinas argued that the very possibility of a world of causes and effects requires the existence of a divine Uncaused Cause which continuously imparts to things their causal power. But then, if they are correct, the existence of God follows from the very assumptions that also underlie science.

Indeed, Aristotle and Aquinas took the view that since we can know a fair amount about the existence and nature of God through reason alone, philosophical theology *itself* constitutes a kind of science. For they would not agree with the narrow conception of "science" on which a discipline is only "scientific" to the extent that it approximates the mathematical modeling techniques and predictive methods of physics. For Aristotle and Aquinas, the truths of philosophical theology may not be expressible in mathematical language and are not based on specific predictions or experiments, but that does not make them less certain than the claims of physics. On the contrary, they are more certain, because they rest on strict demonstrations which begin from premises that any possible physical science must take for granted.

Obviously that is all highly controversial, but the point does not ride on the truth or falsity of Aristotelian-Thomistic natural theology. The point is rather that if the advocate of scientism defines "science" so broadly that anything for which we might give a rational philosophical argument counts as "scientific," then he has no non-arbitrary reason for denying that a philosophically grounded theology or indeed any other aspect of traditional metaphysics could in principle count as a science. Yet the whole point of scientism -- or so it would seem given the rhetoric of its adherents -- was supposed to be to provide a weapon by which fields of inquiry like traditional metaphysics might be dismissed as unscientific. Hence if the advocate of scientism can avoid making his doctrine self-defeating only by defining "science" this broadly, then the view becomes completely vacuous. Certainly it is no longer available as a magic bullet by which to take down the rational credentials of traditional metaphysics.

0.2.2 The descriptive limits of science

The second main problem facing scientism, I have said, is that science cannot in principle provide a complete description of reality. Indeed, it cannot in principle provide a complete description even of *physical* reality. The reason, paradoxical as it sounds, has to do precisely with the method that has made the predictive and technological achievements of modern physics possible. Physics insists upon a purely *quantitative* description of the world, regarding mathematics as the language in which the "Book of Nature" is written (as Galileo famously put it). Hence it is hardly surprising that physics, more than other disciplines, has discovered those aspects of reality susceptible of the prediction and control characteristic of quantifiable phenomena. Those are the only aspects to which the physicist will allow himself to pay any attention in the first place. Everything else necessarily falls through his methodological net.

Now our ordinary experience of nature is of course *qualitative* through and through. We perceive colors, sounds, flavors, odors, warmth and coolness, pains and itches, thoughts and choices, purposes and meanings. Physics abstracts from these rich concrete details, ignoring whatever cannot be expressed in terms of equations and the like and thereby radically simplifying the natural order. There is nothing wrong with such an abstractive procedure as long as we keep in mind what we are doing and why we are doing it. Indeed, what the physicist does is just an extension of the sort of thing we do every day when solving practical problems. For example, when figuring out how many people of average weight can be carried on an airplane, engineers deal with abstractions. For one thing, they ignore every aspect of actual, concrete human beings except their weight; for another, they ignore even their actual weight, since it could in principle turn out that there is no specific human being who has exactly whatever the average weight turns out to be. This is extremely useful for the specific purposes at hand. But of course it would be ludicrous for those responsible for planning the flight entertainment or meals to rely solely on the considerations the engineers are concerned with. It would be even more ludicrous for them to insist that unless evidence of meal and movie preferences can be gleaned from the engineers' data, there just is no fact of the matter about what meals and movies actual human beings would prefer. Such evidence is missing precisely because the engineers' abstractive method guarantees that it will be missing.

The description of the world physics gives us is no less abstract than the one the engineers make use of. Physics simply does not give us material systems in all their concrete reality, any more than the aircraft engineers' description gives us human beings in all their concrete reality. It focuses, as I have said, only on those aspects of a system that are susceptible of prediction and control, and thus on those aspects which can be modeled mathematically. Hence it would be no less ludicrous to suggest that if the description physics gives us of the world does not make reference to some feature familiar to us in ordinary experience, then it follows that the feature in question doesn't exist. The success of the aircraft engineers' methods doesn't for a moment show that human beings have no features other than weight. And the success of physics doesn't for a moment show that the natural world has no features other than those described in a physics textbook. The reason qualitative features don't show up is not that the method has allowed us to discover that they aren't there but rather that the method has essentially stipulated that they be left out of the description whether they are there or not.

The standard story about how the qualitative features fit into the world is some variation on the distinction between primary and secondary qualities. Colors, sounds, and the like as common sense understands them exist, it is said, only in our perceptual awareness of matter rather than in matter itself, as the qualia of conscious experience. What exists in the external material world is only color as *redefined* by physics (in terms of surface reflectance properties), sound as *redefined* by physics (in terms of compression waves), and so forth. But this only makes the qualitative features *more* rather than less problematic. As Thomas Nagel writes:

> The modern mind-body problem arose out of the scientific revolution of the seventeenth century, as a direct result of the concept of objective physical reality that drove that revolution. Galileo and Descartes made the crucial conceptual division by proposing that physical science should provide a mathematically precise quantitative description of an external reality extended in space and time, a description limited to spatiotemporal primary qualities such as shape, size, and motion, and to laws governing the relations among them. Subjective appearances, on the other hand -- how this physical world appears to human perception -- were assigned to the mind, and the secondary qualities like color, sound, and smell were to be analyzed relationally, in terms of the power of physical things, acting on the senses, to produce those appearances in the minds of observers. It was essential to leave out or subtract subjective appearances and the human mind -- as well as human inten-

tions and purposes -- from the physical world in order to permit this powerful but austere spatiotemporal conception of objective physical reality to develop. (2012, pp. 35-36)

The problem is that this method entails that the mind itself cannot be treated as part of the material world, given how mind and matter are characterized by the method. If matter, including the matter of the brain, is essentially devoid of qualitative features and mind is essentially defined by its possession of qualitative features, then the mind cannot be material. Dualism of a Cartesian sort, with all of its problems (the interaction problem, the problem of other minds, zombies, epiphenomenalism, etc.) follows -- not as a kind of rearguard resistance to the new scientific conception of the world, but precisely as a direct consequence of it.

Erwin Schrödinger saw things far more clearly than his scientistic admirers do when he wrote:

We are thus facing the following strange situation. While all building stones for the [modern scientific] world-picture are furnished by the senses qua organs of the mind, while the world picture itself is and remains for everyone a construct of his mind and apart from it has no demonstrable existence, the mind itself remains a stranger in this picture, it has no place in it, it can nowhere be found in it. (1956, p. 216)

Also more perceptive than contemporary proponents of scientism was another of their heroes, the ancient atomist Democritus, who saw 2400 years ago that excluding qualitative features from the world is fraught with paradox. An imagined dialogue between the atomist's intellect and his senses written by Democritus and quoted by Schrödinger (1956, p. 211) goes as follows:

Intellect: Colour is by convention, sweet by convention, bitter by convention; in truth there are but atoms and the void.

Senses: Wretched mind, from us you are taking the evidence by which you would overthrow us? Your victory is your own fall.

Democritus' point, and Schrödinger's, is that it will not do to take an eliminativist line and deny that the problematic qualitative features really exist at all. For it is only through observation and experiment

-- and thus through conscious experiences defined by these very qualitative features -- that we have evidence for the truth of the scientific theories in the name of which we would be eliminating the qualitative. Such eliminativism is incoherent.

Nor will it do to suggest that further application of the method in question is bound eventually to explain conscious experience in the way it has explained everything else. This is like saying that since we have been able to get rid of the dirt everywhere else in the house by sweeping it under a certain rug, we can surely get rid of the dirt under the rug by applying the same method. That is, of course, the one method that cannot in principle work. And by the same token, stripping away the qualitative features of a phenomenon and redefining it in purely quantitative terms is the one method that cannot in principle work when seeking to explain conscious experience. For conscious experience, the method itself tells us, *just is* the "rug" under which all qualitative features have been swept. Applying the same method to the explanation of qualitative features of conscious experience is thus simply incoherent, and in practice either changes the subject or amounts to a disguised eliminativism. Nagel pointed this problem out long ago (1979), and Schrödinger saw it too:

> Scientific theories serve to facilitate the survey of our observations and experimental findings. Every scientist knows how difficult it is to remember a moderately extended group of facts, before at least some primitive theoretical picture about them has been shaped. It is therefore small wonder, and by no means to be blamed on the authors of original papers or of textbooks, that after a reasonably coherent theory has been formed, they do not describe the bare facts they have found or wish to convey to the reader, but clothe them in the terminology of that theory or theories. This procedure, while very useful for our remembering the facts in a well-ordered pattern, tends to obliterate the distinction between the actual observations and the theory arisen from them. And since the former always are of some sensual quality, theories are easily thought to account for sensual qualities; which, of course, they never do. (1992, pp. 163-64)

The reason that "of course, they never do" is that the scientist's working notion of matter is one that has, by definition, extruded the qualitative from it. Hence when the scientist identifies some physical property or process he finds correlated with the qualitative features of conscious experience -- this or that property of external objects, or this or that process in the brain -- and supposes that in doing so he has explained the qualitative, he is in thrall to an illusion. He is mistaking the theoretical, quantitative re-description of matter he has replaced the qualitative with for the qualitative itself. He may accuse his critic of dualist obscurantism when the critic points out that all the scientist has identified are physical features that are *correlated with* the qualitative, rather than the qualitative itself. But such accusations merely blame the messenger, for it is the scientist's own method that has guaranteed that dualist correlation is all that he will ever discover.

So, the qualitative features of the world cannot in principle be explained scientifically nor coherently eliminated, and a Cartesian account of their relation to matter is, the Scholastic agrees (Feser 2008, Chapter 5), unacceptable. But a purely quantitative conception of matter is problematic even apart from these considerations. Bertrand Russell (yet another hero of contemporary naturalists who saw things more clearly than they do) indicates how:

> It is not always realised how exceedingly abstract is the information that theoretical physics has to give. It lays down certain fundamental equations which enable it to deal with the logical structure of events, while leaving it completely unknown what is the intrinsic character of the events that have the structure... All that physics gives us is certain equations giving abstract properties of their changes. But as to what it is that changes, and what it changes from and to – as to this, physics is silent. (1985, p. 13)

Now if, as Russell emphasized, physics gives us the abstract structure of the material world but does not tell us the intrinsic nature of that which has that structure, then not only does physics not tell us everything about physical reality, but it tells us that there must be something more to physical reality than what it has to say. For there is no such thing as a structure all by itself; there must be something that has the structure. By the very fact that physics tells us that an abstract structure of such-and-such a mathematically describable character exists, then, physics implies that there is more to reality than that structure itself, and thus more to reality than what physics can reveal.

Russell's own position tried to kill two birds with one stone, solving both the problem of fitting qualitative features into nature and the problem of finding the intrinsic properties of matter by identifying the qualitative features themselves as the intrinsic properties of matter. There are serious problems with this sort of view (Feser 1998, 2006b), and as we will see, the Scholastic's own approach to understanding the nature of material substances is in any event simply incommensurable with the entire post-Cartesian framework within which Russell, Schrödinger, and most other modern commentators on these matters are working. The point to emphasize for present purposes is that, however one solves them, the problems described are philosophical rather than scientific, and they show that science is nowhere close to giving us an exhaustive description of reality. On the contrary, the very nature of scientific method shows that there exist aspects of reality it will not capture.

0.2.3 The explanatory limits of science

If there are limits to what science can *describe*, there are also limits to what science can *explain*. This brings us to the third problem I have claimed faces scientism -- the fact that the "laws of nature" in terms of which science explains phenomena cannot in principle provide an *ultimate* explanation of reality.

To see the problem, consider physicist Lawrence Krauss's recent book *A Universe from Nothing* (2012). Krauss initially gives his readers the impression that he is going to give a complete explanation, in purely scientific terms, of why anything exists at all rather than nothing. The bulk of the book is devoted to exploring how the energy present in otherwise empty space, together with the laws of physics, might have given rise to the universe as it exists today. This is at first treated as if it were highly relevant to the question of how the universe might have come from nothing, until Krauss acknowledges toward the end of the book that energy, space, and the laws of physics don't really count as "nothing" after all. Then it is proposed that the laws of physics alone might do the trick, though these too, as Krauss implicitly allows, don't really count as "nothing" either. Krauss's final proposal is that "there may be no fundamental theory at all" but just layer upon layer of laws of physics, which we can probe until we get bored (p. 177).

Now the problem here is not only that this is a bait and switch -- though it is that, since an endless regress of laws is hardly "nothing," and vaguely speculating on the basis of no evidence whatsoever that there may be such a regress hardly counts as a serious explanation. The deeper problem is that Krauss not only *does not* deliver on his promise but that he *could not* have done so. For any appeal to laws of nature (or a series of "layers" of such laws) simply raises questions about *what* a law of nature *is* in the first place, *how* it has any efficacy, and *where* it (or the series of "layers") comes from. And these are questions which the scientific mode of explanation, which *presupposes* such laws, cannot in principle answer.

The status of laws of nature is a topic we will have reason to consider at some length later on in this book, but for the moment we can merely note that none of the standard approaches gives any aid or comfort to scientism. We might hold, for example, that to speak of the "laws of nature" that govern some material thing or system is simply a shorthand way of describing the manner in which that thing or system will operate given its nature or essence. This, as we will see, is the Scholastic approach to understanding physical laws. But on this view the "laws of nature" *presuppose* the existence and operations of the physical things that follow the laws. And in that case the laws cannot possibly *explain* the existence or operations of the material things themselves. In particular, and contrary to writers like Krauss, since the ultimate laws of nature presuppose the existence of the physical universe, they cannot intelligibly be appealed to as a way of explaining the existence of the universe.

A second view of what "laws of nature" are and how they operate is the one endorsed by early modern thinkers like Descartes and Newton, who sought to overthrow the Aristotelian-Scholastic philosophy that dominated the Middle Ages. On their view, the notion of a "law of nature" is irreducibly theological, a shorthand for the idea that God has set the world up so as to behave in the regular way described by the laws. On this view it is really God's action that strictly does the explaining and neither material things nor the laws they follow really explain anything. But for obvious reasons, this too is not a view that gives any help to scientism, which is as hostile to theological explanations as it is to traditional metaphysics in general.

A third possibility is to hold that "laws of nature" are really nothing more than a description or summary of the regular patterns we happen to find in the natural world. They don't tell us anything about the natures of material things, and they don't reflect the will of God. To say that it is a law of nature that A is followed by B is on this view simply to say that A's tend to be followed by B's in a regular way, and that's that. But on this view, laws tell us only *that* such-and-such a regularity exists, and not *why* it exists. That is to say, on this view a law of nature (or at least the ultimate laws of nature) don't *explain* a regularity, but merely *re-describe* it in a different jargon. Needless to say, then, this sort of view hardly supports the claim that science can provide an ultimate explanation of the world.

A further possibility would be to interpret "laws of nature" as abstract objects, something comparable to Plato's Forms, existing in a realm beyond the material world, and where physical things somehow "participate in" the laws in something like the way Plato thought that every tree participates in the Form of Tree or every triangle participates in the Form of Triangle. Here too an appeal to laws of nature doesn't really provide an ultimate explanation of anything. For given this view we would still need to know how it comes to be that there is a physical world that "participates in" the laws in the first place, why it participates in these laws rather than others, and so on. And that requires an appeal to something other than the laws.

Again, we will have reason to consider this issue in greater depth later on, but the point to emphasize for the moment is that once again we have questions which of their nature cannot be answered by science but only by philosophy, because they deal precisely with what any possible scientific explanation must take for granted. Nor will it do to suggest that ultimate explanation is not to be had anyway, so that science cannot be faulted for failing to provide it.

For one thing, this is itself a philosophical claim rather than a scientific one. For another, the claim is false, as we will see later in this book when discussing the principle of sufficient reason.

0.2.4 A bad argument for scientism

Now if scientism faces such grave difficulties, why are so many intelligent people drawn to it? The answer – to paraphrase a remark made by Wittgenstein in another context – is that "a picture holds them captive." Hypnotized by the unparalleled predictive and technological successes of modern science, they infer that scientism must be true, and that anything that follows from scientism – however fantastic or even seemingly incoherent – must also be true.

Consider the argument for scientism given by Alex Rosenberg in his book *The Atheist's Guide to Reality* (2011). He writes:

The technological success of physics is by itself enough to convince anyone with anxiety about scientism that if physics isn't "finished," it certainly has the broad outlines of reality well understood. (p. 23)

And it's not just the correctness of the predictions and the reliability of technology that requires us to place our confidence in physics' description of reality. Because physics' predictions are so accurate, the methods that produced the description must be equally reliable. Otherwise, our technological powers would be a miracle. We have the best of reasons to believe that the methods of physics -- combining controlled experiment and careful observation with mainly mathematical requirements on the shape theories can take -- are the right ones for acquiring all knowledge. Carving out some area of "inquiry" or "belief" as exempt from exploration by the methods of physics is special pleading or self-deception. (p. 24)

The phenomenal accuracy of its prediction, the unimaginable power of its technological application, and the breathtaking extent and detail of its explanations are powerful reasons to believe that physics is the whole truth about reality. (p. 25)

Of course, many proponents of scientism would regard Rosenberg's physics-only version as too restrictive. They would regard sciences like chemistry, biology, and the like as genuine sources of knowledge even if it turned out that they are irreducible to physics. But they would agree with Rosenberg's main point that the "success" of science, broadly construed, supports scientism. Rosenberg's argument, suitably modified in a way that would make it acceptable to other defenders of scientism, is essentially this:

1. The predictive power and technological applications of science are unparalleled by those of any other purported source of knowledge.

2. Therefore what science reveals to us is probably all that is real.

Now this, I maintain, is a bad argument. How bad is it? About as bad as this one:

1. Metal detectors have had far greater success in finding coins and other metallic objects in more places than any other method has.

2. Therefore what metal detectors reveal to us (coins and other metallic objects) is probably all that is real.

Metal detectors are keyed to those aspects of the natural world susceptible of detection via electromagnetic means (or whatever). But however well they perform this task -- indeed, even if they succeeded on every single occasion they were deployed -- that simply wouldn't make it even probable that there are no aspects of the natural world other than the ones they are sensitive to. Similarly, what physics does (and there is no doubt that it does it brilliantly) is to capture those aspects of the natural world susceptible of the mathematical modeling that makes precise prediction and technological application possible. But here too, it simply doesn't follow that there are no other aspects of the natural world.

Rosenberg adds to his argument the suggestion that those who reject scientism do not do so consistently. He writes:

"Scientism" is the pejorative label given to our positive view by those who really want to have their theistic cake and dine at the table of science's bounties, too. Opponents of scientism would never charge their cardiologists or auto mechanics or software engineers with "scientism" when their health, travel plans, or Web surfing are in danger. But just try subjecting their nonscientific mores and norms, their music or metaphysics, their literary theories or politics to scientific scrutiny. The immediate response of outraged humane letters is "scientism." (p. 6)

So, according to Rosenberg, unless you agree that science is the *only* genuine source of knowledge, you cannot consistently believe that it gives us *any* genuine knowledge. But this is about as plausible as saying that unless you think metal detectors *alone* can detect physical objects, then you cannot consistently believe that they detect *any* physical objects at all. Those beholden to scientism are bound to protest that the analogy is no good, on the grounds that metal detectors detect only part of reality while science detects the whole of it. But such a reply would simply beg the question, for whether science really does describe the *whole* of reality is precisely what is at issue.

The non sequitur is very common but it is a non sequitur all the same. It is implicit every time a defender of scientism demands to know the predictive successes and technological applications of metaphysics or theology, and supposes he has won a great victory when his critic is unable to list any. (Cf. Ladyman, Ross, Spurrett and Collier 2007, pp. 7 and 16) This is about as impressive as demanding a list of the metal-detecting successes of gardening, cooking, and painting, and then concluding from the fact that no such list is forthcoming that spades, spatulas, and paint brushes are all useless and ought to be discarded and replaced with metal detectors. The fallacy is the same in both cases. That a method is especially useful for certain purposes simply does not entail that there are no other purposes worth pursuing nor other methods more suitable to those other purposes. In particular, if a certain method affords us a high degree of predictive and technological power, what that shows is that the method is useful for dealing with those aspects of the world that are predictable and controllable. But it simply does *not* show us that those aspects *exhaust* nature, that there is nothing more to the natural world than what the method reveals. Those who suppose otherwise are like the proverbial drunk who assumes that, because the area under the street lamp is the only place he would be able to see the keys he has lost, there must be no other place worth searching for them and no other method by which they might be found.

At this point some advocates of scientism might admit that there are questions science cannot answer and even that there are other methods for dealing with those questions, such as those provided by philosophy. But they might still insist that there is little point in pursuing these questions or methods, on the grounds that the questions are not susceptible of the crisp and definitive answers that science affords and that the methods do not generate the technologies that science provides us with. On this view, the superiority of science is evidenced by its *practical value* and by the fact that it achieves *consensus*, or at least something approaching consensus. Philosophy, by contrast, is notoriously controversial and impractical. So, even if science can't tell us everything, it does tell us everything worth knowing about.

But a moment's reflection shows that this fallback position will not work. For one thing, to take this sort of position is like avoiding classes you know you won't do well in and then appealing to your high grade point average as evidence of your superior intelligence. If you will *allow to count* as "scientific" only what is predictable and controllable and thus susceptible of consensus answers and technological application, then naturally -- but trivially -- science is going to be one long success story. But this no more shows that the questions that fall through science's methodological net are not worthy of attention than the fact that you've only taken courses you knew you would excel in shows that the other classes aren't worth taking. For another thing, the claim that only questions susceptible of scientific investigation, consensus answers, and technological application are worth investigating is itself not a scientific claim, but a philosophical claim, and thus one that requires a philosophical defense. Once again the very attempt to avoid going beyond science implicates one in doing so.

0.3 Against "conceptual analysis"

The advocate of scientism will insist that unless metaphysics is "naturalized" by making of it nothing more than science's bookkeeping department, then the only thing left for it to be is a kind of "conceptual analysis." And the trouble with this, we are told, is that we have no guarantee that the "intuitions" or "folk notions" the conceptual analyst appeals to really track reality, and indeed good reason to think they do not insofar as science often presents us with descriptions of reality radically different from what common sense supposes it to be like. (Cf. Ladyman, Ross, Spurrett, and Collier 2007, Chapter 1)

Now, one problem with this sort of argument is that it fallaciously takes science's *methodological exclusion* of certain commonsense features from its picture of the natural world as a *discovery* that those features don't really exist there. To take just one example, given its purely quantitative methods, physics excludes any reference to teleological features. But to conclude from this that the natural world has no inherent teleological features is, again, like concluding from the predictive and technological success of the aircraft engineers' methods that passengers' entertainment and meal preferences don't exist, since the methods make no reference to them. Claims about what science has "shown" vis-à-vis this or that metaphysical question invariably merely *presuppose*, rather than demonstrate, a certain metaphysical interpretation of science. The absence of a certain feature from the scientist's description of reality gives us reason to doubt that feature's existence *only* given a further argument which must be metaphysical rather than scientific in nature. And as we will see in the course of this book, in general such arguments are no good. Indeed, there are severe limits on what might coherently be eliminated from our commonsense picture of the world in the name of science. As I have argued elsewhere (2008, Chapter 6; 2013a) there is, eliminative materialists' glib dismissal of the incoherence problem notwithstanding, no way in principle coherently to deny the existence of intentional thought processes. We will see in the course of this book that it is also impossible coherently to deny, in the name of science, the existence of change, causation, teleology, substance, essence, and other basic metaphysical realities.

But putting that aside, there is a no less fundamental problem with the objection under consideration, which is that it rests on a false alternative. While there are metaphysicians whose method is that of "conceptual analysis" (e.g. Jackson 1998), Scholastics are not among them. The supposition that if you are not doing natural science then the only other thing you could be doing is "conceptual analysis" is essentially a variation on Hume's Fork, the thesis that "all the objects of human reason or enquiry may naturally be divided into two kinds, to wit, *Relations of Ideas*, and *Matters of Fact*" (Hume, *Enquiry Concerning Human Understanding*, Section IV, Part I). Now Hume's Fork is notoriously self-refuting, since it is not itself either a conceptual truth (a matter of the "relations of ideas") or empirically testable (a "matter of fact"). The Scholastic is happy in this case to follow Hume's advice and commit it to the flames. But the supposition made by the contemporary naturalist is no better. The claim that "all the objects of human reason or enquiry" are or ought to be either matters of "conceptual analysis" or matters of natural science is itself neither a conceptual truth nor a proposition for which you will find, or could find, the slightest evidence in natural science. It is a proposition as metaphysical as any a Scholastic would assert, differing from the latter only in being self-refuting. (The naturalist might claim that neuroscience or cognitive science supports his case, but if so he is deluding himself. For neuroscience and cognitive science, when they touch on matters of metaphysical import, are rife with tendentious and unexamined metaphysical assumptions (Bennett and Hacker 2003). And insofar as such assumptions are *naturalist* assumptions, the naturalist merely begs the question in appealing to them.)

Now that fact alone suffices to show that it is possible to take a cognitive stance toward the world that is neither that of natural science, nor merely a matter of tracing out conceptual relations in a network of ideas that might float entirely free of mind-independent reality (as "conceptual analysts" are accused of doing). The naturalist takes this third stance in the very act of denying that it can be taken. But more can be said. It is hardly news that there are truths -- namely those of logic and mathematics -- that do not plausibly fit into either of the two categories Hume and his naturalist descendents would, in Procrustean fashion, try to fit all knowledge into. Truths of logic and mathematics have a *necessity* that propositions of natural science lack and an *objectivity* that mere "conceptual analysis," at least as that is typically understood these days, would seem unable to guarantee. Some naturalists would try to find ways of showing that logical and mathematical truths are not really necessary or objective after all, but there are notorious difficulties with such proposals. Moreover, it would obviously beg the question to propose denying either the necessity or objectivity of logic and mathematics merely because they don't sit well with naturalism. Nor will it do for naturalists simply to shrug their shoulders and write off the necessity and objectivity of logic and mathematics as a mere unresolved problem that eventually will -- someday, somehow, by someone -- be solved by whatever "our best science" turns out to be a century or three hence. We may, with poetic justice, quote their hero David Hume against them: "But here we may observe, that nothing can be more absurd, than this custom of calling a difficulty what pretends to be a demonstration, and endeavoring by that means to elude its force and evidence" (*Treatise of Human Nature*, Book I, Part II, Section II).

Now as we will see, the Scholastic maintains that there are truths of a *metaphysical* nature which (like the truths of logic and mathematics) are necessary and objective but which also (like the truths of logic and mathematics) are not plausibly regarded as propositions either of natural science or of mere "conceptual analysis." Like logic and mathematics, and like the naturalist's own basic epistemological assumption, they simply fall between the tines of Hume's Fork. The naturalist might not understand how such knowledge is possible, but that is his problem, not the Scholastic's. The naturalist already has oceans of knowledge for which he cannot account -- again, the truths of logic and mathematics, and his own metaphysical variation on Hume's Fork -- and thus has no business questioning the epistemological credentials of Scholastic metaphysics. He is like a thief caught red handed with the loot, who demands that the police who have apprehended him produce the pink slip for their cruiser.

This situation illustrates what is for the Scholastic a basic philosophical truth, which is that *metaphysics is prior to epistemology*. One way in which this is the case is that absolutely every epistemological theory rests on metaphysical assumptions -- including Hume's when he begins with the supposition that there are impressions and ideas, and including the naturalist's when he supposes that our cognitive faculties are at least reliable enough to make natural science an objective enterprise. Naturally, these metaphysical assumptions cannot be justified by reference to the epistemological claims they support without begging the question. When the critic of metaphysics insists that the metaphysician establish his epistemological credentials before making any metaphysical assertions, he is making a demand that is incoherent and to which he does not submit himself.

Another way in which metaphysics is prior to epistemology is that our knowledge of various metaphysical truths is something with which a sound epistemology must be consistent, so that if an epistemological theory is *not* consistent with our having knowledge of these truths then it must be rejected. In the limiting case, an epistemological theory that was inconsistent with its *own* metaphysical assumptions would obviously be for that reason something we must reject. Now elsewhere I have (following James Ross) argued that our capacity to grasp abstract concepts and to reason in accordance with formally valid patterns of inference is something incompatible with naturalism, and that the naturalist cannot evade the problem by attempting to deny that we really possess such concepts or reason in such ways (Ross 1992 and 2008, Chapter 6; Feser 2013a). That alone is reason to reject any naturalist epistemology. But we will see in the course of this book that there are other metaphysical truths which cannot coherently be denied, so that if scientism or naturalism is incompatible with our knowing such truths, what follows is not that we don't know such truths but rather that scientism or naturalism is false.

Naturalists do not see the force of these difficulties because they presuppose too narrow a range of epistemological options. In particular, they tend at least implicitly to operate within a framework of assumptions inherited from the early moderns. The rationalists held that certain metaphysical concepts and truths are innate. The empiricist tradition, denying that there are any innate concepts or knowledge, ended up denying also that we really have the metaphysical concepts in question, or at least that we can know that the concepts correspond to anything in mind-independent reality. Splitting the difference between rationalism and empiricism, Kant held that the concepts in question are innate, but reflect only the way the mind must carve up reality and correspond to nothing in reality itself. His successors claimed that even this is too ambitious -- that the concepts in question do not reflect even any necessary features of cognition as such, but only the contingent way in which cognition has been molded by evolution, or even merely by historical and cultural circumstances. Naturally, metaphysics as "conceptual analysis" or as "descriptive" (Strawson 1959) comes to seem about as relevant to discovering objective truth as lexicography is. The latter tells us only how we *talk* about reality, and not about language-independent reality itself. The former tells us only about how we *conceive* of reality, and not about mind-independent reality itself.

But the Scholastic simply rejects the entire rationalist/empiricist/Kantian dialectic and insists on maintaining an epistemological position that predated these views, and against which they reacted. The Scholastic agrees with the rationalist that there are necessary metaphysical truths that we can know with certainty, but does not take them to be innate. The Scholastic agrees with the empiricist that all of our concepts must be derived from experience and that our knowledge must be grounded in experience, but he does not accept either the early modern empiricist's desiccated notion of "experience" or his tendency to collapse intellect into sensation, as e.g. Hume does when characterizing "ideas" as faint copies of impressions. (This is an issue I will have reason to address later on in the book.) Thus the Scholastic does not accept the basic assumptions that made Kantianism and its contemporary "naturalized" or "descriptive" successors seem the only alternatives to a rationalist or empiricist position.

Thus, when some recent advocates of "naturalized metaphysics" dismiss contemporary "conceptual analysis" based metaphysics as "neo-scholastic" (Ladyman, Ross, Spurrett, and Collier 2007), they demonstrate only their ignorance of what Scholastics actually thought. The Scholastic maintains that though "there is nothing in the intellect that was not first in the senses" (to cite a famous Scholastic maxim), the intellect can nevertheless come to know, via the abstraction from particulars of universal essences and via demonstrative rather than merely probabilistic arguments, aspects of reality beyond what can be experienced. I will have reason to address this topic briefly in the last chapter of this book, but spelling out in detail how this all works would require a long excursus in Scholastic philosophical psychology and epistemology. (Cf. Bittle 1936; Coffey 1958a and 1958b; Van Steenberghen 1949; Wilhelmsen 1956; O'Callaghan 2003; McInerny 2007; Ross 2008, Chapter 5; Groarke 2009) But such an excursus is, for the reasons given, in no way necessary here as a prolegomenon to metaphysics. For epistemology and philosophical psychology themselves presuppose metaphysics. Vis-à-vis epistemology and psychology ("naturalized" or otherwise) -- and vis-à-vis natural science too, *where* (though *only* where) it touches on the most fundamental issues about substance, causation, essence, and the like -- metaphysics wears the trousers.

1. Act and potency

1.1 The general theory

1.1.1 Origins of the distinction

The first of the famous twenty-four Thomistic theses reads:

> Potency and act are a complete division of being. Hence, whatever is must be either pure act or a unit composed of potency and act as its primary and intrinsic principles. (Wuellner 1956, p. 120)

The distinction between potency and act is fundamental not only to Thomism but to Scholastic philosophy in general (though as we will see, Scotists and Suarezians disagree with Thomists about how to interpret the distinction). It is absolutely crucial to the Scholastic approach to questions about the metaphysics of substance, essence, and causation (and for that matter to Scholastic philosophy of nature, philosophical psychology, natural theology, and even ethics). We would do well to begin, then, with an outline of the theory of act and potency. Subsequent sections of this chapter and the next will develop and defend key aspects of the theory as they apply to causation. In later chapters we will see how the theory applies to other metaphysical issues.

The theory has its origins in Aristotle's account of where the Eleatics on the one hand, and Heraclitus on the other, went wrong in their respective positions vis-à-vis *change versus permanence* -- an account that was extended by Scholastic writers to a critique of the Eleatic and Heraclitean positions vis-à-vis *multiplicity versus unity*.

Parmenides and Zeno denied the reality of change. Parmenides' position is essentially that (1) change would require being to arise out of non-being or nothingness, but (2) from non-being or nothingness, nothing can arise, so that (3) change is impossible. Zeno aimed to reduce the notion of local motion to absurdity via paradoxes some of which presuppose that traversing a finite distance would require traversing an infinite number of shorter distances. For example, in the dichotomy paradox, Zeno suggests that a runner can get from point A to point B only if he first reaches the midpoint between A and B; but he can reach that midpoint only if he first reaches the point midway between A and the midpoint, and so on *ad infinitum*. Hence he can never reach B, and indeed can never even move beyond A.

A natural first response to such arguments would be to apply the method of retorsion and argue that those who deny the reality of change are led thereby into a performative self-contradiction. The Eleatic philosopher has to move his lips or pen in order to put his argument forward; if he bites the bullet and denies that even his lips and pen are really moving or that he is really trying to change the minds of his listeners or readers, he still has to go through the steps of his reasoning in his own mind, and that involves change. The reality of change is not *self*-evident, insofar as it is not a necessary truth that any change ever actually occurs. But it is still *evident* insofar as we have to acknowledge it in order to argue for anything at all. (Cf. Smith and Kendzierski 1961, p. 16)

This tells us at most *that* something has gone wrong in the Eleatic arguments, but not *what*, exactly, has gone wrong. The problem with Parmenides' reasoning, in Aristotle's view, is neither in the inference from (1) and (2) to (3), nor with premise (2), with which Aristotle agrees. It is rather with premise (1), the thesis that change would involve being arising from non-being. For there is, according to Aristotle, an alternative analysis of change, on which it involves, not being arising from non-being, but rather one *kind* of being arising from another kind. In particular, there is *being-in-act* -- the ways a thing *actually* is; and there is *being-in-potency* -- the ways a thing could *potentially* be. For instance, a given rubber ball might "in act" or actually be spherical, solid, smooth to the touch, red in color, and sitting motionless in a drawer. But "in potency" or potentially it is flat and squishy (if melted), rough to the touch (if worn out through use), light pink (if left out in the sun too long), and rolling across the ground (if dropped).

These potentialities or potencies are real features of the ball itself even if they are not actualities. The ball's potential flatness, squishiness, roughness, etc. are not *nothing*, even if they do not have the *kind* of being that the ball's roundness, solidity, smoothness, etc. currently have. That is why the ball can *become* flat, squishy, and rough in a way it *cannot* become sentient, or eloquent, or capable of doing arithmetic. Being-in-potency is thus a middle ground between being-in-act on the one hand, and sheer nothingness or non-being on the other. And change is not a matter of being arising from non-being, but rather of being-in-act arising from being-in-potency. It is the *actualization of a potential* -- of something previously *non*-actual but still *real.*

Zeno too overlooks the distinction between being-in-act and being-in-potency. The infinite number of smaller distances in the interval between two points A and B are indeed there, but only potentially rather than actually. Hence there is no actually infinitely large number of distances the runner must traverse, and Zeno's purported *reductio* fails.

Heraclitus had (on a traditional interpretation, anyway) gone to the opposite extreme from that of the Eleatics, holding that there is no being but only endless becoming. Change and change *alone* is real -- the implication being that there is no stability or persistence of even a temporary sort, nothing that corresponds to Aristotle's notion of being-in-act. Here too the method of retorsion might be deployed. If there is no stability of *any* sort, how could the Heraclitean philosopher so much as reason through the steps of his own argument so as to be convinced by it? For there will on the Heraclitean view be no persisting subject, so that the person who reaches the conclusion will not be the same as the person who entertained the premises. (Cf. Geisler 1997, pp. 65-66) Nor will there be any such thing as "the" argument for his conclusion -- some single, stable pattern of reasoning which the Heraclitean might rehearse in his attempts to convince his critics, or even repeat to himself on future occasions.

Nor is there, in the Aristotelian view, any sense to be made of change in the first place except as change *toward* some outcome, even if only a temporary outcome. The ball melts, but this is not merely a move away from roundness and solidity; it is a move in the direction of squishiness and flatness, and thus in the direction of new actualities. Moreover, such changes occur in repeatable patterns. This or that particular instance of roundness or flatness comes and goes, but new instances of the same features can and do arise. Hence the changes that occur in the world in fact reflect a degree of stability that belies Heraclitus' doctrine of flux, even though it does not approach the absolute stasis of the Eleatics.

The Eleatic and Heraclitean extremes vis-à-vis change and permanence are paralleled by similar extremes on the question of multiplicity versus unity. Parmenides denies that there can possibly be more than one being. For if a being A and a purportedly distinct being B really were distinct, there would have to be something to differentiate them. But since A and B both are, by hypothesis, beings, the only thing that could do so would be non-being; and non-being, since it is just nothingness, does not exist and thus cannot differentiate them.

Zeno reaches a similar conclusion via his paradox of parts. If there is more than one being, then either these multiple beings have size or they do not. If they do not, then since things of no size can, even when combined, never yield anything with size, it would follow that there is nothing of any size at all, which is absurd. But if these multiple beings do have size, then they are infinitely divisible and thus have an infinite number of parts. And if they have an infinite number of parts, then they must all be of infinite size, which is also absurd. So there cannot be more than one being.

The Heraclitean position, by contrast, when pushed to the extreme would entail that there is only multiplicity and no unity in the world, nothing to tie together the diverse objects of our experience. There is this particular thing we call "round," that one, and a third one, but no one thing, *roundness*, that they all instantiate; there is this perceptual experience of what we call a "ball," that one, and a third one, but no one thing, that ball itself, that these experiences are all experiences of, and no one subject, the perceiving self, which has the various perceptual experiences. (To be sure, Heraclitus himself adopted a kind of monism on which there is one thing, the world itself, which is the subject of endless change -- a *dynamic monism* rather than the *static monism* of the Eleatics. Still, none of what J. L. Austin called the "middle-sized dry goods" of everyday experience could count as unified subjects on this view.)

Once again the method of retorsion might be deployed against such views. If, as the Eleatics claim, there is in no sense more than one being, then how can the Eleatic so much as distinguish between himself and his interlocutor, or his premises and his conclusion? How can he distinguish between the *reality* that his philosophy is supposed to reveal to us and the false *appearance* of things that it is intended to dispel? If, as the Heraclitean claims, there is no unity to the things of ordinary experience but only multiplicity, then there can be no one self who abides through the stages of a chain of reasoning -- in which case how can the Heraclitean ever validly draw a conclusion from his premises, as he needs to do in order to make his case? And how could he even state his thesis unless there were stable, recurring patterns -- roundness, flatness, melting, etc. -- in terms of which to characterize change or becoming?

The distinction between act and potency can be applied to a critique of the Eleatics' denial of multiplicity, as much as to a critique of their denial of change. Contra Parmenides, non-being or nothingness is not the only candidate for a principle by which two beings A and B could be differentiated. For despite their both being *actual*, they can yet be differentiated by reference to their *potencies*. Two balls A and B might both be actually round and red, but differ insofar as A is actually rolling while B is rolling only potentially, B is actually in the drawer while A is in the drawer only potentially, and so forth. Zeno, meanwhile, supposes that the infinite number of parts a thing with size has are all in it actually, when in fact they are in it only insofar as a thing and its parts could each *potentially* be divided and divided again.

We have, then, the following basic argument for the distinction between potency and act: That change and permanence, multiplicity and unity, are all real features of the world cannot coherently be denied; but they can be real features of the world only if there is a distinction in things between what they are *in act* and what they are *in potency*; therefore there *is* a distinction to be made in things between what they are in act and what they are in potency.

To this basic argument, Scholastic philosophy of nature would add a consideration from the success of modern science. Science would be impossible if either the Eleatic position or its Heraclitean opposite were true. If Parmenides and Zeno were correct, there would be no world of distinct, changing things and events for the physicist, chemist, or biologist to study; and perceptual experience, which forms the evidential basis for modern science but which consists precisely in a series of distinct and changing perceptual episodes, would be entirely illusory. If the opposite, Heraclitean position were correct, there would be no stable, repeatable patterns for the scientist to uncover -- no laws of physics, no periodic table of elements, no biological species -- and thus no way to infer from the observed to the unobserved. On either of these views, the ontological and epistemological presuppositions of science would be undermined. Yet there is no way to avoid the Eleatic and Heraclitean extremes without affirming the distinction between act and potency. So we must affirm it given the success of science.

1.1.2 The relationship between act and potency

If act and potency are distinct features of a thing, we must still address the question of what *kind* of distinction we are talking about. For Scholastic writers commonly differentiate between *real* distinctions and *logical* distinctions, where the former reflect differences in extra-mental reality itself and the latter differences in our ways of thinking about extra-mental reality. Scotists add to this classification the notion of a *formal* distinction as something intermediate between a real and a logical distinction. Thomists regard the distinction between act and potency as a real distinction, while Scotists and Suarezians regard it as a formal distinction. We will return to this issue below.

Thomists also differ with Scotists and Suarezians about whether anything other than potency limits act. Take the roundness of a certain rubber ball, which is actual, but in a limited way insofar as roundness as such is perfect roundness yet the ball's roundness is not perfect (since there is always at least a slight imperfection in even the most carefully made ball), and insofar as roundness, which is of itself a universal, comes to be instantiated in this particular object and in that sense limited to a particular time and place. The Thomist position is that it is only potency which can ultimately account for these limitations on a thing's actuality. Indeed, this is the second of the twenty-four Thomistic theses:

> Because act is perfection, it is limited only by potency which is a capacity for perfection. Hence, a pure act in any order of being exists only as unlimited and unique; but wherever it (act) is finite and multiplied, there it unites in true composition with potency. (Wuellner 1956, p. 120)

In particular, it is the potency of rubber qua material substance to take on different forms that limits the roundness currently in it to being only an approximation of perfect roundness; matter as such lacks the fixity or determinacy to realize more than such an approximation. It is also matter which limits the roundness to *this* rather than *that* particular time and place; and this too reflects matter's potency, insofar as a given parcel of matter is always potentially at some other point in time and space even if actually at this one.

Scotists and Suarezians, by contrast, hold that the limitations of a thing's actuality can be accounted for by reference to the thing's cause. The ball's roundness is imperfect because the ball's cause put, as it were, only so much roundness into it; the roundness is limited to this particular time and place because that is when and where the ball's cause put it into the ball. For the Thomist, however, such an *extrinsic* principle of limitation is possible only if there is an *intrinsic* principle -- something in the limited thing itself by virtue of which its cause is able to limit its actuality -- and this can only be potency. Hence the cause of the ball can put a limited degree of roundness into it precisely because the ball has the potency to be something other than perfectly round; and it can cause the roundness to be instantiated here and now rather than some other time and place precisely because the rubber which takes on that form has the potency to be at various times and places. (Cf. Clarke 1994; Phillips 1950, pp. 187-91; Renard 1946, pp. 30-39)

This dispute is closely related to the dispute over whether the distinction between act and potency is a real distinction, to which, again, we will return below; and to the dispute over whether the distinction between a thing's essence and its existence is a real distinction, which will be addressed in chapter 4.

Even those who regard the distinction between act and potency as real emphasize that act is prior to or more fundamental than potency in several crucial respects. For one thing, any potency is always defined in relation to act. For instance, a rubber ball's potency for melting, becoming flat, etc. just is a potency for being *actual* in those ways -- for being melted *in act*, flat *in act*, and so on.

Second, a thing's potencies are *grounded in* its actualities. It is because the ball is actually made of rubber rather than either granite or butter that it has a potency for melting at just the temperature it does rather than at some higher or lower temperature.

Third, a potency can be actualized only by what is already actual. For instance, the ball's potential flatness and squishiness cannot actualize themselves, precisely because they are merely potential rather than actual; and neither, for the same reason, can anything else that is merely potential be what actualizes them. If they are to be actualized, it can only be something already actual, like the heat of an oven, which actualizes them. This is one version of the Scholastic *principle of causality*, which will be examined in chapter 2.

Finally, act is prior to potency insofar as while there can be nothing that is pure potency -- since, if a thing were *purely* potential and in no way actual, it would not exist -- there can be something which is pure act. The notion of that which is absolutely pure actuality or *actus purus* is the core of Scholastic philosophy's conception of God, and its existence is the upshot of the key Scholastic arguments for God's existence. (Cf. Feser 2009, chapter 3; Feser 2011)

1.1.3 Divisions of act and potency

Given the distinction between act and potency, quite a few subdistinctions can be made and commonly are made by Scholastic writers. Consider first the divisions of potency. The first distinction to be made here is between *pure* or *logical possibility* on the one hand and *real potency* on the other. Unicorns would be examples of the logically possible insofar as there is no such thing as a unicorn but also no contradiction in the notion of a unicorn; such pure or logical possibilities are also called *objective potencies* insofar as they are possible *qua* objects of thought. This distinguishes them from real potencies, which are grounded in the natures of real things, as a ball's potential for melting at a certain temperature is grounded in the nature of the rubber out of which it is made. It is real potencies that are regarded by Scholastic writers as potencies in the proper sense, and they are sometimes called *subjective potencies* insofar as they are grounded in a real subject, rather than merely existing as objects of thought. (Note that these senses of "objective" and "subjective" are nearly the reverse of the contemporary philosopher's use of "objective" to refer to what exists mind-independently and of "subjective" to refer to what exists only as an object of consciousness.)

On the side of real or subjective potencies a further distinction is made between *active potency*, which is the capacity to bring about an effect, and *passive potency*, which is the capacity to be affected. Fire's capacity to melt rubber is an active potency, whereas rubber's capacity to be melted is a passive potency. An active potency is a *power*; a passive potency is a *potentiality* in the strict sense. (Cf. Coffey 1970, p. 56)

We will have much to say about active potency in the next section. For the moment let us note that for the Scholastic, active potency is, strictly speaking, a kind of act or actuality (in particular, what is called a "first actuality"); more precisely, it is a kind of act relative to the substance possessing it, though a kind of potency relative to the action it grounds (Koren 1955, p. 59). By "potency" what is usually meant is passive potency. (Cf. Koren 1960, p. 122; Renard 1946, p. 29) Pure active potency or power unmixed with any passive potency or potentiality is just pure actuality, and identified by the Scholastics with God; in everything other than God active potency is mixed with passive potency. This difference is marked by the Scholastic distinction between *uncreated* active potency and *created* active potency.

Several distinctions are also to be made in the category of passive potency. We can distinguish first between passive potency considered in relation to the thing that has it, and passive potency considered in relation to the agent which brings about an effect in the thing that has it. In the first case, we can make a further distinction between passive potency considered in relation to the *essence* of a thing, and passive potency considered in relation to its *existence*. (As we will see in chapter 4, for the Scholastic the essence of a thing is in potency relative to the thing's existence.) Where the essence of material things is concerned, we can in turn distinguish further between *prime matter*, which is pure potentiality for the reception of form, and *second matter*, which is matter which has taken on some substantial form but is in potency relative to the reception of accidental forms. (More on this in chapter 3.)

Where the second case (passive potency considered in relation to the agent that brings about an effect in the thing that has it) is concerned, we can distinguish between *natural* passive potency and *supernatural* or *obediential* passive potency. A natural passive potency points to an outcome that can be realized given only a thing's natural capacities, and can be actualized by some agent that is itself a mixture of active and passive potency. A supernatural or obediential potency points to an outcome that cannot be realized given only a thing's natural capacities, and requires as an agent a purely actual divine cause. In human beings, potencies for eating, sleeping, walking, talking, thinking, willing, writing poems or doing science, and even coming to know the truths of natural theology and natural law are for the Scholastic all natural potencies; whereas the capacity to attain the Beatific Vision is an obediential potency.

Turning to the divisions of act or actuality, the first distinction to be made is between *pure* act and *mixed* act. *Actus purus* or act utterly unmixed with any potentiality is, as has been said, the core of Scholastic philosophy's conception of God. Everything else is act in some way mixed with potency. Sometimes a distinction is made between *absolutely pure* act and *relatively pure* act. For Aquinas an angel is a relatively pure act insofar as it is a form without matter (where, as we will see in chapter 3, form corresponds to act and matter to potency). However, its essence is still in potency relative to its existence, so that it is not *absolutely* pure act. Only God is that.

In the category of mixed act we can distinguish further between *operative* act and *entitative* act. Operative act concerns a thing's operations or activities, whereas entitative act concerns what it is statically speaking. Under entitative act, we can distinguish a thing's *essential* act -- its essence or nature, *what* it is -- from its *existential* act -- its existence, or *that* it is. (Here I follow Gardeil's (1967) usage. To avoid confusion, however, it should be noted that some authors use the expression "entitative act" to refer to what I'm calling "existential act." See Koren (1955, p. 121) and Phillips (1950, p. 185), who distinguish "entitative act" in their sense from "formal act," which is what I'm calling "essential act.")

Under essential act, we can distinguish between a thing's *substantial form*, that which makes it the kind of substance it is, and an *accidental form*, which modifies an already existing substance. A thing's substantial form is sometimes called its "first act," and an accidental form a "second act." However, the expressions "first act" and "second act" are also often used in a different way, to distinguish a *power* from the *operation* of a power. For example, the power of speech is a first act or actuality, and using this power or speaking on a particular occasion would be a second act or actuality.

Combining these senses of the expressions, we can illustrate their relationship as follows. A man's having the substantial form of a rational animal is a first actuality; his having the power of speech is a second actuality relative to this first actuality. Having the power of speech is however itself a first actuality relative to the actual exercise of that power, which is a second actuality relative to the mere having of the power. Similar distinctions can be made vis-à-vis potentiality. Someone who knows no English has the potential to speak it insofar as he might learn English. That is a "first potentiality" for speaking English. Once he does learn the language he has a kind of standing ability to speak it on particular occasions if he wishes to. That is a "second potentiality" for speaking English. (This second potentiality is in turn a first actuality insofar as it is a power that can be distinguished from the exercise of the power. The actual exercise of the power to speak English would, accordingly, be in turn a second actuality.)

1.2 Causal powers

1.2.1 Powers in Scholastic philosophy

With this conceptual and terminological framework in hand, we now turn to the analysis of causation. Aristotelians famously distinguish four causes: *formal, material, efficient,* and *final.* In contemporary analytic philosophy, however, terms like "cause," "causality," and "causation" are generally used to refer to efficient causality almost exclusively. Occasionally final causality is discussed (even if, usually, only to reject the notion). Formal and material causes are not treated as causes at all. Partly for this reason, but also and more substantively because of the natural flow of the order of exposition chosen for this book, the present chapter and the next will treat of efficient and final causality alone. Formal and material causes will be dealt with in the context of the discussion of substance in chapter 3.

An *efficient cause* (also called an *agent* in Scholastic philosophy) is that which brings something into being or changes it in some way. An efficient cause thus actualizes a potency, and it does so by exercising its own active potencies or powers. In arguing for the existence of active potencies or causal powers, Scholastic writers emphasize the point that a cause is not always bringing about its characteristic effect. For instance, as the author of this book I am its efficient cause. But I am not always actually writing it. I am doing so at the moment I type this sentence, but I was not doing so three hours ago and I will not be doing so three hours from now. My *power* to write must therefore be distinguished from this or that actual, particular *action* of writing, as a standing precondition of the latter. For that matter, on the side of the patient or thing being affected (such as my computer screen, on which words appear as I write), its passive potency or potential for being changed (the correlate of the active potency or power of the efficient cause or agent) must be distinguished between this or that actual, particular instance of change, again as a standing precondition of the latter.

The distinctions between, on the one hand, a causal power or active potency and its actual exercise on any particular occasion, and on the other a passive potency or potentiality and its actualization on any particular occasion, can be seen as applications of the account of change given by the theory of act and potency. For if we were to hold instead that only actual, particular, instances of causation and actual, particular effects are real -- that there are no such things as powers and potentialities, active and passive potencies -- then we would in effect be saying that act alone is real and potency unreal. But in that case change would be impossible. (Cf. Coffey 1970, pp. 55-56; Klubertanz 1963, p. 128)

We noted above that the theory of act and potency is also applied by Scholastics to the problem of multiplicity versus unity, and in general to the explanation of how what is of itself unlimited comes to be limited. The notion of a causal power can be seen as a special case of the limitation of act by potency. Other than what is pure actuality, any cause only ever has a certain specific range of effects. It is not *unlimited* in what it may produce (pace Hume, whose views will be addressed below). A magnet can attract metal in a way a piece of wood cannot; a piece of wood can make a noise when it hits another solid object in a way that smoke cannot; and so on. A causal power qua potency just is that which limits efficacy, of itself actual and unlimited, to a specific range of outcomes. Wood has the *power* to generate noise under certain circumstances, but not the power to attract metal. (Cf. Hart 1959, pp. 230; McInerny 2004, p. 210)

As the explanatory role powers play vis-à-vis change and limitation indicates, the common charge that the Scholastic notion of powers is vacuous and explanatorily useless is unjust. The alleged problem with powers is famously summed up in Molière's joke about the doctor who explained why opium causes sleep by attributing to it a "dormitive power." Since "dormitive power" means "a power to cause sleep," the doctor's explanation amounts to saying "Opium causes sleep because it has a power to cause sleep." This, so it is claimed, is a mere tautology and thus explains nothing. But though the statement is not very informative, it is not in fact a tautology. To say "Opium causes sleep because it causes sleep" *would* be a tautology, but the statement in question says more than that. In attributing a sleep-inducing *power* to opium, it tells us that the fact that sleep tends to follow the taking of opium is not merely an accidental feature of this or that sample of opium, but belongs to the nature of opium as such. That this is not a tautology is evidenced by the fact that critics of the Scholastic notion of powers regard the attribution of a dormitive power to opium as false rather than (as they should regard it if it were a tautology) trivially true. The critics do not say: "Yes, opium has the power to cause sleep, but that is too obvious to be worth mentioning." Rather, they say: "No, opium has no such power, because there are no such things as powers in the Scholastic sense." (Cf. Martin 1997, pp. 188-90)

Acknowledging this point, Stephen Mumford notes that a critic might still object that appeal to a dormitive power is uninformative, since while it tells us that there is something about the opium itself that causes sleep, it does not tell us exactly what that is. (Mumford 1998, pp. 136-41) But this does not by itself give us any reason to doubt or deny the existence of powers. As Mumford goes on to point out, we have to distinguish between *causal relations* and *causal explanations*. Whether identifying A as the cause of B provides an informative explanation depends on our background knowledge and on the modes of presentation under which A and B are identified. But that is a separate issue from whether A is in fact causally related to B. Indeed, the latter issue is in a sense more fundamental insofar as A cannot enter into a true causal explanation of B in the first place unless A really is causally related to B.

To be sure, while the weakness of an explanation does not by itself show that the *explanans* is false, it is certainly not unreasonable to regard explanatory power as a mark of truth. But as I have indicated, that powers do play an important explanatory role is precisely why Scholastic writers affirm their existence. And it is crucial to be clear about exactly what it is they are intended to explain, if we are seriously going to address the question of whether the explanation they provide is informative. Here it cannot be emphasized too strongly that the Scholastic affirmation of causal powers is not in competition with the sorts of explanations put forward in empirical science. To say that opium has a dormitive power, for example, is not to make an assertion that conflicts with anything we know about opium from modern chemistry, because the Scholastic metaphysician is simply not addressing the same question the chemist is. The Scholastic philosopher is addressing a *deeper* question than the chemist is -- a question, not about opium *per se*, but about the necessary preconditions of there being any causality at all, whether in the case of opium and sleep or in any other case. He is claiming that in order to make sense of the facts that a cause is not constantly bringing about its characteristic effects, that its efficacy involves real change, and that its efficacy is limited in just the ways it is, we have to affirm the existence of active potencies or causal powers. *How* precisely does this or that particular cause -- opium, say -- bring about its characteristic effects? That is a question for the chemist, and the Scholastic metaphysician qua metaphysician does not claim to have an answer to it. His claim is merely that, whatever the details turn out to be, they will involve the operation of real powers.

That the attribution to opium of a dormitive power is minimally informative is, in any event, something the critic of Scholasticism cannot object to without special pleading. For the approaches the critic would pit against the Scholastic position (even if they are in fact not necessarily in competition with it) are also, considered by themselves, minimally informative. To say, as Boyle or Locke might have, "Opium causes sleep because the corpuscular constitution of opium is such that, when ingested, sleep results" -- or, to use more modern language, to say "Opium causes sleep because the chemical structure of opium is such that, when ingested, sleep results" -- is hardly more informative than saying "Opium causes sleep because it has a dormitive power." (Cf. Des Chene 1996, p. 24, n. 5; Woolhouse 1983, p. 112) If the former statements are neither tautologies nor completely uninformative -- and they are not -- then neither is the latter. Of course, the critic might reply that statements of the former sort are not intended by themselves to provide a complete explanation, but simply to make a general point about what a correct explanation will have to involve, whatever the empirical details turn out to be. But as I have said, the same thing is true of the attribution of causal powers.

There is this difference, though. As Anthony Kenny notes, we need to distinguish between the *possessor* of a power, the *power* itself, the *vehicle* of the power, and the actual *exercise* of the power (Kenny 1989, pp. 73-74). In the case of opium, its specific chemical properties are the vehicle by which its dormitive power is exercised; other substances with the power to cause sleep may do so via other specific chemical properties and thus different vehicles. The difference between the metaphysician and the chemist, then, is essentially that the former is concerned with powers and the latter with vehicles. As Kenny points out, the attempt to reduce powers to their vehicles (as the critic who takes Molière's joke to show that we can do away with powers in favor of chemistry alone proposes doing) is like the attempt to reduce powers to their actual exercise, in constituting an attempted reduction of potentiality to actuality. But just as reducing powers to their actual exercise would make act alone real, implicitly deny the reality of potency, and thus entail that change is impossible, so too would reducing powers to their vehicles have the same implication. To affirm that change is real, then, entails affirming the reality of powers as distinct from either their exercise or the vehicles by which they operate.

Some Scholastics, though, would effectively reduce powers to their *possessors*. For while Thomists take the distinction between a substance and its powers to be a real distinction rather than a merely formal or logical one, other Scholastics do not. (Cf. Coffey 1970, pp. 246-51 and 298-305; Hart 1959, pp. 226-28) We will return to this issue below.

For Scholastic philosophers in general, though, it is the possessors of powers that are causes in the strict sense. Powers are accidents of substances, not substances in their own right. It is not powers which bring about effects, but rather substances which do so, by way of their powers. Similarly, it is, primarily, not events which are causes but rather the substances that enter into events that are causes. An event involves the actualization of a potency; hence while there is a sense in which an event might be said to be a cause, since events themselves presuppose causality they cannot be the fundamental kind of cause. Neither, for the Scholastic, is it correct to analyze causality in terms of regularities or counterfactual conditions. These are *consequences* of causal relations between substances, so that to define causal relations in terms of regularities or counterfactuals is to put the cart before the horse.

Naturally, then, to understand the Scholastic position on causality requires an account of Scholastic views about substance, which is the subject of chapter 3. There is much that can be said short of that, however, and it is best approached through a consideration of recent criticisms of the post-Humean theories of causation that developed in the wake of the early modern philosophers' rejection of Scholasticism.

1.2.2 Powers in recent analytic philosophy

Contemporary analytic philosophy has seen a revival of interest in powers, dispositions, capacities, and related notions. That this is essentially a recapitulation of Scholastic themes usually thought passé has not gone unnoticed by commentators (Des Chene 1996, p. 24; Lamont 2007; Ott 2009, pp. 29-30; Runggaldier 2012). Certainly the recent arguments reinforce those made within the Scholastic tradition, while that tradition, with its own battery of arguments and fine distinctions hammered out over the course of centuries, has much to contribute to the current debate. As Mumford has noted in a useful overview of the literature (2009), recent work can be divided into that which is motivated by considerations from general metaphysics, and that which is motivated by considerations from philosophy of science. We will consider each in turn. First, however, some historical stage-setting is in order.

1.2.2.1 Historical background

The views against which analytic powers theorists have reacted were developed in the context of assumptions inherited from David Hume, who has dominated modern philosophical thinking about causation. Hume's work had itself brought to a climax a series of developments whose immediate origins lie in the debate about causation initiated by Descartes and the other early moderns who sought to overthrow Scholasticism, but which has precursors in Scholastic writers like William of Ockham and Nicholas of Autrecourt.

Ockham's theological voluntarism -- the view that the divine will is prior to the divine intellect -- led him to resist the idea that there is anything in the nature of things that might put limits on what God could command. This is what motivated his anti-realism about universals (variously interpreted as either nominalist or conceptualist). For if a thing instantiates a universal essence or nature, this would seem to imply limits on what God could will for it. For instance, if there is a universal human nature that determines that among the things that are good for us are loving God and avoiding adultery, then even God could not will for us to hate him or to commit adultery, consistent with willing what is good for us. But for

Ockham, God *could* in principle command us to do these things, and if he did so these things really would be good for us.

More to the present point, for Ockham God could also break the causal connections that ordinarily hold between things:

> Whatever God produces by the mediation of secondary causes, he can immediately produce and conserve in the absence of such causes... Every effect that God is able to produce by the mediation of a secondary cause he is able to produce immediately by himself. (*Quodlibet* 6, q. 6, in William of Ockham 1991, at p. 506)

> It follows from this that it cannot be demonstrated that any effect is produced by a secondary cause. For even though when fire is close to combustible material, combustion always follows, this fact is, nevertheless, consistent with fire's not being the cause of it. For God could have ordained that whenever fire is present to a close-by patient, the sun would cause combustion [in the patient]... Thus, there is no effect through which it can be proved that anyone is a human being – especially through no effect that is clear to us. For an angel can produce in a body everything that we see in a human being – e.g. eating, drinking, and the like... Therefore, it is not surprising if it is impossible to demonstrate that anything is a cause... (*Opera Theologica* V, 72-93, quoted in Adams 1987, p. 750)

This would seem to entail that causes and effects are inherently "loose and separate," as Hume would later put it. So too does this passage:

> Between a cause and its effect there is an eminently essential order and dependence, and yet the simple knowledge of one of them does not entail the simple knowledge of the other. And this also is something which everybody experiences within himself: that however perfectly he may know a certain thing, he will never be able to excogitate the simple and proper notion of another thing, which he has never before perceived either by sense or by intellect. (*In I Sent.*, q. 3, fol. D2, recto. F, quoted in Gilson 1999, pp. 70-71)

Indeed, Ockham also says things that seem to imply a "regularity" theory of causation, as when he writes that:

> That is the cause of something which, not being posited, the thing does not exist, and being posited, the thing exists. (*Expositio in Libros Physicorum*, fol. 123c, 203a, quoted in Weinberg 1964, p. 260)

Accordingly, some have attributed to Ockham a proto-Humean conception of causation. (See e.g. Gilson 1999 and chapter 1 of Klocker 1968.) To be sure, as Marilyn McCord Adams has argued, when all the textual evidence is considered it is clear that things are more complicated than this, and it would be a mistake to characterize Ockham's position as "Humean," full stop. (See chapter 18 of Adams 1987.) Still, there are in Ockham's voluntarism and anti-essentialism the seeds of doubt about our ability to know objective causal connections. And proto-Humean views about causality are more explicit in later Ockhamite thinkers like Autrecourt (Copleston 1993, p. 142), who argues that no proposition about a causal relation between A and its purported effect B is certain, because there is no logically necessary connection between A and B; and that the reason we regard A and B as causally related is that we have found A to produce B in the past, but cannot be certain that it will do so in the future (Marenbon 2009, pp. 49-51; Weinberg 1964, pp. 272-75).

The notion of a "secondary cause," to which Ockham refers above, is that of something which has its causal power only in a secondary or derivative way. A stock example is a stick which has the power to move a stone only insofar as it is used by someone as an instrument for moving the stone. The standard Scholastic view is that relative to God, who as pure actuality is the source of all causal power, everything else that exists is a secondary cause. But secondary causes nevertheless are true causes. However, some medieval Islamic theologians took the view that they are *not* true causes, and that only God ever causes anything. This "occasionalist" position held that no purported cause A really generates its apparent effect B, but rather that God causes B on the occasion when A is present. Autrecourt seems to have been acquainted with the arguments for this view, which relied in part on the claim that there are no necessary connections between purported causes and effects. (It is not clear, though, that Autrecourt himself was an occasionalist.)

Occasionalism would have an enormous influence on early modern philosophy. According to some interpreters, Descartes took an occasionalist view vis-à-vis the apparent causal relations between material objects (e.g. Huenemann 2008, p. 33; see Garber 1992, pp. 299-305 for detailed consideration of the evidence). Whether or not he did, his broader metaphysical commitments made such a position difficult to avoid. Given his conception of matter as pure extension, it is hard to see how force or power, by which one material object might move another, could be a property of such objects. Given his view that God is the total efficient cause of motion and that he recreates the material world from moment to moment, it is hard to see what is left for material objects to do. And of course, Malebranche and other followers of Descartes explicitly took an occasionalist line.

Berkeley, for whom physical objects are just collections of ideas and ideas are entirely passive, also adopted an occasionalist position vis-à-vis their causality. Though Leibniz did not, he did explain (what he regarded as) the false appearance of causality in physical objects by attributing it to a divinely pre-established harmony between them. Very different from the idealism of Berkeley and Leibniz was the atomistic materialism of Hobbes and Gassendi. Yet like Descartes, they had difficulty accounting for motion given their conception of matter. If the only properties of atoms are size, shape, solidity, and the like, then how can they have any force or power to move other atoms? Gassendi took motion to be imparted and preserved by God.

In general, the tendency of the early moderns was to take what Walter Ott has called a "top-down" approach to understanding the order that exists in the world (Ott 2009, pp. 5-6) and what Brian Ellis has called a "passivist" view of matter (Ellis 2002, p. 2). Aquinas and other mainstream Scholastics attributed active causal powers to material substances, and accordingly regarded the immediate source of the order they exhibit as immanent to them, their orderly behavior arising from the "bottom-up" as it were. Rejecting Scholastic powers, the early moderns came to see matter as instead entirely passive and devoid of any inner principle of change. Laws of nature, conceived of as divine decrees imposed on matter from outside and above, were Descartes' and Malebranche's alternative source of order, and other moderns would adopt a similar approach. (Cf. Osler 1996) Locke and Boyle are partial exceptions to this trend, attempting as they do to develop a notion of powers stripped of Aristotelian features like final causality and consistent with their empiricist epistemology (see Part III of Ott 2009). But for reasons we will be considering, it is doubtful that any doctrine of powers could be made consistent with these strictures, and it is no surprise that their position did not catch on.

As Kenneth Clatterbaugh notes in his study of the development of early modern thinking about causation from Descartes to Hume, at the beginning of this debate, which lasted about a century, ten propositions inherited from the Scholastics were widely accepted:

(1) There are four kinds of causation -- material, efficient, formal, and final.

(2) Forms preexist in efficient causes.

(3) Causation requires that something is "communicated" from the cause to the effect.

(4) Proper explanations are deductively inferential.

(5) Cause and effect are necessarily linked.

(6) Causes and effects are substances.

(7) Some substances are active (self-moving causes).

(8) Causation may be instantaneous.

(9) Proper explanations are in terms of the true or proper causes of change.

(10) God is the total efficient cause of everything. (Clatterbaugh 1999, p. 15)

(Clatterbaugh's proposition (10) needs qualification. As Clatterbaugh recognizes, while the Scholastics regarded God as the ultimate source of all causal power, they did not in general follow occasionalism in denying that secondary causes are true causes.)

As Clatterbaugh goes on to note:

> Each of these key propositions is abandoned in the course of the debate; only proposition (9) survives by the end of the debate, but what counts as true or proper cause is significantly changed by 1739. (Clatterbaugh 1999, p. 15)

In particular, what were regarded as true and proper causes are those identified by empirical science. But the understanding of causation Hume leaves us with, rejecting as it does both the "bottom-up" and "top-down" approaches of his predecessors, is inadequate to account for what science reveals to us. If matter is inherently passive, then causation seems to disappear altogether as an objective feature of the natural world; and if divine decree is rejected as an alternative source of the regularity that exists in nature, that regularity seems to be a brute fact, without any explanation at all.

Hume embraces both of these implications, or at least denies that we can have any real knowledge of causes or of the source of the world's regularity. Echoing Autrecourt, he holds in *An Enquiry Concerning Human Understanding* that the "constant conjunction of two objects" in our experience is what leads us to regard them as causally related, but that objectively "all events seem entirely loose and separate" rather than being necessarily connected. In principle, any effect or none might follow from any cause. The efficacy we think we perceive in things is really just a projection of our expectations onto the world. (Whether Hume actually denies outright the reality of objective causal relations or is rather a "skeptical realist" about them has, of course, been a matter of debate in recent Hume scholarship, but that is not an issue that needs to be settled for our purposes. Cf. Read and Richman 2007.)

Ockham began, Autrecourt furthered, and the early modern occasionalists completed the removal of real causality from the world and its relocation into God. Hume's position is essentially the result of removing God from the picture as well. Nor, where Hume agrees with his predecessors, is the resemblance accidental. As Ott writes, "Hume... [was] directly influenced by Malebranche... to the point of all but plagiarizing from his copy of Thomas Taylor's translation of *The Search After Truth*" (Ott 2009, p. 3). "The old saw that Hume is occasionalism minus God is," Ott judges, "not too far off the mark" (Ott 2009, p. 195).

We consider below Hume's arguments and, on the other side, the reasons Scholastic philosophers are committed to propositions like the ones identified by Clatterbaugh. Suffice it for the moment to make the following point. Contemporary accounts of causation -- regularity theories, counterfactual theories, and so forth -- have taken an essentially Humean problematic as their starting point. The tendency has, until recently, been implicitly to suppose that serious debate must take place within the boundaries Hume established. Yet the philosophical trends that culminated in Hume's analysis were both historically contingent and largely motivated by theological assumptions that neither the mainstream, non-Ockhamite Scholastic tradition nor Hume's secular admirers would accept. Those tempted to suppose that the Humean approach somehow has the burden of proof in its favor should keep this in mind. There is no *objective* reason to regard Hume's assumptions as the default ones. And as contemporary philosophers with no Scholastic ax to grind have argued, there is good reason to question them.

1.2.2.2 Considerations from metaphysics

In his *Enquiry*, Hume offers the following definition: "We may define a cause to be *an object, followed by another, and where all the objects similar to the first, are followed by objects similar to the second*" (section VII). *Regularity theories* of causation are developments of this basic idea. (See Psillos 2009 for an overview.) The thought is that the causal relationship between A and its effect B can be entirely captured in terms of the regular correlation that exists between them. No reference need be made to a power in A by which it generates B, or to any necessary connection between A and B. Causation reduces to a Humean, purely contingent "constant conjunction" of inherently "loose and separate" items.

But regularity theories are subject to several objections. (Cf. Collins, Hall, and Paul 2004b) For one thing, they have difficulty in accounting for the asymmetry between causes and effects. A regular correlation between A and B does not by itself entail that A is the cause of B, rather than B being the cause of A. Nor will adding a condition to the effect that a cause A must temporally precede its effect B easily solve the problem, since (as we will see below) some causes and effects are simultaneous. Furthermore, there are cases that the regularity approach cannot seem to handle even if we do add the condition in question. Suppose a stone is thrown into a pond, followed first by a splashing sound and ripples in the water, and a few moments later by the motion of a leaf floating in the pond a few feet away. Events similar to the leaf's motion are regularity correlated with temporally prior events like the splashing sound and ripples in water. The regularity theory would therefore seem to entail that the splashing sound and the ripples are equally plausible candidates for being the cause of the leaf's motion. But of course, in fact it is only the ripples, and not the sound, that is the cause.

A third difficulty can be seen if we add to the example the detail that a second stone is thrown toward the pond but is caught before it hits the water. Since the throwing of such stones is regularly followed temporally by events like the motion of the leaf, the regularity theory would seem to entail that the throwing of this second stone is the cause of the leaf's motion. But of course, in fact it is the throwing of the first stone alone that caused the motion, since the second stone was prevented from having any such effect.

But it is widely thought that an alternative account of causation, still Humean in spirit but immune to such objections, can be defended. Following the *Enquiry*'s definition of "cause" quoted above, Hume immediately goes on to write: "Or in other words, where, if the first object had not been, the second never had existed." Despite the "in other words," Hume here adds a condition that goes beyond regularity, a condition that forms the core of *counterfactual theories*, the most prominent defender of which is David Lewis (1973). Such theories hold that causality is essentially a matter of counterfactual dependence. It's not just that whenever A occurs, B also occurs; what makes for a causal connection between A and B is that if A had not occurred, B would not have occurred either. (See Paul 2009 for an overview and Collins, Hall, and Paul 2004a for a collection of key essays.)

Following Robert Koons (2000, pp. 21-22) and ignoring the technical details, we can summarize Lewis's counterfactual analysis of the relation of causal dependence between event tokens A and B as follows:

1. If A had not occurred, B would not have occurred.

2. If A had occurred, B would have occurred.

3. A and B both occurred.

Condition (1) states that A is a *necessary* condition (at least in the actual circumstances if not absolutely), and condition (2) that it is a *sufficient* condition, for the occurrence of B.

This sort of account, it is held, captures the asymmetry between a cause A and its effect B insofar as B depends counterfactually on A in a way A does not depend on B. Neither does the account seem threatened by examples like those involving the stone. The leaf would not have moved if the ripples had not been made by the stone, though it would still have moved had the splashing sound somehow been prevented. Hence the counterfactual account captures the fact that it was the ripples, and not the sound, which moved the leaf. And the leaf would still have moved even if the second stone had never been thrown in the first place. Hence the counterfactual account captures the fact that it was the first stone rather than the second that was causally responsible for the motion.

Such an account is nevertheless essentially Humean insofar as, like the regularity theory, it "hold[s] that causal facts are to be explained in terms of -- or more ambitiously, shown to reduce to -- facts about *what happens*, together with facts about the *fundamental laws* that govern what happens" (Collins, Hall, and Paul 2004b, emphasis in original). The difference from the regularity theory is just that the relevant laws are taken to incorporate counterfactual conditions. To say that the account analyzes causation in terms of "facts about *what happens*" is essentially to say that the analysis is entirely in terms of *actualities* rather than potentialities or powers. To say that the relevant actualities are related by "facts about... *fundamental laws*" is to say that they have no *intrinsic* or *necessary* connection to one another but are related only *extrinsically* and *contingently*. It is to say that causes are (as Ellis would put it) "passive" rather than having any active tendency to bring about their effects, and that (as Ott would put it) the connection between causes and effects is therefore imposed "top-down" via laws that could have been other than they are. Inherently, causes and effects are "loose and separate" and the "constant conjunction" enshrined in the laws that connect them reflects mere nomological necessity rather than metaphysical necessity. As with Ockham, Autrecourt, and the Islamic and early modern occasionalists, the order we find in the natural world is in no way inherent to it but is entirely imposed from outside. The difference is that this external source of order is to be identified with a set of contingent laws rather than with God.

There are problems with the counterfactual approach too, however, and they are among the reasons why some analytic metaphysicians have opted to return to an ontology of powers. C. B. Martin's "electro-fink" example has been particularly influential (Martin 2008, chapter 2). Consider a live wire, which if touched by a conductor will cause electricity to flow into it. If the counterfactual analysis were correct, then anything we might want to say about the causal relation in question here would be captured in a conditional such as the following:

If the wire is touched by a conductor, then electrical current flows from the wire to the conductor.

But suppose the wire is attached to an *electro-fink*, which is a device which renders a dead wire live when it touches a conductor or, when run in reverse cycle, renders a live wire dead when it touches a conductor. Then the conditional above will *not* be true of a wire when it is live, but *will* be true of a wire when it is dead. In particular, when the wire is live, current will not flow from it to the conductor, because it will be prevented from doing so by the electro-fink; hence the conditional fails to give necessary conditions for the wire's being live, since a wire could be live even when it is not true that it will transmit current to a conductor. And when the wire is dead, current will still flow from it to the conductor, because it will be made live by the electro-fink; hence the conditional fails to give sufficient conditions for the wire's being live, since a wire could in fact be dead even when it will transmit current to a conductor. The proper way to characterize the wire, in Martin's view, is to say that it has a *power* when it is live which is prevented from operating by the electro-fink, and lacks such a power when it is dead but is then given this power by the electro-fink -- a power the wire's having of which cannot, as Martin's example shows, simply be reduced to the obtaining of certain counterfactual conditions. An ontology of real powers, in short, captures a crucial aspect of the causal situation that the counterfactual analysis cannot capture.

Lewis attempts to solve the difficulty posed by "finks" (as examples like Martin's have come to be known in the literature) by proposing the following "Reformed Conditional Analysis" (Lewis 1997):

(RCA) Something x is disposed at time t to give response r to stimulus s if, for some intrinsic property b that x has at t, for some time t' after t, if x were to undergo stimulus s at time t and retain property b until t', s and x's having of b would jointly be an x-complete cause of x's giving response y,

where an x-complete cause of y is one that includes all the intrinsic properties of x which contribute causally to y's occurrence. The idea is that the problem in the electro-fink example is that there is at least a brief time lag between the conductor's touching the wire and the current's flowing to the conductor, a lag during which the flow is blocked by the electro-fink. But if the wire has some property b that *would* at *some* time t' *have* caused the current to flow when the stimulus of the conductor is present if the electro-fink hadn't operated as quickly as it does, then the RCA will still be true. The notion of "cause" involved in the RCA can (so it is claimed) in turn be analyzed in terms of a further counterfactual statement, giving us in effect a "double counterfactual" analysis (Nolan 2005, p. 104). Hence talk of powers can, so it is held, at the end of the day be cashed out in terms of counterfactuals.

However, finks are not the only problem cases facing the counterfactual analysis, and examples of another sort -- called "antidotes" or "masks" in the literature -- have been raised against the RCA. To borrow an example from Alexander Bird (2007, pp. 27-29), consider a fatal poison for which someone who has ingested it has also taken an antidote. Suppose the antidote works by changing the body's physiology so that the poison does not have its typical effect. This is different from "finkish" cases insofar as the poison (unlike the wire in the electro-fink example) is not changed; it is rather the environment in which it operates that changes. And the example is such that while the antecedent of the RCA is true of it, the consequent is not.

That is to say, it is true that the poison retains at *t'* the intrinsic properties that give it a disposition to kill the one ingesting it, but it is nevertheless false that at *t'* those properties result in the death of the one ingesting it. Hence we have a counterexample to the RCA.

As further counterexamples, George Molnar cites "intrinsic maskers," powers the operation of which constitute an antidote for or mask the operation of other powers (Molnar 2003, p. 93). For instance, King Midas had the power to nourish himself, but this power was masked by his power of turning everything he touched into gold. The RCA does not capture his having the first power, since though Midas always retains the intrinsic properties by virtue of which he could nourish himself, his turning the food he touches into gold prevents them from ever causing him to be nourished. Molnar also points out that conditional analyses cannot capture powers that operate continuously and unconditionally. He writes:

> Rest mass is such a power according to General Relativity. Massive objects are spontaneously manifesting their gravitational power in continuous interaction with space-time.

> Note that this line of criticism does not depend on reference to actual cases of unconditionally manifesting powers. The mere possibility of the existence of spontaneous manifestations is enough to refute relational analyses of powers in which the relation is conditionalized on some triggering event. (2003, p. 87)

Earlier it was noted that Scholastic writers argue that a thing's power to produce a certain effect has to be distinguished from its actually producing it on particular occasions, as a standing precondition of the latter, on pain of implicitly denying the distinction between potency and act and thus the possibility of change. Recent analytic powers theorists also insist on this distinction, on the basis of arguments like the following. First, powers must be distinct from their manifestations insofar as it can be possible for a thing to produce a certain outcome even though it never in fact produces it. For instance, it is possible for the phosphorus in the head of a match to generate flame and heat if the match is struck, and this is true even if the match is never in fact struck and is destroyed without ever having been used. The power of the phosphorus to generate flame and heat is what grounds this possibility.

Humeans may insist, on empiricist grounds, that there must be some observable test situation in which the manifestation would actually occur. But there could be cases where the test itself guarantees that the manifestation will *not* occur. D. H. Mellor (1974) gives the example of a nuclear reactor which has the power to cause an explosion, but never does so precisely because the safety mechanism which monitors for possible explosions shuts the reactor down before one can occur. Yet had the reactor not had the power to cause an explosion, the safety device would not have been needed in the first place.

A second argument is that a power must be distinct from any of its manifestations because they simply belong to different ontological categories. Mumford, following Ryle (1949), notes that while the manifestation of a power is a kind of *event*, a power is a kind of *state* (Mumford 2009, p. 270). Mumford adds a third argument to the effect that a power must be distinct from a manifestation insofar as at least some powers do not persist through their manifestations. (Mumford gives the example of *solubility*, which a soluble substance will not retain after it has dissolved. This would seem, however, to be an example of what Scholastics call a passive potency rather than a power or active potency in the strict sense. An example involving an active potency or power might be that of a match, which loses its power to generate flame and heat once it is struck and actually generates it.)

It is worth pausing at this point to address a terminological issue. Arguments of the sort we've been considering are often stated in terms of "dispositions" rather than "powers." This is not a difference that always makes a difference, as some writers use the terms interchangeably (e.g. Mumford and Anjum 2011, p. 4). However, not all do, and Bird insists that the verbal difference marks a genuine distinction (Bird 2013; Cf. Oderberg 2007, pp. 131-32). Whether there are powers is in Bird's view a question of what he calls fundamental metaphysics, whereas the need for a dispositional account of some phenomenon is a question of non-fundamental metaphysics. A Humean like Lewis could, Bird says, accept a dispositional analysis of some phenomenon without affirming the existence of powers. Bird's point seems to be that someone could regard a dispositional analysis as correct but still reducible (to, say, a counterfactual analysis). Powers would (if I understand Bird correctly) be dispositions which are *not* reducible via an analysis that makes no reference to dispositions.

The point is well-taken, but having noted it we can for the most part ignore it for present purposes. Metaphysics as such is concerned with the questions of what powers are, whether there must be powers of at least some sort, and if so what the implications of there being any would be. Whether irreducible powers (as opposed to mere reducible dispositions) exist in some specific corner of reality (for example, where human beings are concerned, or animals and plants, or inorganic phenomena of various sorts) would be a question for various disciplines less general than metaphysics -- philosophical anthropology and philosophy of mind, philosophy of biology, philosophy of chemistry, philosophy of physics and philosophy of nature.

According to some powers theorists, among the implications of there being powers is that a ground exists for causality that other, non-powers approaches cannot provide. Causation is just the manifestation of a power. More precisely, and as Molnar emphasizes (2003, pp. 194-98), an effect is typically "polygenic" in the sense of being a combination of the manifestations of several powers operating in tandem. Molnar gives the example of two horses pulling a barge from either side of a canal. Each horse pulls the barge in a direction at an angle from the canal, but the effect of this combination of manifested powers is that the barge moves straight ahead down the canal. This example also illustrates how powers are "pleiotropic" in the sense of making contributions to different kinds of effect. The pulling action of horse A, taken in tandem with that of horse B, may produce motion in a northerly direction, but the very same pulling action will result in motion in a different direction in other contexts.

This account allows us to see that the relationship between causation and necessity is more complicated than is often recognized. On the one hand, contemporary powers theorists typically hold that there is a necessary connection between a power and its manifestation. A stock example would be how solubility necessarily has dissolving as its manifestation. (Here we need once again to note that this seems to be an example of a passive potency rather than an active one, but examples of the latter can be substituted. For instance, the power of being a solvent necessarily has the dissolving of something else as its manifestation. Note that, for the reasons considered when discussing Molière's "dormitive power" example, to attribute the power of being a solvent to something is not trivial even if it is admittedly only minimally informative.)

On the other hand, precisely because powers are pleiotropic and an effect is typically polygenic, there are bound to be examples of cause and effect relations that are not necessary. We often say things like "Throwing the stone caused the window to shatter," but of course shattered windows don't always and necessarily result from thrown stones. The reason is that even if there is a necessary connection between a power and its manifestation, effects are typically the result of *several* active (and passive) potencies operating in tandem -- in this case, the solidity of a particular stone, the brittleness of a particular pane of glass, the strength of a particular person's arm, etc. are all relevant to the actual outcome -- and if some of these potencies are absent (or if a "fink" or "mask" is present), an effect that *would* follow when a certain power is operating in their presence (or when the fink or mask is absent) would *not* in this case follow. Drawing an analogy with forces as understood in physics, Mumford and Rani Lill Anjum (2011) characterize powers as "vectors" which combine in various ways to produce divergent outcomes. (Though Mumford and Anjum do not regard even the relationship between powers and their manifestations as either necessary or contingent, but as a *tending towards* which in their view constitutes an irreducible modality intermediate between contingency and necessity.)

This sort of account also enables us to see why counterfactual analyses of causation are at least superficially plausible but also ultimately inadequate. Given the way certain powers regularly operate in tandem and thus regularly generate the same effect, some counterfactual description of the causal situation will naturally seem correct at least initially. But given the polygeny of effects, there is bound to be some factor the addition or deletion of which will change the outcome, so that "finkish" and "masking" counterexamples will sink attempts to *reduce* causality to counterfactual dependence. The problem with Humean analyses is not so much that regularity and counterfactual dependence are not real aspects of causation, but that they are the *consequences of* causal relationships rather than being *constitutive of* causal relationships. What *is* constitutive is what can only be captured in the language of powers and their manifestations.

There are also instances of causation for which the Humean model of distinct and temporally separated events is not even prima facie plausible, but which the powers approach has no difficulty handling. Mumford cites the examples of two books leaning against one another and keeping each other from falling over, and a refrigerator magnet sitting motionless in place (2009, pp. 275-76). In such cases we have causation -- the books cause each other to stay up and the magnetic pull keeps the magnet from falling to the ground -- but it is not plausible to regard them as involving distinct and temporally separated events. For instance, it is not that the one book holds the other up and then in a later, separate event, the second book is held up. Rather, the holding up and being held up are two aspects of a single event -- or rather, not an *event* at all (since as Mumford says, "in a sense, nothing is happening") but a continuous state. And even where it is appropriate to speak of events, causation does not always involve *distinct* events. To borrow an example from Kenny, "sugar's tasting sweet to me is one and the same event as my tasting the sweetness of the sugar" (1993, p. 35; Cf. Kenny 1989, p. 102). The same point can be made even with respect to the stone breaking the window. The stone's pushing through the glass and the glass's giving way to the stone are distinct aspects of the causal situation, but they are not "loose and separate" events. They are rather two aspects of a single event. And the aspects in question are most plausibly just the ones a powers analysis would identify: the stone's active potency or power to shatter glass, and the glass's passive potency or power to be shattered. Similarly, the books, the magnet, the sugar, and the person tasting the sugar all plausibly manifest various powers even if the examples in question do not plausibly involve distinct and temporally separated events.

We have, then, a battery of arguments from contemporary analytic metaphysics that support the thesis that causal powers are real features of the world: The standard Humean alternatives are inadequate; the powers analysis captures what is correct in those alternatives and also explains why they are subject to counterexamples of the finkish and masking sort; it accounts for instances of causation for which the Humean approach is not even a prima facie plausible analysis in the first place; it explains why it is possible for a cause to generate a certain effect even if it never in fact does so; the notions of the pleiotropic and "vector"-like nature of powers and the polygenic nature of effects capture the complexity of actual causal situations (in a way Humean analyses, relying as they often do on simplistic examples of the billiard ball sort, do not); and so forth.

To be sure, there are further issues that have arisen in the contemporary debate over powers, such as how powers ever get manifested, the relationship between "dispositional" properties and "categorical" ones, and the role a power's purported "directedness" toward a manifestation plays in explaining its necessary connection to the latter. We will address these issues below. Before doing so, let us look at how considerations from the philosophy of science have also contributed to a revival of the notion of causal powers.

1.2.2.3 Considerations from philosophy of science

Nancy Cartwright argues that an ontology of powers (or "capacities," as she usually calls them) makes better sense of the analytic method employed in sciences like physics than Humean approaches can (1989; 1992, reprinted in a slightly shortened form as chapter 4 of Cartwright 1999). Controlled experiments aim to determine what effect a factor will have in idealized circumstances, acting alone in a way it does not in the ordinary course of things. For instance:

> Consider Coulomb's law of electrostatic attraction and repulsion. Coulomb's law says that the force between two objects of charge q_1 and q_2 is equal to q_1q_2/r^2. Yet, this is not the force the bodies experience; they are also subject to the law of gravity. ... Coulomb's is not the force that actually occurs; rather, it is a hypothetical power hidden away in the actual force. ...
>
> Coulomb's law tells not what force charged particles experience but rather what is in their nature, qua charged, to experience. Natures are something like powers. To say it is in their nature to experience a force of q_1q_2/r^2 is to say at least that they *can* experience this force if only the right conditions occur for the power to exercise itself; for instance, if they have very small

masses so that gravitational effects are negligible. (Cartwright 1992, p. 48)

A Humean counterfactual analysis would hold that Coulomb's law tells us the force two bodies *would* experience *if* their masses were equal to zero. But there are, as Cartwright notes, several problems with this suggestion. First, the antecedent of this conditional can never in fact be instantiated, which doesn't sit well with the Humean's insistence on analyzing causation in terms of actualities or "facts about what happens." Second, the appeal to what would happen if the masses were equal to zero suggests an interest in "what the total force would be, were there no other forces at work" (Cartwright 1992, p. 49). The counterfactual analysis itself thus seems implicitly to assume that there are powers whose operations can affect and be affected by each other. Third, that the focus is, specifically, on what would happen in circumstances where no other forces are at work -- as opposed to all the other circumstances in which a charged body might operate -- suggests a commitment to there being a specific behavior that charged bodies will by nature exhibit on their own and try to exhibit even when impeded. We have, that is to say, an implicit recognition that a power makes a unique contribution to an overall outcome -- what Molnar calls the "pleiotropic" character of powers, and what Mumford and Anjum call their "vector"-like operation.

The causal regularities the Humean would make fundamental are, in Cartwright's view, in fact an artifact of what she calls "nomological machines," relatively stable arrangements of components whose capacities or powers in combination give rise to relatively stable patterns of behavior (Cartwright 1999, chapter 3; Cartwright and Pemberton 2013). Even the fundamental laws of physics, Cartwright holds, only operate in a *ceteris paribus* way. Newton's law of inertia holds only in circumstances where no forces act on a body, circumstances which never actually obtain. Kepler tells us that planets move in ellipses, but this is only approximately true insofar as planets are always acted upon by the gravitational pull of other bodies. Kepler's law holds to the extent that it does only because the solar system constitutes a kind of nomological machine, whose components and their powers are arranged in a stable enough way that they give rise to behavior that approximates the law. Most nomological machines are, unlike the solar system, artificial, the product of experimental conditions.

Within the domain of scientific evidence for causal claims, Cartwright and John Pemberton distinguish between what they call "what-evidence," which concerns the things that enter into causal relations, and their arrangements (as in nomological machines); "how-evidence," or information about the processes these things and their arrangements are involved in; and "that-evidence," which concerns the regularities that result (Cartwright and Pemberton 2013). The trouble with Humean approaches to causation is that they deal only with "that-evidence" and cannot plausibly account (as the powers approach can) for the underlying "what-evidence" and "how evidence." Empirical science involves activities like: identifying arrangements of things in the world into nomological machines and predicting their future states; constructing arrangements so as to control future events (as when setting up experiments or making artifacts); intervening in preexisting arrangements so as to alter the usual outcomes; building up knowledge of the markers of the presence of certain powers (such as a thing's having a certain microstructure); knowledge of the particular contributions such powers make to various outcomes; and knowledge of how these contributions combine in the processes found in various nomological machines (Cartwright and Pemberton 2013, p. 104).

The Humean has to insist that all of this can somehow be captured in a set of laws connecting certain stating features of a causal situation with certain effects. Even for a simple context like the flushing of a toilet, where the powers theorist would make reference to the way the causal powers of the various component parts combine or are impeded given the circumstances and the arrangements of the parts, the Humean has to posit a complex network of laws connecting (say) the exact shape of this specific part, the exact shape of that specific part, the exact arrangement they happen to be in, the vibrations caused by nearby passing objects, etc., with exactly the sort of outcome that occurs in such-and-such a particular case. But the number and complexity of such laws that would have to be postulated is immense; the suggestion that they can be reduced to some smaller set of laws is an unbacked promissory note; and appeal to such laws is neither necessary nor what actually characterizes our practice (Cartwright and Pemberton 2013, pp. 106-108).

Stathis Psillos notes that the Humean could object that we need to appeal to regularities or Humean laws in order to identify what capacities a thing has in the first place (Psillos 2008; Cf. Psillos 2002, pp. 190-96). He might say, for instance, that we can attribute to aspirin the capacity to make a headache go away only after we have established a regular association between taking aspirin and headaches going away. But then (so the argument goes), pace Cartwright, capacities are not more fundamental than Humean law-like regularities.

Cartwright's response (2008) is that the "laws" that enter into identifying capacities are not of the Humean sort, viz. regular associations between occurrent properties (that is, actualities or "facts about what happens," as I referred to them earlier). Rather, they will be laws which themselves make reference to capacities. An example of such a law might be: *If an object of mass* m *manifests its capacity to attract an object of mass* M *a distance* r *away and nothing interferes, the second object will have an acceleration* Gm/r^2 -- where the capacity is ascribed to a property we have other ways to identify and where we have a claim about what behavior occurs when the capacity is manifested. Even if there is a sense in which "a given capacity is what it is because of the laws it participates in" (Cartwright 2008, p. 195), it is not a sense that vindicates the Humean position.

Anjan Chakravartty argues that an ontology of powers (he uses the term "dispositions") is especially useful in defending *scientific realism* (2013; Cf. Chakravartty 2007). Scientific realism is the view that our best scientific theories correctly describe mind-independent reality (as opposed, say, to being merely useful instruments for making predictions). The main consideration in its favor is, as Hilary Putnam famously put it, that "it is the only philosophy that doesn't make the success of science a miracle" (1975, p. 73). But scientific realism comes in different varieties. *Entity realism* holds that the theoretical entities posited by our best scientific theories really exist; *structural realism*, by contrast, holds that it is the structure of relations between the entities posited by such theories, rather than the entities themselves, which really exists. These are alternative ways of dealing with the problem that many scientific theories of the past have turned out to be mistaken, and currently accepted scientific theories may turn out to be mistaken too. The entity realist accommodates this fact by affirming only the existence of certain entities posited by our best scientific theories, and not necessarily the other aspects of the theories. The structural realist holds instead that it is only the relations between the entities posited by the theories that the realist need affirm, while allowing that the other aspects may be false.

One virtue of a powers ontology, in Chakravartty's view, is that it allows the scientific realist to combine insights from both of these versions of realism. The strength of entity realism is its emphasis on the idea that causal knowledge of a putative entity that allows us to manipulate it gives us grounds for believing that it is real. The strength of structural realism is its emphasis on the idea that the relational features of a theory are the ones most likely to survive theory change. Now as Chakravartty writes:

> The behaviours that entities manifest in virtue of the dispositions [or powers] they possess are generally described by scientific theories in terms of relations, often in the form of mathematical equations relating variables whose values are determinate magnitudes of the properties in question. (2013, p. 117)

To attribute *powers* to a thing, then, is both to identify its *causal* features and to do so precisely by reference to its *relations*. This unifies what would otherwise seem competing elements of the two versions of scientific realism in question.

A second unifying job a powers ontology performs, in Chakravartty's view, concerns the relationship between causation, laws, and natural kinds. All three notions commonly play a role in defenses of scientific realism, and all three are controversial. Defending them is easier when they can be shown to be tightly integrated, as they are on a powers ontology. For to attribute powers to a thing is precisely to attribute to it certain causal properties; these properties are commonly regarded as typical of the kind to which it belongs; and laws of nature can be understood as descriptions of the behavioral regularities that follow upon the manifestation of the causal powers a thing has by virtue of being the kind of thing it is.

Finally, a powers ontology affords, in Chakravartty's view, a way of dealing with a skeptical objection to scientific realism, to the effect that realism cannot account for the way that explanatory models that are equally successful but incompatible can apply to the same systems. For instance, in studies of fluid flow, it is sometimes useful to model a fluid as a continuous medium, and sometimes as a collection of discrete particles in motion. Since it cannot be both continuous and a collection of discrete particles, this might seem to pose a problem for realism. But the problem is avoided, Chakravartty argues, if we think in terms of attributing certain powers or dispositions to fluids. For a power manifests itself in different ways in different circumstances. (Recall Molnar's point about the "pleiotropic" character of powers and the "polygenic" nature of effects, and Mumford and Anjum's treatment of powers as "vectors.") We should not be surprised, then, that a fluid will by virtue of its powers behave in some circumstances in ways that makes it useful to describe it as if it were continuous, and in other circumstances in ways that make it useful to describe it in terms of discrete particles.

Other writers approaching our topic from a philosophy of science perspective have revived the Scholastic distinction between active and passive potencies -- characterizing it instead as a distinction between *powers* and *liabilities*, or between *active causal powers* and *passive causal powers* (Harré and Madden 1975; Swinburne 1979, pp. 42-44; Bhaskar 2008, p. 87; Ellis 2001, p. 110) -- and have argued that it is implicit in what science tells us the world is like. Brian Ellis writes:

> Scientists today certainly talk about inanimate things as though they believed they had such powers. Negatively charged particles have the power to attract positively charged ones. Electrostatic fields have the power to modify spectral lines. Sulfuric acid has the power to dissolve copper. (Ellis 2001, p. 109)

Of course, the Humean will insist that such talk can be cashed out in terms of laws of nature or the like. But the writers in question respond that this has things precisely backwards -- that laws of nature themselves must be explained in terms of powers and liabilities. Powers are what Ellis calls the "truth-makers" for laws of nature (Ellis 2001, pp. 112 and 222; Cf. Bhaskar pp. 45-56).

1.2.2.4 Powers and laws of nature

Here the concerns of the metaphysicians and the philosophers of science dovetail. Here we also come full circle, back around to the key notion with which the early moderns, who began the long intellectual trajectory against which recent analytic powers theorists are rebelling, sought to replace the Scholastic notion of causal powers. As noted already, because the early moderns came to regard matter as essentially passive, some of them relocated the source of activity in the world in divine decrees. Laws of nature were descriptions of how the world operated given these decrees. The idea of laws of nature was, then, originally theological. Of course, most contemporary philosophers and scientists who appeal to laws of nature don't think of them in theological terms, but it is at least an open question whether laws can be made sense of apart from God. At least one contemporary philosopher with no theological ax to grind thinks not (Cartwright 2005).

Be that as it may, it is certainly difficult to see how laws of nature, understood non-theologically, can plausibly *replace* causal powers. For what is a law of nature if it is not a divine decree? There are four main candidate answers. Empiricists maintain that a law is a regularity to be found in nature. (There are different accounts of what sort of regularity counts as a law, but that is a complication we can ignore for present purposes.) There are several objections that can be raised against this sort of view (Cf. Mumford 2004), one of them being Cartwright's point that the *ceteris paribus* character of regularities is more naturally interpreted in terms of the operation of powers rather than laws. But the point to emphasize here is that if a law is just a regularity, then it doesn't *explain* anything. For what we need to know is *why* there are just the regularities that exist in nature, rather than some other regularities or no regularities at all. We might regard some given level of regularities as a special case of deeper regularities, but this will still leave the deepest regularities unaccounted for. Calling these regularities "laws" would merely be to *re-describe* them rather than to explain them. The powers theorist, by contrast, has an explanation of these regularities, and of why they hold in a *ceteris paribus* way: they are the "pleiotropic" or "vector"-like manifestations of the powers things have by virtue of their essences. Of course, the Humean may shrug his shoulders and say the basic regularities just exist without any explanation, but that is hardly to give a *reason* for preferring laws of nature to causal powers.

Another approach would be to interpret laws *instrumentally* rather than realistically. Laws are just useful tools for making predictions, developing technologies, and the like. But this faces the Putnamesque objection that it makes a miracle of the success of science's use of the notion of a law of nature. We need an explanation of *why* laws are such useful instruments if they are not real.

One realist alternative is to regard laws as relations between universals, with universals conceived of in terms of either Platonic realism or Aristotelian realism (Dretske 1977, Tooley 1977, Armstrong 1983). It might seem that this sort of view can explain the regularities that exist in nature, without resort to powers. Things in the world are related in the regular ways that they are because they are instances of universals, which are related in parallel ways. But if we interpret this approach in a Platonic way, then we need an explanation of *how* laws conceived of as abstract entities existing outside the natural world come to have any influence on it, which merely pushes the problem back a stage. (Cf. Cartwright 2005) Yet if, following David Armstrong, we interpret it in an Aristotelian way, then the laws will depend for their existence on their instances, in which case they cannot be the explanation of those instances. (Cf. Mumford 2004, pp. 101-3). One might suggest, in the Platonic case, that the laws operate by virtue of God's using them as a blueprint when creating the world; or, in line with the standard Scholastic development of Aristotelian realism, that they pre-exist their instantiation in individual things as ideas in the divine intellect. But of course, in either case we will have brought God back into the picture, when the point was to find a non-theological account of laws.

A further objection to Armstrong's version of this position is put forward by Alexander Bird (2007). Armstrong takes universals to be related by "nomic necessitation." This is a move away from the Humean conception of things as entirely "loose and separate," but is still "semi-Humean" insofar as it relates things in such a way that they are only contingently necessary. *Given* the laws of nature which necessarily connect being an F with being a G, every individual F will be a G; but being an F and being a G could have been related by different laws instead. So, where N is nomic necessitation, given that N(F,G), it will be true that ∀x (Fx → Gx).

But, asks Bird, is it *necessary* (in a fully anti-Humean sense that goes beyond mere nomic necessitation) that if N(F,G), then ∀x (Fx → Gx)? If not, then the relationship between N(F,G) and ∀x (Fx → Gx) is either accidental, in which case we do not have an explanation after all; or it is a relation of nomic necessitation, in which case we have a vicious regress. On the other hand, if N(F,G) and ∀x (Fx → Gx) are related in a strongly necessary, anti-Humean way, then N is essentially like the relationship between powers (Bird uses the term "potencies") and their manifestations -- and thus not really a true alternative to the powers account at all. (See chapter 3 of Mumford 2007 for a useful survey of the debate over Armstrong's position.)

This brings us, finally, to the account of laws that some recent powers theorists have adopted. For Ellis (2001, 2002), a law is just a matter of a natural kind's having an essential property; and a causal law is just a matter of a natural kind's essentially having a certain dispositional property or causal power. On this view, laws of nature are necessary in the strong, metaphysical, anti-Humean sense that Armstrong's position shrinks from. Other powers theorists (such as Mumford) have opted to abandon the notion of laws as unnecessary once one rejects the passivist, anti-Aristotelian conception of nature that made the early moderns see a need for them. But even some Scholastic writers have refrained from going that far, one of them defining a law of nature or physical law in essentially Aristotelian terms as follows:

physical law, 1. an intrinsic tendency in a natural body or other nature to produce definite effects proper to its nature in a definite uniform way and measure or by determinate means...

2. the scientific or mathematical expression of this constant way in which a natural body or other nature acts... (Wuellner 1956a, p. 70; cf. Bittle 1941, p. 422, and Smith 1950, pp. 97-99)

More recently, David Oderberg (whose influences are no less Scholastic than analytic) has endorsed something like Ellis's view, holding that the laws of nature are the laws of the natures of things, the ways things will behave give their essences (2007, pp. 143-51).

Naturally, laws thus understood can hardly *replace* causal powers and the rest of the anti-Humean metaphysical apparatus, since thus understood they *presuppose* the latter. Nor does there seem to be any principled reason for affirming laws of nature if they are not to be understood in either this Aristotelian, "bottom-up" way (to borrow Ott's terminology) or the theological, "top-down" way. As Ott notes, laws understood in neither of these ways seem to be "brute facts" (2009, p. 7) -- and, he suspects, "either vacuous or incoherent" (p. 249). Certainly it is difficult to see any motivation for them, other than their provision of an *ad hoc* way of avoiding a commitment to either Aristotelian causal powers or theism.

As this lengthy excursus on contemporary analytic metaphysics and philosophy of science shows, despite the long dominance of Humeanism, an essentially Scholastic notion of causal powers is very much alive, and supported by a wide range of arguments. We will see that the same thing is true of the other main elements of the Scholastic approach to causation.

1.3 Real distinctions?

We noted above that there is disagreement among Scholastics about whether the distinctions between act and potency, and between a substance and its powers, are real distinctions. These disputes are paralleled by recent debate within analytic philosophy over the relationship between *categorical* and *dispositional* properties (where "categorical" properties correspond roughly to actualities and "dispositional" ones roughly to potencies). Properly to understand the issues requires making a number of distinctions between kinds of distinctions. (Cf. Bittle 1939, chapter XII; Coffey 1970, pp. 104-7 and 139-57; De Raeymaeker 1954, pp. 62-69; Harper 1940, volume I, pp.342-60; Koren 1955, pp. 70-74)

1.3.1 The Scholastic theory of distinctions

Scholastics define a *real* distinction as one that reflects a difference in extra-mental reality and a *logical* distinction (or "distinction of reason") as one that reflects only a difference in ways of thinking about extra-mental reality. A logical distinction can be either *purely logical* or *virtual*. It is purely logical when it is merely verbal, without any foundation in reality. The distinction between "human being" and "rational animal" is (given the Aristotelian definition of a human being) a distinction of this sort. It is virtual when it has some foundation in reality. For example, a man's nature as a rational animal is (given the Thomistic account of essence, to be discussed in chapter 4) in reality one thing, not two. But we can view it either under the aspect of rationality or under the aspect of animality, for we know of instances when animality exists apart from rationality. Hence there is a virtual distinction between the two aspects. A virtual distinction can in turn be either *major* or *minor* (or *perfect* or *imperfect*). It is major or perfect when the concepts expressing the different aspects do not include one another, as is the case with animality and rationality since (again) there are cases when the one exists without the other even though they are united in human beings. It is minor or imperfect when the concepts do include one another implicitly, as in the case of "being" and "substance," since "being" covers everything that exists, including substances, and a "substance" is a kind of being.

A real distinction, which holds entirely apart from the way the intellect conceives of a thing, can also be either *major* or *minor* (or *absolute* versus *modal*). A major or absolute real distinction is a distinction between entities, though the entities may be of different types. Most obviously, individual objects like people, dogs, trees, and stones are really distinct. Also really distinct are parts of an individual object, such as two halves of a stone, an apple and the tree it hangs from, and the paw and leg of a dog. A third instance of a major real distinction would be that between a substance and its positive accidents -- for instance, between a stone and its color. A fourth would be the distinction between accidents themselves, such as the distinction between quantity and quality. A minor or modal real distinction would be a distinction not between things but between a thing and its modes, understood as features that have no being apart from the thing. An example would the distinction between a material object on the one hand and its location or state of rest or motion on the other.

Among the marks of a real distinction, the clearest is *separability*. Hence we regard two dogs, or a dog and its leg, as really distinct because they can exist apart from each other. We regard an object and its location as really distinct because the former continues to exist even when the latter changes. But separability is not the only mark of a real distinction. Another is *contrariety of the concepts* under which things fall, i.e. an incompatibility between some of the elements of these concepts. For example, *being material* and *being immaterial* obviously exclude one another, so that there must be a real distinction between a material thing and an immaterial thing. A third mark sometimes suggested is *efficient causality* -- the idea being that if A is the efficient cause of B, then A and B must be really distinct -- though one writer objects that such a causal claim arguably presupposes, and thus cannot ground a claim about, a real distinction between A and B (Coffey 1970, p. 148).

A major or perfect virtual distinction may appear at first glance hard to distinguish from a real distinction. But the key to understanding the difference between any logical distinction and a real one is this: If the intellect's activity is essential to making sense of a distinction, it is logical; if not, it is real. Consider again the example of man's nature as a rational animal, or an animal's nature as a sentient corporeal substance. On the one hand, a man and an animal are each one thing. A particular animal's sentience is not really distinct from its corporeality, nor is either really distinct from its substancehood. It is a single substance which is at once corporeal and sentient. A particular man's rationality is not really distinct from his animality; nor, for that matter, are the sentience, corporeality, and substancehood he has by virtue of being an animal really distinct. He is a single substance which is at once corporeal, sentient, and rational. All the same, there are animals that lack rationality, corporeal substances that lack sentience, and (more controversially) substances that lack corporeality. An intellect that knows all this can therefore distinguish a man's rationality from his animality, an animal's sentience from its corporeality, and a corporeal thing's corporeality from its substancehood. Because there are animals that are not rational, corporeal things that are not sentient, etc., these distinctions have a foundation in reality. But because these things are not really distinct in men and animals themselves, and the distinction arises only when the intellect notes that there are animals without rationality, etc., the distinction is a logical one (specifically, a major virtual one) rather than a real one.

Here we come to some matters famously in dispute among Scholastics. If separability is not the only mark of a real distinction, is it nevertheless a necessary condition? Is a distinction between A and B real only if A and B are separable? Thomists answer in the negative, and thus draw a further distinction between a real *physical* distinction (which entails separability of the really distinct aspects) and a real *metaphysical* distinction (which does not entail separability). But Scotus and Suarez answer in the affirmative, maintaining that a distinction is real only when it entails separability. (Or at least this is so in created things; the Persons of the Trinity are held to be distinct but inseparable. Cf. Cross 2005, p. 109.)

Scotus also adds to the distinction between real and logical distinctions a third and intermediate kind, the *formal* distinction. (Cf. in addition to the literature on the theory of distinctions cited above: Ingham and Dreyer 2004, pp. 33-38; King 2003, pp. 22-25) Consider yet again a man's rationality and animality. Scotus agrees that there is no real distinction between them. However, the animality of a man is the same thing as the animality of a dog or any other non-human animal, and the animality of a dog is distinct from rationality (since, of course, it exists entirely apart from rationality). So the animality of a man must be distinct from his rationality. But though this distinction is not a real one, neither is it a logical one, since it reflects a difference that exists even apart from the intellect's consideration. Scotists call it a distinction between "formalities" -- the formality of animality and the formality of rationality -- and the distinction, purportedly neither real nor logical, is accordingly labeled a formal distinction.

The trouble with the notion of a formal distinction is that it is hard to see how it can avoid collapsing into either a real distinction or a virtual (and thus logical) distinction. For either the intellect plays some role in the distinction or it does not. If a man's rationality and animality are distinct *entirely* apart from the consideration of the intellect, then what we have is just a real distinction. Whereas if they are distinct because the intellect separates out the animality and the rationality on the basis of the existence of dogs and the like, then we have a logical distinction with a foundation in reality, namely a virtual distinction. There just doesn't seem to be some third, "formal" kind of distinction. However, some Scotists would argue that Scotus's formal distinction is in fact essentially the same as a virtual distinction, the difference with Aquinas being one of emphasis. A virtual distinction requires the operation of the intellect, but has a foundation in reality. Thomists emphasize the first element, thus labeling the distinction "logical." Scotus, on this interpretation, is merely concerned to emphasize the second element, the fact that virtual distinctions are grounded in mind-independent "formalities."

It is also worth noting that the motivation for drawing a purportedly intermediate formal distinction seems to disappear if we acknowledge, with Aquinas, that a real distinction need not entail separability. Since Scotus takes A and B to be really distinct only if they are separable, any two aspects of a thing that are not separable but which are evidently distinct even apart from the intellect's consideration of them will seem to be neither really distinct nor merely logically distinct, but something intermediate. This suggests an argument in favor of Aquinas's position on separability and against that of Scotus and Suarez: If every real distinction entailed separability, then there would have to be some intermediate, "formal" distinction between a real distinction and a virtual distinction; but there is no such distinction, since the formal distinction collapses on analysis into either a real distinction or a virtual distinction; so not every real distinction entails separability.

As Oderberg suggests, the claim that a real distinction entails separability is also subject to counterexamples. He writes:

> Consider a circle. It has both a radius and a circumference. There is obviously a real distinction between the properties *having a radius* and *having a circumference*. This is not because, when confining ourselves to circles, *having a radius* can ever exist apart from *having a circumference*...
>
> The radius of a circle is really distinct from its circumference, as proved by the fact that the latter is twice the former multiplied by *pi*. Since the radius is *part* of the property *having a radius* and the circumference is part of the property *having a circumference*, the properties themselves are really distinct though inseparable... [T]he same is true for triangularity and trilaterality. (2009, p. 677)

As Oderberg points out, what explains inseparability in cases like these is not identity or the absence of a real distinction, but rather the essence or nature either of the really distinct things A and B or (where A and B are qualities of a thing) of the thing whose qualities they are. "When it comes to circles (and triangles) there are mathematical laws, expressing their natures, that ensure inseparability" (p. 678).

1.3.2 Aquinas versus Scotus and Suarez

As we noted earlier in the chapter, while Aquinas regards the distinction between act and potency as a real distinction, Scotus considers it a formal distinction and Suarez a virtual distinction. Aquinas also takes the distinction between a substance and its causal powers to be a real distinction, while Scotus takes it too to be a formal distinction, and other Scholastics a virtual distinction.

A natural way to think about these disputes is as follows. Potency, all Scholastics agree, cannot exist on its own but is grounded in a thing's actualities. A rubber ball has the passive potency to be melted at a certain temperature because it is actually made of rubber; a hammer has the active potency or power to shatter glass because it is actually made of steel. Now suppose we assume, with Scotus and Suarez, that a real distinction entails separability. Then for potency to be really distinct from act, it would have to be separable from act at least in principle. But, it is generally agreed, it is not separable. Therefore, the distinction between them must not be real, but only formal or virtual. And since a causal power is a kind of potency and the substance of which it is the power is a kind of act, the distinction between them must also be formal or virtual rather than real.

The Thomist, however, can reply to this as follows. First, for the reasons already given, the notion of a formal distinction intermediate between a real and a virtual distinction is dubious; the formal distinction collapses either into a real distinction or a virtual one. If it is real, then there is no genuine disagreement with Aquinas about the nature of the distinctions between act and potency or substances and their powers. If it is virtual, then there is a genuine disagreement. If the distinctions between act and potency and a substance and its powers are not real but only virtual, however, then since change and causation involve the actualization of potency, it seems to follow that change and causation are not real features of the world. That leaves us with an essentially Parmenidean view of reality. (Cf. Coffey 1970, p. 303; Phillips 1950, p. 182) But for the reasons given earlier, the Parmenidean view is incoherent. Therefore we must conclude that since change is real, the distinction between act and potency is real; and into the bargain, we have a further argument for the conclusion that a real distinction does not entail separability.

Further arguments for the real distinction between act and potency are as follows. (Cf. Gardeil 1967, pp. 197-98) First, an act or actuality involves completeness or perfection, while a potency is a mere capacity for completeness or perfection. But clearly a perfection and a mere capacity for that perfection are really distinct. For example, being spherical (as a child's rubber ball might be) is clearly really distinct from having the mere capacity to become spherical (as a parcel of molten rubber in a toy factory might have). Hence act and potency are really distinct. A second, related argument is that if a thing already has a potency (for having a spherical shape, say), but requires a cause distinct from it in order for it to come to have the corresponding actuality, then the potency and the actuality must be really distinct.

One argument for the real distinction between a substance and its powers goes as follows. Certain powers possessed by the same substance are clearly really distinct from each other. For example, the power of seeing is really distinct from the power of hearing, as is evident from the fact that an animal can exercise its power of sight without exercising its power of hearing, and vice versa. But if these powers weren't really distinct from the substance whose powers they are, then they couldn't be really distinct from each other either. Hence they must be really distinct from the substance which possesses them. (Cf. Coffey 1970, pp. 304-305; Hart 1959, pp. 227-28)

Two further arguments go as follows. (Cf. Aquinas, *Summa Theologiae* I.77.1; Koren 1955, p. 57; Koren 1962, p. 158) First, if a substance and its powers are not really distinct, then the latter will be actualized whenever the former is. Now a substance is actual as long as it exists, but its active potencies or powers are not necessarily actualized as long as it exists. For example, the phosphorus in the head of a match obviously exists even when its active potency or power of generating flame is not being actualized, and indeed even if it is never actualized. Hence the active potency or power must be really distinct from the substance. The second, related argument is that to deny a real distinction between a power and the substance that possesses it is essentially to commit a category mistake. A power is a kind of accident, and accident is just a different category from substance (cf. the discussion to come in chapter 3). Hence a substance and its powers must be really distinct.

1.3.3 Categorical versus dispositional properties in analytic metaphysics

This dispute among Scholastic metaphysicians illuminates and is illuminated by the debate over the relationship between categorical and dispositional properties in recent analytic philosophy. We noted above that while "disposition" and "power" are sometimes used interchangeably, there is another usage on which some philosophers would accept that there are dispositions but not that there are powers. The idea is this. We can think of a *dispositional* property as one that a thing has when a certain *conditional* statement is true of it, viz. the statement that if a certain *stimulus* is present to it, then a certain *manifestation* will follow. Stock examples would be fragility, which something has when, given that it is struck by a hard object, it will shatter; or solubility, which a thing has when, given that it is submerged in water, it will dissolve. Now a philosopher who thinks there are powers or potencies in the sense operative in this chapter obviously thinks there are dispositional properties. But a philosopher could deny that there are such powers or potencies and still affirm that there are dispositions, so long as he took them to be reducible to something that was not a power or potency. He could accept that conditionals of the sort in question are true, but argue that they are made true by *non*-dispositional or *categorical* properties -- properties that a thing simply has, *un*conditionally as it were.

Stock examples of categorical properties would be shape, or having a certain structure, or spatiotemporal properties. The view that all dispositional properties can be reduced to categorical ones is called *categoricalism*. For a glass to be fragile, on this view, would just be (say) for the particles that compose it to bear a certain structural relationship to one another and for there to hold certain laws of nature governing particles bearing such a relationship. Opposing this position in recent analytic metaphysics is the *property dualist* view that there are irreducibly dispositional properties alongside the irreducibly categorical ones. And then there is *pan-dispositionalism*, which holds that all properties are *dispositional* and that there are no irreducibly categorical ones. Finally, there are monistic views which hold that there is only one kind of property but that it can be described either as categorical or dispositional. When this sort of view regards the categorical and dispositional aspects as being really there in this one kind of property, it might be labeled a *two-sided* brand of monism (also known as the *limit view* insofar as it sees the categorical and the dispositional as limits on opposite sides of a single continuum). When it regards this one fundamental property as at bottom neither categorical nor dispositional -- its categorical and dispositional aspects being just different ways we might describe it -- then it might be labeled *neutral monism*. (See Mumford 2007, chapter 5, for a useful overview of the debate between these views. Cf. Armstrong, Martin, and Place 1996; Damschen, Schnepf, and Stüber 2009; Groff and Greco 2013; Handfield 2009; Kistler and Gnassounou 2007; Marmodoro 2010; and Mumford 1998)

Armstrong, whose views on laws of nature we considered above, is a chief proponent of the view that dispositions are real but also reducible to categorical properties. He agrees that dispositions cannot be given a purely conditional analysis. There must be some "truthmaker" which accounts for *why* a conditional of the sort in question holds. But the truthmaker can in his view be identified with the categorical properties of a thing together with the laws of nature governing those properties. Given the relationship of "nomic necessitation" holding between salt's molecular structure together with the circumstance of being immersed in water, on the one hand, with dissolving on the other, it follows that if salt is put in water, it will dissolve. That is all there is to salt's having the dispositional property of solubility: categorical properties plus laws of nature. No irreducible powers or potencies need be posited. (Cf. Armstrong 1996a)

Of course, one objection to this account is that the view about laws of nature that it rests on is itself seriously problematic. In particular, and as we saw Bird object, Armstrong's conception of laws either makes of them non-explanatory brute facts, or leads to a vicious regress, or implicitly presupposes a power-like relationship between properties of precisely the sort Armstrong was trying to avoid. Another objection that has been raised against Armstrong is that categorical properties are essentially epiphenomenal, making no causal difference to the world. Their causal features are entirely extrinsic, depending on the laws that Armstrong takes to govern them only contingently; had the laws been different, the very same properties would have been associated with entirely different dispositions. What is the point, then, of positing such categorical properties if they don't do anything?

This consideration provides a motivation for pan-dispositionalism, which is defended by Mumford and Anjum (Mumford 2013; Mumford and Anjum 2011). If dispositional properties alone ever do anything, then perhaps they are the only kinds that exist in the first place. Nor, in Mumford and Anjum's view, are alleged examples of purely categorical properties compelling. Consider shape. Superficially, having a certain shape might seem to confer no dispositions on a thing, but in fact it does. It is because of the difference in shape between a knife and a ball that the former can cut things and the latter cannot. Being round, the latter has a disposition to roll that a cube does not have. And so forth. A purported counterexample Mumford and Anjum attribute to E. J. Lowe would be a soap bubble, which is round but, it is suggested, does not have a disposition to roll; another alleged counterexample is Peter Unger's case of a soft sphere which squashes flat instead of rolling (Unger 2006, p. 269). But these, Mumford and Anjum insist, are not true counterexamples at all. The soft sphere fails to roll precisely because it loses its shape, and the bubble fails to roll because while it has a disposition to do so, it also has a disposition to stick to surfaces, which counteracts the first disposition. Yet as Lowe points out, that sphericity *confers* a power or disposition still doesn't entail that it *is* a power or disposition (2006, p. 138).

An objection to pan-dispositionalism raised by Armstrong is that its account of causality seems to lead either in a circle or a vicious regress. A disposition is the disposition it is only by reference to its characteristic manifestation. But if all properties are dispositions, then a manifestation will itself be a further disposition. The disposition to produce A will just be the disposition to produce the disposition to produce B, which will in turn be the disposition to produce the disposition to produce C, and so on. Writes Armstrong:

> All serious distinction between powers and the manifestation of powers gets lost... Causality becomes the mere passing around of powers from particulars to further particulars. To put it scholastically, the world never passes from potency to act... *nothing ever happens...* There may not be a contradiction here, but it is position that I find unbelievable. (Armstrong 2005)

Mumford replies that a "passing around" is a kind of event, so that something plausibly *is* happening on the pan-dispositionalist analysis. Armstrong's chief complaint, in Mumford's view, is really that he finds irreducibly dispositional properties "mysterious" (Armstrong 1996b, p. 91). Writes Mumford:

> Indeed, it appears that he thinks that the things that are passed around are not real at all. Pure powers... are thought of by Armstrong as mere potencies: potential rather than actual.... [But the] realist about dispositions or causal powers will accept such powers to be real enough... [Powers] are certainly assumed as actual in their own right, whether or not they are manifested... When I ascribe a disposition I ascribe it actually and unconditionally. Passing round of powers would be for the realist, therefore, the passing round of something actual. (Mumford 2007, p. 88; Cf. Mumford and Anjum 2011, p. 6)

As Lowe points out, though, the trouble with the threat of regress or circularity is not merely Armstrong's concern about whether anything can ever happen on such an account. It is that no property can get its identity fixed on a pan-dispositionalist account (2006, p. 138; Cf. Robinson 1982, pp. 114-15). The nature of a property A will be determined by reference to a property B, whose nature will be determined by reference to a property C, whose nature will be determined by reference to D, and so on either ad infinitum or in a way that leads us back to A. So what is the nature of A? If we say that the series goes on to infinity, then we never actually give the nature of A but just keep deferring the question forever; if we say that the series loops around back to A, then we give the nature of A by reference to the nature of A, which is no answer at all. Bird, who also defends pan-dispositionalism, suggests that the problem can be solved by appealing to the mathematical field of graph theory (2007, chapter 6). A power or dispositional property can be uniquely identified by the position it occupies in an asymmetric graph. As Oderberg argues in reply, though, even when a node in such a graph can be given a unique definition, the definition will still be circular, so that the problem is not really solved at all (2012a; Cf. Oderberg 2011 and 2012b).

The "two-sided" or "limit view" version of monism has been defended by Martin (Martin 1996), and the "neutral monist" version by, at one point, Mumford (1998). Mumford has, under the influence of Molnar (2003), since given the latter view up as insufficiently realist about dispositions (Mumford 2013). And Armstrong poses a dilemma for Martin's version. Is the relationship between the categorical and dispositional "sides" of properties contingent or necessary? If it is contingent, then the categorical "side" could have been associated instead with different dispositions or even with no disposition. But in that case, what does it amount to to call the disposition a "side" of this property? If, on the other hand, the disposition is necessarily connected to the categorical side, then whatever causal work is supposed to be done by the dispositional "side" will necessarily flow from the categorical "side" to which it is connected. And in that case we might as well "cut out the middleman" and take the categorical to be what produces effects (Armstrong 1996b, pp. 95-96; cf. Mumford 2007, p. 85).

This leaves the property dualist view that categorical and dispositional properties are distinct and equally fundamental. It has been defended by Ellis (2001), Molnar, (2003), and U. T. Place (1996). Against the categoricalist claim that the causal powers of a thing can be accounted for in terms of categorical properties like structure, Ellis and Caroline Lierse object:

> [T]he causal powers of things cannot be explained, except with reference to things that themselves have causal powers. Structures are not casual powers, so no causal powers can be ex-

plained just by reference to structures. For example, the existence of planes in a crystal structure does not by itself explain its brittleness, unless these planes are cleavage planes -- that is, regions of structural weakness along which the crystal is disposed to crack. But the property of having such a structural weakness is a dispositional property that depends on the fact that the bonding forces between the crystal faces at this plane are less than those that act elsewhere to hold the crystal together. Therefore the dispositional property of brittleness in a crystal depends not only on the crystal's structure, but also on the cohesive powers of its atomic or molecular constituents. However, cohesive powers are causal powers. (Ellis 2001, pp. 115-16; adapted from Ellis and Lierse 1994).

Here the considerations raised by Armstrong and Mumford against the other views might seem to pose a dilemma for the dualist. Are categorical properties themselves efficacious or not? If so, then it is hard to see why distinct dispositional properties are needed in order to account for causality, in which case we might as well opt for Armstrong's categoricalism. But if they are not, then they are epiphenomenal and do no explanatory work, in which case we might as well opt for Mumford and Anjum's pan-dispositionalism. (Cf. Mumford 2007, p. 83) But Ellis and Lierse hold that though spatial, temporal, and other categorical properties are not causal powers, we know they are there because they enter into the laws that describe the operation of causal powers. For instance, spatial separation will be relevant to the strength of gravitational attraction or electrical repulsion. (Cf. Ellis 2001, pp. 137-38; Cf. Ellis 2002, pp. 171-76) Molnar too argues that the operation of powers is "location-sensitive" -- citing, like Ellis and Lierse, the role distance plays in the operation of a force -- so that for a categorical property like location to be causally inert is not for it to be causally irrelevant (2003, pp. 162-65). Place (1996) argues that there is a sense in which a categorical property causes a disposition -- the structure of a crystal is, after all, what makes it brittle. A manifestation might be seen, then, as the *direct* effect of a disposition and the *indirect* effect of the underlying categorical basis of the disposition (which causes both the disposition and, through it, the manifestation). In these different ways, the property dualist can defend the claim that both categorical and dispositional properties do real explanatory work.

Naturally, Scholastic philosophers will tend to sympathize less with categoricalism than with those views which affirm irreducible dispositions, as marking a welcome departure from Humean orthodoxy and a rediscovery of potency as a real feature of the world. They might also favor property dualism over the various monistic brands of dispositionalism, as closer to the Scholastic insistence on the reality of both act and potency. However, they are also bound to regard the recent debate, however salutary, as still too beholden to Humean metaphysical assumptions and insufficiently nuanced in the distinctions it presupposes.

For example, as the passage quoted above indicates, Mumford essentially agrees with Armstrong that everything real must be actual. Armstrong's view is that since irreducible dispositions or powers are not actual, they are therefore not real; while Mumford argues that since they are real, they are actual. Yet the whole point of the Aristotelian theory of act and potency is that, contrary to Parmenides' assumption, actuality does not exhaust reality -- that *being-in-potency* is a middle ground between *being-in-actuality* and sheer nothingness or non-being. Similarly, Molnar claims that a power is an "actual property" rather than an "unrealized possibility" (2003, p. 126), while Martin says:

> Dispositions are actual though their manifestations may not be. It is a common but elementary confusion to think of unmanifesting dispositions as unactualised *possibilia*; though that may characterize unmanifested manifestations. Armstrong appears to be guilty of this confusion in his reference to 'potential being'... (Martin 1996b, p. 176)

This too is a false dichotomy and misses the Scholastic philosopher's point. As we have seen, Scholastics distinguish between *logical or objective* potencies on the one hand and *real or subjective* potencies on the other. Unrealized possibilities or *possibilia* would fall into the former category, but causal powers fall, not into the class of actualities, but rather into the class of real or subjective potencies -- potencies that are in a real, concrete subject rather than being mere abstract possibilities. Galen Strawson (2008), who argues for the identification of the dispositional and the categorical, presupposes that there can be no real distinction between A and B unless A and B can exist apart. But this, of course, simply begs the question against the Thomistic view that a real distinction does not entail separability. (Cf. Oderberg 2009)

Ellis seems at least to hint at the needed distinctions and at a more thoroughgoing challenge to prevailing suppositions when he says that dispositions need be grounded only in "occurrent" rather than categorical properties, and notes that the idea that the fundamental occurrent properties must be causally impotent and thus categorical rather than dispositional reflects a Humean set of assumptions (2001, pp. 116-17; on "occurrent," cf. Lowe 2006, p. 139 and Oderberg 2007, p. 132). As this indicates, the notion of the "categorical" is not exactly the same as the Scholastic notion of "actuality," since Scholastics by no means regard actualities as per se causally impotent. Nor, as we have seen, is the notion of the "dispositional" exactly the same as the Scholastics' notion of potency, insofar as some dispositionalists take dispositions to be actualities. "Categorical" and "dispositional" properties are also often spoken of as if they could at least in principle exist apart from one another. As Oderberg points out, from the point of view of the theory of act and potency, this just gets things fundamentally wrong. There is no such thing as potency without act, and (apart from God, who is pure act) no such thing as act without potency (Oderberg 2007, p. 138). Potency always presupposes some actuality that shapes or circumscribes it. A power is a power to generate *this* particular manifestation rather than *that* one, and reflects the form of the substance having the power, a form which actualizes its otherwise indeterminate prime matter. (See chapter 3.) Act, in any finite and changing substance, always presupposes some potency as the principle which limits it and accounts for its changeability. Potency and act are both *really distinct* and *inseparable*. Certainly, merely to suppose otherwise is to beg the question against the Scholastic position rather than to refute it. Or at least, it is to beg the question against the Thomistic version of the Scholastic position.

In particular, the categoricalist and the pan-dispositionalist essentially presuppose, with Scotus, Suarez, and Descartes, that a real distinction between what they call categorical and dispositional properties would entail separability. The categoricalist starts with the idea that dispositional properties cannot exist apart from the categorical properties in which they are grounded, and concludes that they must be reducible to categorical properties. The pandispositionalist starts with the idea that we should take purported categorical properties seriously only insofar as they have causal power, and concludes that if they have it then they are really just powers or dispositional properties. The "two-sided" and "neutral monist" views allow for both the categorical and dispositional only insofar as they are really just aspects of the same property. But if a real distinction does not entail separability, then we need not infer from the dependence of the "dispositional" on the "categorical" that the former is reducible to the latter, or from the efficacy of the "categorical" that it must really be "dispositional," or from the reality of both the "dispositional" and the "categorical" that they must really in some sense be the same property. Nor, from the real distinction between the "dispositional" and the "categorical," would we need to infer to a form of property dualism on which they could exist apart from one another.

Given the baggage associated with "categorical" and "dispositional" in contemporary philosophy, the Scholastic will in any event prefer to stick to the traditional jargon of act and potency. He might also be forgiven for thinking that while each side of the current debate has grasped an important part of the truth that the theory of act and potency seeks to capture -- the categoricalist, the insight that actuality is fundamental to reality; the various brands of dispositionalism, the insight that we cannot make sense of causation without potency -- both sides have also missed the larger picture, the set of problems that spawned the development of the theory of act and potency in the first place. Making all of reality "categorical" or actual entails a return to Parmenidean static monism; making all of reality "dispositional" or potential threatens a return to Heraclitean dynamic monism. But neither the Parmenidean nor the Heraclitean extremes are ultimately coherent, and the only way to avoid them is to affirm both act and potency as really distinct, even if inseparable, aspects of reality.

2. Causation

2.1 Efficient versus final causality

Aristotelians famously distinguish between *efficient* and *final* causes. An efficient cause is that which brings something into existence or changes it in some way. It is also called an "agent" or "agent cause" in Scholastic philosophy. It is, more or less, what is usually meant by "cause" in contemporary philosophy. A final cause is an end, goal, or purpose, "that for the sake of which" something exists or occurs (Aristotle, *Metaphysics*, Book V, Chapter 2). Final causality is sometimes referred to as "teleological causation" in contemporary philosophy.

Where final causality or teleology is concerned, several crucial distinctions need to be kept in mind so that common misunderstandings are avoided. (See Feser 2010 for a detailed discussion.) First, we need to distinguish *intrinsic* finality from *extrinsic* finality. That the parts of a watch are directed toward the end of telling time has nothing to do with the nature of the parts themselves. The time-telling function is imposed on the parts entirely from outside, by the watchmaker and the users of the watch. The finality here is thus extrinsic. By contrast, the tendency of an acorn to grow into an oak is intrinsic to it in the sense that it is just in the nature of an acorn to grow into an oak. Whereas the metal bits of a watch would still be metal bits whether or not they played a role in a timepiece, an acorn would not be an acorn if it did not have a tendency to develop into an oak. (This distinction is very closely connected to the Aristotelian distinction between artifacts and true substances, which will be examined in chapter 3.)

As this indicates, there is also a second distinction to be drawn between an *end or goal* on the one hand, and a thing's *directedness toward* that end or goal on the other. Hence there is a difference between the end of telling time, and the parts of a watch functioning together so as to realize that end; and there is a difference between the end of becoming an oak, and an acorn's pointing to that end. An end or goal is itself always extrinsic to a thing. Actually telling time is different from the parts of a watch having the function of telling time. Actually being an oak is different from an acorn's having a tendency to become an oak. But the *directedness toward* an end is not always extrinsic. Sometimes it is extrinsic, as in the case of the watch parts, but sometimes it is intrinsic, as in the case of the acorn.

We need to distinguish, third, between the question of *whether* finality exists in a thing and the question of what the *source* of a thing's finality is. These are sometimes conflated. In particular, atheists and theists alike often conflate the question of whether there is finality or directedness toward an end in nature with the question of whether there is a divine intelligent cause of such directedness. These questions, though obviously related, are distinct, and several possible views need to be differentiated. There is, first of all, the view that there is such directedness in nature and that its direct source is the divine intellect. This sort of view can be found in Anaxagoras, Plato (in the *Timaeus*), Newton, and William Paley. Christopher Shields (2007, p. 74) labels it *teleological intentionalism*, and André Ariew (2002, 2007) has called it *Platonic teleology*. They contrast it with *Aristotelian teleology*, according to which there is directedness toward an end in natural objects, but that it is the nature of those objects that is the source of this directedness. An acorn is directed toward becoming an oak simply because that is what it is to be an acorn, not because a divine intelligence so directs it.

The view is called "Aristotelian" because while Aristotle affirmed the existence of a divine Unmoved Mover, as commonly interpreted he did not think the finality of things as such needed a divine or any other intelligent cause (cf. Johnson 2005). Their natures alone sufficed to explain their directedness toward an end. (The idea of natural teleology without a divine source has recently been defended in Nagel 2012.) But there is a middle ground position between Aristotle's view so interpreted and the Platonic view, which is the Scholastic or at least Thomistic view of teleology. On this view, the *proximate* source of natural teleology is the nature of the things themselves, while the *distal* source is the divine ordering intellect. This is the view defended in Aquinas's Fifth Way, which affirms the Aristotelian view that finality is intrinsic to natural phenomena while nevertheless arguing that it must ultimately depend on God (Feser 2009, pp. 110-20; Feser 2013b). (This parallels Aquinas's concurrentist view of efficient causality, on which things have -- contra occasionalism -- real causal power, but that divine concurrence is nevertheless necessary for any cause to be efficacious.)

An implication of the Thomistic view is that the question of whether natural teleology exists can be bracketed off from the question of whether it has a divine source. While the Thomist holds that natural teleology depends necessarily on God, he also holds that this thesis requires further argumentation, beyond the argumentation required to establish that natural finality exists in the first place. Hence the naturalist metaphysician cannot dismiss the idea of natural teleology merely on the basis of his atheism.

The question of whether finality exists in nature must also be distinguished from the question of whether irreducible teleology exists in the biological realm. For the Scholastic philosopher of nature, the key to the difference between living and non-living things lies in the distinction between *immanent* and *transeunt* (or "transient") causation (Klubertanz 1953, pp. 47-50; Koren 1955, chapter 1; Oderberg 2007, pp. 194-7; Oderberg 2013). Immanent causation begins and remains within the agent or cause (though it may also and at the same time have some external effects); and typically it in some way involves the fulfillment or perfection of the cause. Transeunt causation, by contrast, is directed entirely outwardly, from the cause to an external effect. An animal's digestion of a meal would be an example of immanent causation, since the process begins and remains within the animal and serves to fulfill or perfect it by allowing it to stay alive and grow. One rock knocking another one off the side of a cliff would be an example of transeunt causation. Living things can serve as transeunt causes, but what is characteristic of them is that they are also capable of immanent causation in a way that non-living things are not. A living thing can undertake activity that is *perfective* of it, that *fulfills* it or *furthers its own good*, while non-living things cannot do this.

In this way a living thing aims at a unique kind of end or goal. But it is only its having this specific *sort* of end or goal, and not the having of an end or goal as such, that makes it a living thing. For the

Scholastic metaphysician, finality is not confined to the biological realm and it is therefore not to be identified with immanent causation or biological function, which represent only one kind of finality. There is also finality or teleology in inorganic systems insofar as they are cyclical or tend toward certain end-states (Oderberg 2008; Cf. Hawthorne and Nolan 2006 for a sympathetic non-Scholastic treatment). More generally, there is finality wherever there is efficient causation of even the simplest sort.

That efficient and final causality go hand in hand is already implicit in the theory of act and potency. Efficient causation is just the actualization of a potency. But a potency is always a potency *for* some specific outcome or range of outcomes, and in that sense entails finality or directedness. Indeed, while early modern philosophers like Bacon and Descartes minimized the importance of final causes and later moderns would come to deny their reality altogether, for Scholastics like Aquinas, efficient causality, and indeed all of Aristotle's four causes, *presuppose* final causality. Hence in the *Commentary on Aristotle's Metaphysics*, Aquinas writes:

[E]ven though the end is the last thing to come into being in some cases, it is always prior in causality. Hence it is called the cause of causes, because it is the cause of the causality of all causes. For it is the cause of efficient causality, as has already been pointed out... and the efficient cause is the cause of the causality of both the matter and the form, because by its motion it causes matter to be receptive of form and makes form exist in matter. Therefore the final cause is also the cause of the causality of both the matter and the form. Hence in those cases in which something is done for an end (as occurs in the realm of natural things, in that of moral matters, and in that of art), the most forceful demonstrations are derived from the final cause. (V.3.782)

This indicates that formal and material causes depend on final causes by way of efficient causes, but Aquinas asserts an even more direct link in *De principiis naturae*:

[T]he end does not cause that which is the efficient cause, rather, it is a cause of the efficient cause's being an efficient cause. For health -- and I mean the health resulting from the physician's ministrations -- does not make a physician to be a physician; it causes him to be an efficient cause. Hence, the end is the cause of the causality of the efficient cause, for it makes the efficient cause be an efficient cause. Similarly, it makes the matter be matter, and form be form, since matter receives a form only for some end, and a form perfects matter only for an end. Wherefore the end is said to be the cause of causes, inasmuch as it is the cause of the causality of all the causes. (IV.24; Cf. *Commentary on Aristotle's Physics* II.5.186)

We will consider the nature of efficient causality in more detail below, and examine formal and material causes in chapter 3. For the moment let us consider why in Aquinas's view the reality of efficient causality entails the reality of final causality.

2.2 The principle of finality

2.2.1 Aquinas's argument

Consider an ice cube's tendency to cause the liquid or air surrounding it to grow cooler, or the tendency of the phosphorus in the head of a match to generate flame and heat when the match is struck. These, specifically, are the effects the ice cube or phosphorus will reliably bring about unless somehow impeded (for instance, by melting the ice cube before it has a chance to cool its surroundings, or by damaging the match by submerging it in water). The ice cube will cool the surrounding air *rather than* heating it, or causing it to become toxic, or having no effect at all; the phosphorus will cause flame and heat *rather than* frost and cold, or the smell of lilacs, or no effect at all. That the ice cube and phosphorus have just the specific effects they do in fact have rather than some others or none at all – or, counterfactually, that they would have had those specific effects had they not been impeded – is in Aquinas's view explicable only if we suppose that there is something in them that is *directed at* or *points to* precisely those outcomes rather than any others, as to an end or goal. In short, if A is by nature an *efficient* cause of B, then generating B must be the *final* cause of A. As Aquinas says, "every agent [i.e. efficient cause] acts for an end: otherwise one thing would not follow more than another from the action of the agent, unless it were by chance" (*Summa theologiae* I.44.4; Cf. *Summa theologiae* I-II.1.2 and *Summa contra gentiles*

III.2). Later Scholastics would come to refer to this as the *principle of finality*. (See Bittle 1939, chapter XXXIII; Coffey 1970, chapter XV; De Raeymaeker 1954, pp. 270-75; Hart 1959, chapter XII; Klubertanz 1963, chapter VIII; Koren 1960, chapter 14; Phillips 1950b, pp. 245-54; Renard 1946, pp. 144-61; Smith and Kendzierski 1961, chapter VIII; and for a recent defense from outside the Scholastic camp, Hoffman 2009)

Aquinas is not to be read as regarding chance as an alternative explanation, however. For one thing, that A generates B in a *regular* way tells against the connection being a chance one. As Aquinas says in the first stage of the Fifth Way:

We see that there are things that have no knowledge, like physical bodies, but which act for the sake of an end.

This is clear in that they always, or for the most part, act in the same way, and achieve what is best. This shows that they reach their end not by chance but in virtue of some tendency. (*Summa theologiae* I.2.3, as translated in C. F. J. Martin 1997, p. 179)

For another thing, in Aquinas's view chance *presupposes* finality, and so provides no genuine alternative at all. Chance is nothing more than the accidental convergence of non-accidental lines of causation. To take a stock example from Boethius, suppose a farmer discovers treasure buried in the field he is plowing (*Consolations of Philosophy*, Book V, Chapter 1. Cf. Aristotle, *Physics*, Book II, Part 5). The discovery was in no way intended by either the farmer or the person who buried the treasure, nor is there any causal regularity in nature connecting plowing and the discovery of treasure. Still, the farmer did intend to plow, someone did intend to bury the treasure, and there are all sorts of natural causal regularities instantiated when the farmer plows the field and discovers the treasure. These regularities, as well as the actions of the farmer and the burier of the treasure, all involve finality. In Aquinas's view, it would therefore be incoherent to suggest that causal regularity can be accounted for by chance *rather* than finality, since to make sense of chance itself we need to *appeal* to finality.

Now modern philosophers would generally hold that we needn't appeal to chance *or* finality, insofar as efficient causality alone suffices to account for causal regularities in the natural world. Such a view can even be found in some Scholastic thinkers. William of Ockham denied that it could be demonstrated through natural reason that final causes exist in non-rational natural objects. In his view, only agents with free will clearly exhibit teleology:

> [S]omeone who is just following natural reason would claim that the question 'For what reason?' is inappropriate in the case of natural actions. For he would maintain that it is no real question to ask for what reason a fire is generated; rather, this question is appropriate only in the case of voluntary actions. (*Quodlibet* 4, q. 1, in William of Ockham 1991, at p. 249)

To the argument that without final causes, an agent or efficient cause would act by chance rather than reliably generating its associated effect, Ockham responds:

> I reply that this argument goes through for a free agent, which is no more inclined by its nature toward the one effect than toward the other. However, the argument does not go through for a natural agent, since an agent of this sort is by its nature inclined toward one determinate effect in such a way that it is not able to cause an opposite effect. This is evident in the case of fire with respect to heat. (Ibid.)

In general, Ockham held that apart from revelation, we could know very little about teleology:

> If I accepted no authority [i.e. the truths of faith], I would claim that it cannot be proved either from propositions known per se or from experience that every effect has a final cause that is either distinct or not distinct from its efficient cause. For it cannot be sufficiently proved that every effect has a final cause. (Ibid., p. 246)

The tendency to associate teleology only with rational agents is even more pronounced in the work of John Buridan. As Dennis Des Chene writes:

> Ockham had already argued, following Avicenna, that the final cause acts only by virtue of existing in the intellect of an agent; to which Buridan added that when it acts thus, it acts as an effi-

cient cause, and that where the agent is not such as to conceive the ends by which it acts, there is no final cause at all, only efficient causes. To the argument that if there were no ends in nature, then one thing would follow from another haphazardly, Buridan replies (as we would) that efficient causes suffice. (1996, pp. 186-87)

Des Chene himself develops this objection to the argument for the principle of finality as follows:

The [Aristotelian] argument is, on its face, unconvincing. Everyone agrees that efficient causes necessitate their effects ("if the cause is given, so is the effect," writes Eustachius with his usual brevity...). So people will not emerge from the sea ever if they do not always: one does not need ends to account for that regularity. Given that we have not seen any such occurrence, and that the sea remains constant in composition, there is no reason to expect that the weird event will occur. Likewise, if people have always given birth to people, and birds to birds, and if they remain constant in composition, then there is no reason to expect that people will bear birds or birds people. So if the regularity to be explained is 'people give birth only to people, and no other kind of thing does', then an appeal to the necessity of efficient causes seems to suffice. (Ibid., p. 178)

But the objection fails. For we need to know what it *means* to say that efficient causes necessitate their effects, and we need an *explanation* of this necessitation. Now the necessitation either involves something intrinsic to the causes and effects, or it does not; and either possibility poses grave problems for the view that efficient causation suffices to account for regularity.

Consider first the possibility that necessitation involves something *extrinsic* to the causes and effects themselves. On this view, that an efficient cause A necessitates its effect B has nothing to do with A or B themselves, but with something else. But what is this something else? One option is to hold that *God* ensures that B follows upon A. But that just raises the question of *how* God does so. If we answer that He efficiently causes B merely by necessitating it, then we have simply pushed the problem back a stage rather than solved it. If we answer instead that He causes B by virtue of having it in view as an *end*, then we will have resorted to finality after all and given up the view that efficient causation alone suffices to account for regularity. (The proposal also has an obvious theological drawback insofar as it seems to entail occasionalism.)

Rather than appeal to God, though, might we not say that it is a "law of nature" that B follows upon A? Yet as we noted earlier, the appeal to "laws of nature" *by itself* hardly suffices to explain anything, for it just raises the question of what "laws of nature" are and why they hold. Now if we say that a law of nature is simply a kind of regularity, then we are led into either a vicious circle or a vicious regress, since the regularity of the connection between A and B is what we're trying to explain in the first place. For to explain regularities in nature in terms of efficient causal necessitation, efficient causal necessitation in terms of laws of nature, and laws of nature in terms of regularities, would be to go around in a circle; while if, to avoid this circularity, we say that the regularity enshrined in a law of nature is of a *higher order* than the sort we started out trying to explain, then we will now need an account of this higher-order regularity, and will thereby merely have pushed the problem back a stage rather than solved it.

To explain "laws of nature," then, we cannot appeal to regularity. And if, to explain them, we appeal instead either to higher-order instances of efficient causal necessitation or higher-order laws of nature, we will once again merely have pushed the problem back a stage rather than solved it. While if we explain laws of nature by reference to God, we will merely have reintroduced at a higher level the very problems the appeal to laws of nature was supposed to help us avoid. The only remaining alternative would seem to be to appeal instead to the Aristotelian idea that "laws of nature" are really a shorthand for a description of how things act given their natures. But this would be to concede that there is, after all, something *intrinsic* to A and B that explains the efficient causal relations holding between them, and thus to abandon the suggestion that the necessitation we've been discussing is *extrinsic* to causes and effects.

So, treating causal necessitation as grounded in something *extrinsic* to causes and effects would seem a hopeless strategy for anyone who wants to defend the view of Ockham, Buridan, and Des

Chene that efficient causation suffices to explain regularity. The only realistic option is to treat the necessitation as grounded in something *intrinsic* to the causes and effects. In particular, since an effect B doesn't even exist until generated by its efficient cause A, the necessitation will have to be grounded in something *intrinsic to A*. But what can this intrinsic feature be if it is not the very inclination to an end that Aquinas affirms and that the view in question is trying to avoid? What can it possibly be for A to be such that it *necessitates* the generation of B, other than that there is something in A that *inherently "points"* to the generation of B *specifically*, even before it actually generates B? It seems the only possible alternative intrinsic explanatory feature would be some further instance of efficient causal necessitation internal to A. But this would just raise the same questions all over again – and it would, yet again, thus lead the purported explanation of regularity in terms of efficient causes alone into either vicious regress or vicious circularity. (Cf. Garrigou-Lagrange 1939, pp. 356-58)

There seems, then, to be no way to avoid Aquinas's conclusion that to make efficient causal regularities intelligible we need to attribute finality to efficient causes. Every attempt to avoid doing so merely raises further puzzles which cannot be solved except by admitting finality. But it might seem that the defender of the view that efficient causes alone suffice to account for regularity has one more arrow in his quiver. For isn't Aquinas's position open to the same sorts of objection as his opponent's view is? In particular, if Aquinas holds that efficient causal regularities need to be accounted for by reference to final causes, can it not be said with equal plausibility that final causes in turn need to be accounted for, and that accounting for them will also lead to vicious regress or vicious circularity? Aren't the two positions – Aquinas's on the one hand, and that of Ockham, Buridan, Des Chene, and modern philosophers in general on the other hand – therefore at least at a stalemate?

In fact such a comparison would be spurious. The two views would be on a par only if each made use of its favored notion of causation *to the exclusion* of the other. And Aquinas is doing no such thing. His critic holds that efficient causes *suffice* to explain the regularity that exists in the world, so that no appeal to finality is necessary; indeed, naturalist philosophers typically hold that final causes are ultimately not needed to explain *any* aspect of the natural world (or at least that any teleological notions that are needed can be reduced to non-teleological ones). But Aquinas does not hold that final causality *suffices* to explain either regularity or natural phenomena in general. He merely holds that it is a *necessary part* of a complete explanation. As an Aristotelian, he is committed to the explanatory indispensability of *all* of the traditional four causes – material, formal, efficient, and final – each of which has its place:

> Matter, indeed, is prior to form in generation and time, inasmuch as that to which something is added is prior to that which is added. But form is prior to matter in substance and in fully constituted being, because matter has complete existence only through form. Similarly, the efficient cause is prior to the end in generation and time, since the motion to the end comes about by the efficient cause; but the end is prior to the efficient cause as such in substance and completeness, since the action of the efficient cause is completed only through the end. Therefore, the material and the efficient causes are prior by way of generation, whereas form and end are prior by way of perfection. (*De principiis naturae* IV.25, in Aquinas 1965c)

There is no parity between the view of Aquinas and that of his critic, then. The critic has tried to show that efficient causes suffice to explain regularity, and has failed. Aquinas has not tried to show that final causes suffice to explain it, only that efficient causes do not and that reference to finality is needed as well. In failing to make his own case, the critic has only lent plausibility to Aquinas's.

It would also be a mistake to suppose that the scientific errors or oversimplifications reflected in some purported examples of final causality cast any doubt on the reality of final causality itself. For example, Aristotle and his medieval followers held that heavy objects naturally tend to fall down to the earth, specifically. Of course, that is not correct, for there is nothing special about the gravitational pull of the earth per se. The chemical facts underlying the behavior of phosphorus and ice are much more complicated than the toy examples I gave above would indicate. But none of this is relevant to Aquinas's argument for the principle of finality. For *whatever* the scientific details concerning gravitation, cooling, burning, etc. turn out to be, they will involve patterns of efficient causation (gravitational attraction, molecular interaction, etc.). And these will presuppose finality. Science can tell us whether a particular *example* of finality is a good one, but not whether there *is* such a thing as finality.

The thesis that efficient causality presupposes final causality is certainly lent plausibility by the history of thinking about efficient causes after final causes were deemphasized and then abandoned by the nominalist Scholastics and the early modern philosophers and scientists. Ockham's move away from Aquinas's view of the relationship between the two kinds of cause was part of a package of theses about causality which, as we saw in the previous chapter, culminated in Humean skepticism about causality as a real feature of the world. The crux of this skepticism is the Humean position -- prefigured in Ockham, Autrecourt, and occasionalism -- that causes and effects are inherently "loose and separate" (*Enquiry Concerning Human Understanding*, Section VII, Part II), and that we have "no idea of a power or efficacy in any object" by which it brings about its characteristic effect (*Treatise of Human Nature*, Part III, Section XIV). The power and necessity we see in causes could thus be seen as a mere projection of the mind. Yet causes and effects can be loose and separate only if there is nothing in an efficient cause that inherently *points to* or is *directed toward* its effect. And causes can lack power only if there is no active potency in them, where potency, as we have seen, presupposes finality or directedness toward a characteristic manifestation. Thus, Humean skepticism was plausibly the inevitable sequel to the abandonment of final causes. Conversely, to affirm that efficient causes have real causal power and are necessarily tied to their effects entails affirming that there is after all something in them that points to or is directed at the production of those effects.

Of course, the Humean might also argue that the "conceivability" of a cause existing without its usual effect evidences a lack of necessary connection. I will have more to say about this sort of argument below, but for the moment we can note that it falsely supposes that the necessity in causation has to do with a "constant conjunction" between causes and effects, such that the latter follow invariably upon the former. But as our discussion of "finks," "masks," and the like in the previous chapter indicates, the advocate of causal powers does not hold that a power will *invariably* generate its characteristic manifestation. For it might be frustrated in various ways. As Aquinas writes:

> [A]mong inanimate things the contingency of causes is due to imperfection and deficiency, for by their nature they are determined to one result which they always achieve, unless there be some impediment arising either from a weakness of their power, or on the part of an external agent, or because of the unsuitability of the matter. And for this reason, natural agent causes are not capable of varied results; rather, in most cases, they produce their effect in the same way, failing to do so but rarely. (*Summa contra gentiles* 3.73.2)

The principle of finality tells us the sense in which causes and effects are necessarily connected despite the occasional failure of the latter to follow upon the former. An efficient cause A of its nature *points to* and *tends toward* its characteristic effect B as toward an end or goal. Because B is the object or end toward which A points by its very nature, the connection between them is necessary. But because the relationship is merely one of pointing or tending, the generation of B can be blocked given the presence of finks, masks, and the like.

2.2.2 Physical intentionality in recent analytic metaphysics

This brings us back yet again to the contemporary analytic powers theorists, some of whom have essentially endorsed a return to the principle of finality, and essentially for the reasons Scholastic writers like Aquinas were committed to it. These recent theorists do not use the language of "finality" or "final causality," though. They speak of powers or dispositions as "pointing" or "directed" toward their characteristic manifestations, and they model this directedness or pointing on the "intentionality" of thought. Hence George Molnar speaks of "physical intentionality" (2003, chapter 3), John Heil of "natural intentionality" (2003, pp. 221-22), and U. T. Place of dispositions being "intentional states" (1996).

Molnar especially has explored the respects in which the "physical intentionality" of powers might be said to be like and unlike the intentionality of the mental. Since the time Franz Brentano famously put forward the thesis that intentionality is the mark of the mental, four criteria for the existence of intentionality have, Molnar says (2003, pp. 62-63), come generally to be accepted:

(1) An intentional state is *directed* toward an object. For instance, the thought that *the cat is on the mat* is directed toward the state of affairs of the cat's being on the mat.

(2) The intentional object may or may not exist. For instance, one can have the thought that *the cat is on the mat* even if there is no cat.

(3) The intentional object can be indeterminate, either because it is considered only in a partial way or because it is simply vague. For example, one can have the thought that *there is a cat on the mat* without thinking of the cat's particular color or weight, and the thought that *there is something or other over in that direction* has only a vague object.

(4) Ascriptions of intentional states can exhibit *referential opacity*. For example, if one has the thought that *the cat is on the mat*, then even if the cat's name is Felix, it doesn't follow that one has the thought that *Felix is on the mat*.

Molnar argues that powers exhibit features parallel to these four, and can therefore be said to possess a kind of intentionality (2003, pp. 63-66):

(1) Powers are directed toward their characteristic manifestations. For example, solubility is directed toward dissolving.

(2) The manifestation toward which the power is directed need never in fact exist. For example, a thing is still soluble even if it never in fact dissolves.

(3) A power can have an indeterminate object. For example, there is no particular moment when a given radium atom's disposition to disintegrate must manifest.

(4) Power ascriptions can also exhibit referential opacity. For example, that *acid has the power to turn this piece of litmus paper red* does not entail that *acid has the power to turn this piece of litmus paper the color of Pope Benedict's shoes* (since, though the pope's

shoes were red, he could have decided to wear shoes of a different color).

However, as Alexander Bird argues (2007, pp. 120-26), Molnar's case for powers exhibiting the third and fourth of these features is unconvincing. To take the latter first, there are cases like the one Molnar cites which clearly don't involve anything like intentionality. For example, that *ripe tomatoes are red* does not entail that *ripe tomatoes are the color of Pope Benedict's shoes*, unless we take "the color of Pope Benedict's shoes" to be a rigid designator by virtue of being elliptical for "the *actual* color of Pope Benedict's shoes." But if we read it that way, then from *acid has the power to turn this piece of litmus paper red*, it *does* follow that *acid has the power to turn this piece of litmus paper the color of Pope Benedict's shoes*. Molnar's purported parallel between powers and the referential opacity of ascriptions of intentional states thus breaks down. Neither does Molnar convincingly show that powers are indeterminate in their objects in the way intentional states can be. That there is no particular moment when a given radium atom's disposition to disintegrate must manifest is not a matter of *vagueness*, as a thought might be vague. "The half-life of a radioactive nucleus is perfectly precise, as is the probability of its decaying within a given time interval" (Bird 2007, p. 125). In Bird's view, the most Molnar can plausibly attribute to powers are the first two features he identifies-- directedness toward an object and the possible non-existence of the object. But in the absence of the third and fourth features, the directedness of powers is in Bird's view "neither the same as nor a special case of intentionality" (p. 126).

This is a good reason for preferring the traditional Scholastic language of "finality" to talk of intentionality. Another is that modeling the directedness of causal powers on the intentionality of thought needlessly opens the powers theorist up to the objection that he is committed to a kind of panpsychism, attributing mental properties to all natural causes -- a charge raised against the Scholastics by Descartes and Malebranche (Cf. Ott 2009, pp. 41-2 and 90-2). Molnar responds to this charge in part by noting that it is question-begging, since whether intentionality really entails mind is precisely what is at issue; and partly by suggesting that it is consciousness, rather than intentionality, that is the mark of the mental (2003, p. 71). He also considers the further suggestion that a thing's being directed toward an object entails that it contains a *representation* of that object (2003, pp. 71-80). In reply, Molnar argues that bodily sensations exhibit a kind of intentional directedness without representing the things toward which they are directed. For example, pain is directed toward the bodily location in which it is felt, and its object need not exist (as in phantom limb cases). Yet, Molnar argues (contra representationalist theories of sensation), pain lacks any representational or semantic content.

Obviously, evaluating this dispute would require an extended excursus in contemporary philosophy of mind. It would also require an excursus in Scholastic philosophy of nature and philosophical psychology, because Scholastic writers simply would not carve up the conceptual territory the way contemporary philosophers typically do. What is essential to Aquinas's analysis of efficient causation of the simplest inorganic sort is only what Paul Hoffman (2009) has called a "stripped-down core notion" of finality -- mere directedness toward an end of the sort Bird seems willing to affirm no less than Molnar. Non-sentient forms of life possess that but also exhibit the more complex sort of finality characteristic of the "immanent causation" referred to above. Sentient life, on top of all that, also involves *conscious* pursuit of an end. And *rational* or *human* animals, on top of *that*, are capable of *conceptualizing* their ends, as non-human animals, despite being conscious, cannot.

The trouble with too much contemporary talk about "intentionality" is that it largely runs together these distinct phenomena. If "intentionality" *merely* involves directedness toward an object that may or may not exist, then it cannot be the "mark of the mental," because even the simplest inorganic causes have that. Is consciousness, then, the mark of the mental? If we are using "mental" in a broad sense to include even the perception and mental imagery of which non-human animals are capable, then it is the mark of the mental. But if we are using "mental," "mind," and the like in a narrow sense connoting distinctively intellectual activity of the sort humans are capable of and other animals are not, then consciousness is *not* the mark of the mental. Rather, it is the ability to form abstract concepts, to put them together into propositions, and to reason logically from one proposition to another, that are for the Scholastic the hallmark of mind in this restricted sense (Cf. Feser 2013a).

Directedness exists at all these levels, but at each step beyond the "stripped-down core notion" something *else* is added to mere directedness -- immanent causation in the case of simple organic phenomena, immanent causation and consciousness in the case of animals, and immanent causation, consciousness, and conceptual thought in the case of human beings. So, from the Scholastic point of view, contemporary debates about whether intentionality is the mark of the mental, whether intentionality is necessarily tied to consciousness, whether there is such a thing as "physical intentionality," etc. suffers from a failure clearly to distinguish at the outset of discussion the rich variety of ways in which directedness toward an object might be said to exist in nature. The intentionality of perceptual states and propositional attitudes is too often taken matter-of-factly as the paradigm of directedness, so that the deck is unwittingly stacked in advance in favor of the presumption that there is something inherently "mental" about directedness. And while Molnar and other powers theorists have tried to introduce a broader diet of examples, that directedness is inherently mental is treated as the default position, which believers in "physical intentionality" have the burden of moving us away from. That so treating it merely reflects a historically contingent set of philosophical assumptions derived from the anti-Scholastic revolution of the early moderns -- rather than being the *natural* default position -- is seldom considered.

There is also the distinction between *proximate* and *distal* sources of directedness, as noted above. The Scholastic position, at least as represented by Aquinas, is that the *proximate* source of an inorganic efficient cause's directedness toward its characteristic effect is simply its nature, and that this is something non-conscious and otherwise non-mental. The *distal* source of its directedness, however, is the divine intellect. So, insofar as the recent debate in analytic metaphysics has seen both a tendency to reconsider the possibility of inorganic final causality, and resistance to the idea that the mental can be *entirely* eliminated from an account of final causality, it might be seen as gesturing, however inchoately, at the sort of position Aquinas defended. The trouble, here as in the debate over powers more generally, is that contributors to the discussion have neither entirely freed themselves from the assumptions inherited from the early moderns nor made all the crucial distinctions. Once again we see how Scholastic thinking can shed light on current debates, just as the latter can help elucidate the former.

2.3 The principle of causality

2.3.1 Formulation of the principle

There are several formulations of the principle of causality. Though it is not the most familiar one to contemporary readers, the formulation I take to be fundamental is the one I think it is best to start our discussion with. It is Aquinas's dictum that "nothing can be reduced from potentiality to actuality, except by something in a state of actuality" (*Summa theologiae* I.2.3). An efficient cause, whether of a thing's existence or of some change to it, always actualizes some potency or other. The principle of causality (which is concerned with efficient causality as opposed to final, formal, or material causality) tells us that if a potency is actualized, that can *only* be because some already actual cause actualized it. That is true of passive potencies, like the liability of a glass to be shattered or of salt to be dissolved. It is also true of active potencies or powers, such as a hammer's power to shatter glass. For though an active potency or power is a kind of act or perfection relative to the substance that possesses it, it is in potency or incomplete relative to the activity it underlies (Koren 1955, p. 59). Hence it needs actualization. (The only exception would be the active potencies or powers of what is *pure* actuality -- God -- precisely because it is actuality that is not mixed, as everything else is, with passive potency.)

The basic idea is that since a potency *qua* potency is merely potential rather than actual, it can't do anything. In particular, it can't *actualize* anything, including itself. Hence if it is actualized, something already actual has to be what actualizes it. Other formulations of the principle of causality are essentially just applications of this idea. Hence the theses that *whatever is changed is changed by another* and *whatever comes into existence has a cause* are straightforward applications of the principle, since to change or to come into existence is just to go from potency to act. A contingent thing is such that its existence is distinct from its essence, where its essence is in potency relative to its existence, which actualizes it. (We will explore this topic in a later chapter.) To cause a contingent thing to exist is thus to actualize a potency. Hence the thesis that *whatever is contingent has a cause* is also an application of the principle that a potency can be actualized only by something actual.

Perhaps less obvious an application of the idea is Aquinas's further thesis that "every composite has a cause, for things in themselves different cannot unite unless something causes them to unite" (*Summa theologiae* I.3.7). But as Aquinas goes on to say, "in every composite there must be potentiality and actuality... for either one of the parts actuates another, or at least all the parts are potential to the whole." So for a composite to exist is just for the potency of its parts to comprise the whole to be actualized. Every composite has a cause, then, insofar as only what is already actual can actualize the potency in question.

Then there is Aquinas's thesis that "from the fact that a thing has being by participation, it follows that it is caused" (*Summa theologiae* I.44.1). At least one Thomist proposes *this* as the fundamental formulation of the principle of causality (Hart 1959, pp. 263-64). This proposal seems to reflect the tendency of some twentieth-century Thomists to emphasize the very real Neo-Platonic (as opposed to the well-known Aristotelian) influences on Aquinas, but it seems to me mistaken. For Aquinas fuses the Platonic notion of participation to the Aristotelian theory of act and potency. (Cf. Clarke 1994; Wippel 200, chapter IV) Hence "whatever participates in a thing is compared to the thing participated in as act to potentiality, since by that which is participated the participator is actualized in such and such a way" (*Summa contra gentiles* II.53.4). Furthermore, to participate in being is to have it in only a limited way, and "no act is found to be limited except by a potency that is receptive of the act" (*Compendium theologiae* 18). If participation involves the actualization of potency, though, the formulation of the principle of causality in question seems yet a further application of the idea that a potency can be actualized only by what is already actual.

Occasionally the principle is formulated as *every effect has a cause*. Of course, if "effect" is read as "that which has been caused," then this would be a mere tautology, as Scholastic writers realize (Koren 1960, p. 242; Renard 1946, p. 124; Rickaby 1901, p. 319). But "effect" could be read instead as shorthand for "change," "event," or the like, in which case this formulation is just a variation on some of the others already given. In any event, nothing of substance rides on the question, since this formulation can if desired simply be discarded in favor of the others. Still less is any Scholastic committed to the claim that "*everything* has a cause." A popular straw man familiar from atheist attacks on First Cause arguments for God's existence, the claim that "everything has a cause" is not in fact a premise in such arguments (at least as they have been presented by philosophers), and indeed is a claim that Scholastic philosophers would reject. For Scholastics, in order to be caused (whether caused to exist or caused to undergo some change), a thing must in some way be a mixture of act and potency, since to change or come into being is to go from potency to act. But then what is *pure* actuality and thus devoid of potency not only need not have a cause, but could not have had one. Hence it is false to say that *everything* has a cause. The principle of causality says that what *changes* requires a cause, that what *comes into being* has a cause, that what is *composite, contingent* or merely *participates* in being needs a cause, and in general that *what goes from potency to act* requires a cause. But that is very different from saying that absolutely *everything* has a cause. When the Scholastic says that God is uncaused, that is not because God is being made an arbitrary exception to a general rule. It is rather because God is taken to be pure actuality, non-composite, non-contingent, and so forth.

However it is formulated, the principle of causality (PC) should not be confused with the *principle of sufficient reason* (PSR). PSR has been formulated in many ways by philosophers of diverse metaphysical commitments. Two characteristic Scholastic formulations would be "everything which is, has a sufficient reason for existing" and "everything is intelligible" (both from Garrigou-Lagrange 1939, p. 181). A third is:

> There is a sufficient reason or adequate necessary objective explanation for the being of whatever is and for all attributes of any being. (Wuellner 1956b, p. 15)

There are several important differences between PC and PSR. First, while a cause must be really distinct from its effect, there need not be a real distinction between a sufficient reason and that for which it is a sufficient reason (Koren 1960, pp. 231-32). The reason a cause must be distinct from its effect is that to cause is to actualize a potency, and no potency can actualize itself but must be actualized by something already actual. But the notion of a sufficient reason does not entail the actualization of a potency. Hence though God, as pure actuality, could not have a cause, he does have, in his pure actuality, a sufficient reason for his existence. For that he just *is* pure actuality rather than something needing to be actualized makes his existence intelligible or explicable. Thus while God is not his own cause, he is his own sufficient reason.

A related difference is that while, for the reason given above, not everything has a cause, everything does have a sufficient reason (Reichenbach 1972, pp. 53-56). Everything which has a cause has its sufficient reason in something distinct from it, while that which does not have a cause has its sufficient reason in itself. All causes are reasons in the sense of making the effect intelligible, but not all reasons are causes.

A third difference between PC and PSR is that the former unambiguously concerns mind-independent reality, while the latter, with its references to intelligibility, explanation, and the like, is at least partially concerned with the *intellect's understanding* of mind-independent reality. Causation is an *ontological* notion while explanation is an *epistemological* notion. This difference in emphasis reflects the different metaphysical contexts in which PC and PSR arose -- PC in the context of the Aristotelian theory of act and potency, PSR in the context of modern rationalism. That it concerns intelligibility or explanation has led some critics to object that PSR is the mere expression of a demand that the world conform to our explanatory expectations, and that there is no reason to think the world can meet this demand. Whether this objection is a good one and whether PSR is inherently rationalist in a way that makes it irreconcilable with the Aristotelian commitments of Scholastic philosophy are matters to which we will return in another subsection below.

2.3.2 Objections to the principle

2.3.2.1 Hume's objection

Historically, the most influential critique of the principle of causality has no doubt been Hume's. The key passage reads as follows:

> We can never demonstrate the necessity of a cause to every new existence, or new modification of existence, without shewing at the same time the impossibility there is, that any thing can ever begin to exist without some productive principle; and where the latter proposition cannot be proved, we must despair of ever being able to prove the former. Now that the latter proposition is utterly incapable of a demonstrative proof, we may satisfy ourselves by considering that as all distinct ideas are separable from each other, and as the ideas of cause and effect are evidently distinct, it will be easy for us to conceive any object to be non-existent this moment, and existent the next, without conjoining to it the distinct idea of a cause or productive principle. The separation, therefore, of the idea of a cause from that of a beginning of existence, is plainly possible for the imagination; and consequently the actual separation of these objects is so far possible, that it implies no contradiction nor absurdity; and is therefore incapable of being refuted by any reasoning from mere ideas; without which it is impossible to demonstrate the necessity of a cause. (*Treatise of Human Nature*, Book I, Part III, Section III)

Bruce Reichenbach (1972, p. 56) summarizes Hume's argument thus:

1. Whatever is distinguishable can be conceived to be separate from each other.

2. The cause and effect are distinguishable.

3. Therefore, the cause and effect can be conceived to be separate from each other.

4. Whatever is conceivable is possible in reality.

5. Therefore, the cause and effect can be separate from each other in reality.

The intended implication of (5), in turn, is that any "effect" -- that is to say, any change and the actualization of any contingent, composite, or merely potential thing -- could in principle occur without a cause.

Naturally, given what was said above about the difference between PC and PSR, the Scholastic metaphysician has no problem with premise (2). But premises (1) and (4) are highly problematic. The first problem is that as the reference in the passage to "the imagination" indicates, by "conceivable" Hume means "imaginable." To borrow an example from G. E. M. Anscombe (1981b), what Hume evidently has in mind is something like imagining a rabbit appearing, without imagining at the same time there being a parent rabbit around. But to *imagine* such a thing -- that is to say, to form mental images of the sort in question -- is simply not the same thing as to *conceive* something -- that is to say, to grasp the abstracted, intelligible essence of a thing and determine what is possible for it given that essence.

Hume's procedure reflects the early modern empiricists' conflation of the intellect and the imagination, and Hume's argument (indeed his entire philosophy) is gravely compromised by this conflation. For strictly intellectual activity, which involves the grasp of *concepts*, is just irreducibly different from imagination, which involves the mere entertaining of mental images or phantasms. Concepts are abstract and universal in their reference, while mental images are concrete and particular. For instance, your concept *triangle* applies to every single triangle without exception, whereas a mental image of a triangle is always going to be specifically of an acute, obtuse, or right triangle, of a black, blue, or red triangle, and so forth. Concepts can also be determinate and unambiguous in a way no mental image can be. To borrow a famous example from Descartes, there is no clear and distinct difference between the mental images one can form of a circle, a chiliagon, and a myriagon, but there is a clear and distinct difference between the concepts one can form of these geometrical figures. And even a very clear and simple mental image, such as the image of a triangle, is inherently indeterminate as to its reference. There is, for instance, nothing in such an image itself, or in any set of images, that can determine that it represents triangles in general, or black isosceles triangles in particular, or a dunce cap, or a slice of pizza. Images per se are always susceptible of various alternative interpretations. (See Feser 2013a for a detailed treatment of this issue.)

Since determining what is really possible is, like all philosophical questions, something that presupposes a grasp of the relevant concepts, the fact that we can form mental images of this or that sort is (given the distinction between concepts and images) by itself simply neither here nor there. At the very least the Humean procedure simply begs the question against Scholastics, rationalists, and other philosophers committed to the distinction between intellect and imagination.

But even conceivability in the strict sense that involves the grasp of concepts rather than images doesn't do the work Hume needs it to do. Hume evidently supposes that a real distinction entails separability, but as we saw in the previous chapter, Thomists argue that that is not the case. To conceive of A without conceiving of B simply does not entail that A could exist apart from B even if it shows that A and B are distinct. For example, one can conceive of something's being a triangle without conceiving of its being a trilateral, but any triangle is also a trilateral. We can conceive of a man without conceiving of how tall he is, but it doesn't follow that any man could exist without having some specific height. Or, to borrow an example from Reichenbach, a certain evenly thick plate's being concave on one side and convex on the other are distinct features of it, but they cannot exist apart from each other (1972, pp. 58-59).

Whatever plausibility Hume's separability thesis might seem to have rests in part on his assumption that a cause is always temporally prior to its effect. For if a cause A and its effect B do not exist at the same time, then it might seem to follow that they are separable. But there are two problems with this. First, it is from the Scholastic point of view a mistake to think of a cause and its immediate effect as existing at distinct moments of time. Take the case of a window shattering as a result of a thrown brick hitting it. A Humean might characterize the cause as *the throwing of the brick* and the effect as *the shattering of the glass*. So described we do seem to have "loose and separate" events, since the shattering of glass occurs at least a moment or two after the throwing of the brick and of course we can imagine either one without imagining the other. But for the Scholastic this leaves out the key part of the causal story. For the *immediate* cause is something like *the brick's pushing through the window* and the immediate effect is *the window's giving way to the brick.* These events are *simultaneous*; indeed, they are really just the same event under different descriptions. Now, the cause and the effect themselves are still distinct -- a brick's pushing through glass (the exercise of an active potency) is not the same thing as glass's giving way to the brick (the manifestation of a passive potency) -- but given their simultaneity and reciprocal relationship it is hardly plausible to see them as "loose and separate."

But even when causes and effects do exist at different times, it doesn't follow that they are separable in the relevant sense. For even temporally separated causes and effects can sometimes be accurately described only in an interdependent way. For example, to describe something as a *scar* is to characterize it in a way that relates it to a *wound* as its cause (Walsh 1963, pp. 102-3).

Then there is the problem that the sort of scenario that is supposed to illustrate Hume's point is typically underdescribed. Suppose a rabbit suddenly appeared, "out of nowhere" as it were, on the previously empty table in front of you. Your spontaneous response would likely be to say something like "Where did that come from?" -- a question that implies a *source* or *cause* rather than the lack of one. Of course, that does not by itself show that there is a cause, but it illustrates the point that merely forming a mental image of an object suddenly appearing does not show what Hume seems to think it does, for the image is, like all images, susceptible of alternative interpretations. (Cf. Anscombe 1981b) What exactly makes this a case of imagining something coming into being without a cause, as opposed to a case of imagining a thing coming into being without at the same time imagining its cause, or a case of imagining it coming into being with an unseen or unusual cause? Indeed, what makes it a case of imagining it *coming into being* at all, as opposed to being *transported* from elsewhere (perhaps via a teleportation device of the sort described in science fiction)?

Suppose the Humean tries to add something to the description so that it will show what Hume wants it to show. What could that addition be? As Anscombe notes, it will have to include at the very least a way of distinguishing the rabbit's *coming into being* from its merely being *transported* (by teleportation, say). For if the scenario is not in the first place a case of *coming into being*, it cannot be a case of coming into being *without a cause*. But how can we distinguish the two apart from appeal to a *generating* cause as opposed to a *transporting* cause, as we do in ordinary circumstances? And if we need to bring in the idea of a generating cause in order to show that we are really dealing with a case of *coming into being* in the first place, then we have defeated the whole point of the exercise, which was to get *rid* of the idea of a cause. In short, Humean thought experiments seem to lead us away from the principle of causality only insofar as they are loosely described. The moment we start to make them more precise, they lead us back to the principle. (Cf. Anscombe 1981d; Davies 2004, pp. 50-51)

David Gordon (1984) has a response to Anscombe's argument. Anscombe appeals to everyday examples like the making of a pudding to illustrate the idea of a generating cause as opposed to a transporting cause. We are asked to imagine the case of someone taking certain ingredients, mixing them together, and so forth. But how do we know, Gordon asks, that this process is really what generates the pudding? Perhaps the ingredients simply disappeared and the pudding appeared in its place from somewhere else. If Anscombe can say that the Humean gives no reason to think that the scenario he describes involves coming into being rather than transportation, why can't the same thing be said about Anscombe's examples?

Yet it is hard to see how this threatens Anscombe's main point, which is metaphysical rather than epistemic. She is asking what makes *coming into being* a different thing from *being transported*. And her answer is that it is the difference between the causes of these events that differentiates the events themselves. Gordon, however, is asking how we can *know* whether something has been generated rather than transported. That is a different question. And his very example -- where a pudding either is generated out of ingredients or transported from elsewhere but we don't know which -- presupposes that, whichever of these descriptions is the correct one, it will involve some kind of cause. That is all Anscombe needs to make her point.

Gordon also says that Anscombe has not shown that a transported object would have had a cause when it *did* first come into existence, whenever that was. But this too seems to me to miss the point. For one thing, Anscombe's immediate aim is not the positive one of proving that every coming into being has a cause, but the negative aim of rebutting Hume's attempt to show that a coming into being need *not* have one. To do that she need only argue that Hume's examples don't show what he thinks they do, and she has done that. For another thing, it is no good for Gordon merely to suggest that even if the rabbit of our example was transported from elsewhere, perhaps it had no cause whenever it did come into being. For the question is why we should take seriously in the first place the suggestion that a rabbit or anything else could ever come into being without a cause. Hume's examples were supposed to answer that question, but Anscombe has shown that they do not. Hence to respond to her by saying that the rabbit may nevertheless have come into being without a cause in some scenario *other* than the one we were considering (and which scenario is that, exactly?) merely begs the question.

2.3.2.2 Russell's objection

In his 1913 essay "On the Notion of Cause" (reprinted 2003), Bertrand Russell argued that "the law of causality... is a relic of a bygone age, surviving, like the monarchy, only because it is erroneously supposed to do no harm" (p. 165). Physics, in Russell's view, shows that there is no such thing as causation. For physics describes the world in terms of differential equations describing functional relations between events, and these equations make no reference to causes. "In the motions of mutually gravitating bodies, there is nothing that can be called a cause, and nothing that can be called an effect; there is merely a formula" (pp. 173-74). Moreover, while causes generate effects rather than the other way around, there is nothing in the equations of physics that reflects this asymmetry, since the equations are symmetric and can be run in either direction. Nor, Russell thinks, is there is even an interesting *approximation* to causation to be gleaned from physics. "[T]he word 'cause' is so inextricably bound up with misleading associations as to make its complete extrusion from the philosophical vocabulary desirable" (p. 164).

There are a number of problems with this argument. For one thing, as noted above, the Scholastic would deny that all causes and effects are temporally asymmetric in the first place. The immediate cause of an effect is simultaneous with it. (Cf. Mumford and Anjum 2011, p. 120) For another thing, Russell's argument proves too much. If a thing's absence from the equations of physics suffices to show that it does not exist, then we will have to eliminate not only causation, but all sorts of other fundamental notions as well -- including notions essential to our understanding of science, which Russell needs in order to get his argument off the ground. As Jonathan Schaffer (2007) writes:

> In this respect, "event," "law," "cause," and "explanation" are in the same boat. These nomic concepts serve to allow a systematic understanding of science; they do not themselves appear in the equations. From this perspective, Russell's argument might seem akin to the 'argument' that calculus has eliminated the variable, because the word does not appear in the equations!

A third problem is that it is not clear that physics really is free of causal notions. As C. B. Martin argues, dispositional properties (which, as we saw in the previous chapter, are central to the Scholastic notion of causation) are present at the fundamental level of physical reality:

> [Q]uarks have countless readinesses, countless dispositions for countless (nonactual) manifestations... The readiness of a quark for certain kinds of manifesting with certain kinds of interrelation and interreactivity of quarks and leptons constituting a chimera could exist as a particular readiness of the quark, even though nothing like a chimera ever existed or will ever exist. Even so, the quark has, *actually has*, readinesses for it. The quark is *ready* to go. Dispositionality remains intractable, even down to the ultimate particles of nuclear physics. (Martin 2008, p.50)

Fourth, whether or not causal notions are present in physics, they are certainly present in other sciences. And that the other sciences cannot be reduced to physics is now fairly widely acknowledged in contemporary philosophy. This is true not only of the social sciences, but also of biology (Dupré 1993), and even, some have argued, of chemistry (Van Brakel 2000, chapter 5). But if the other sciences give us genuine knowledge of the world and they make reference to causation, then causation must be a real feature of the world. A related point is that the philosophical naturalism to which Russell himself was committed is in contemporary philosophy typically articulated and defended in terms of causal notions. Naturalists routinely defend causal theories of knowledge, causl theories of perception, causal theories of representational content, and so forth. If causation is central to the articulation and defense of naturalism, though, then naturalists themselves must affirm its existence whether or not physics makes reference to it. A possible reply to such arguments might be to suggest that casual notions are merely *pragmatically* useful, and do not track objective reality (Cf. Price and Corry 2007). But like anti-realism in the philosophy of science more generally, this only raises the problem of explaining *how* these notions are as useful as they are if they don't correspond to reality.

The most basic problem with Russell's argument, however, is that there is simply no reason to suppose that physics gives us anything close to an exhaustive description of reality in the first place. Indeed, there is ample reason to think that it does not. Ironically, Russell himself would later give eloquent expression to the point:

> It is not always realised how exceedingly abstract is the information that theoretical physics has to give. It lays down certain fundamental equations which enable it to deal with the logical structure of events, while leaving it completely unknown what is the intrinsic character of the events that have the structure. We only know the intrinsic character of events when they happen to us. Nothing whatever in theoretical physics enables us to say anything about the intrinsic character of events elsewhere. They may be just like the events that happen to us, or they may be totally different in strictly unimaginable ways. All that physics gives us is certain equations giving abstract properties of their changes. But as to what it is that changes, and what it changes from and to—as to this, physics is silent. (1985, p. 13; Cf. Eddington 1963, pp. 257-60)

Modern physics focuses its attention on those aspects of nature which can be described in the language of mathematics, abstracting away everything else. Its "mathematicizations," as Martin has called them, entail taking what (following Locke) Martin calls only a "partial consideration" of the phenomena studied (Martin 2008, p. 74). That is why physics has achieved such breathtaking precision and predictive success. It simply does not allow into its characterizations of physical phenomena any features that would not be *susceptible* of mathematically precise description and prediction. If there are features of the world that can be captured by this method, then physics has a good shot at finding them. But by the same token, if there are features that cannot be captured by this method, physics is guaranteed *not* to find them. To reason from the predictive success of physics to the conclusion that physics gives us an exhaustive description of reality is therefore to commit a very crude fallacy. It is like reasoning from the success of metal detectors to the conclusion that there are no non-metallic features of reality; or it is like a student's reasoning from the fact that he has taken only classes he knew he would do well in and gotten A's in each, to the conclusion that there is nothing of importance to be learned in other classes; or like a drunk's reasoning from his success in finding things in the light under the lamppost to the conclusion that his lost car keys cannot possibly be anywhere else.

Since the equations of physics are, by themselves, *mere* equations, *mere* abstractions, we know that there must be something more to the world than what they describe. There must be something that makes it the case that the world actually operates in accordance with the equations, rather than some other equations or no equations at all. There must be what the later Russell called an "intrinsic character" to the things related in the ways the equations describe. There must, as he put it be *something* "that changes" and something "it changes from and to," something about which, as Russell admitted, "physics is silent." Now if what the equations describe really is *change*, then as the Scholastic philosopher argues, this change entails the theory of act and potency. That means that among the intrinsic features of the things physics describes must be real potencies -- active and passive, powers and liabilities -- and these are, of course, causal properties.

Even if someone wanted to resist attributing real change and causal powers to mind-independent physical reality, he will still have to attribute them to our *experience* of physical reality, through which we acquire the observational and experimental evidence on which physics is based. One experience gives way to another; for example, the experience of setting up an experiment is followed by the experience of observing the results. That entails (for all Russell has shown) the actualization of a potency, and thus causation. The later Russell himself took us to know the world described by physics only by virtue of the fact that our experiences are causally related to that world. In short, there is no way coherently to appeal to physics in support of the claim that causation is not a real feature of the world.

2.3.2.3 The objection from Newton's law of inertia

Aquinas's First Way of proving the existence of God rests on the premise that "whatever is in motion is put in motion by another," another formulation of (or at least an implication of) the principle of causality (*Summa theologiae* I.2.3). The premise is often claimed to have been refuted by Newton, whose First Law states that "every body continues in its state of rest or of uniform motion in a straight line, unless it is compelled to change that state by forces impressed upon it." If an object continues moving without something moving it, then it might seem that we have motion without a mover, change without a changer, the actualization of potency without anything doing the actualizing. The principle of causality might therefore seem to be falsified. In fact there is no conflict between Aquinas's principle and Newton's, for reasons I have set out at length elsewhere (Feser 2012, and at greater length still in Feser 2013d). Here it will suffice to summarize a few key points.

First, there is no formal contradiction between Aquinas's principle and Newton's, even if we suppose that "motion" is being used in the two principles in the same sense. Newton's law tells us that a body *will* in fact continue its uniform rectilinear motion if it is moving at all, as long as external forces do not prevent this. It does not tell us *why* it will do so. In particular, it does not tell us one way or the other whether there is a "mover" of *some* sort which ensures that an object obeys the First Law, and which is in that sense responsible for its motion. Of course, one might ask what sort of "mover" an object obeying the principle of inertia could have if it is not an "external force" of the sort Newton intended to rule out. One might also ask whether such a mover, whatever it might be, really serves any explanatory purpose, and thus whether we ought to bother with it given Ockham's razor. Those are good questions (which I address in the papers cited above). But they are beside the present point, which is that Aquinas's principle and Newton's do not actually contradict one another, *even if* we assume that they are talking about the same thing when they talk about motion.

A second point, though, is that the two principles are *not* talking about the same thing, or at least not exactly the same thing. Newton's principle is concerned solely with *local* motion, change with respect to place or location. When Scholastic philosophers speak of "motion," they mean change of *any* kind. This would include local motion, but also includes change with respect to quantity, change with respect to quality, and (in an extended sense of "motion") change from one substance to another. More to the point, for the Scholastic all such change involves the actualization of a potency. Hence what Aquinas's principle is saying is that *any potency that is being actualized is being actualized by something else (and in particular by something that is already actual)*. This principle is not in formal contradiction with Newton's law of inertia because they are simply not talking about the same thing. When the Newtonian principle states that a body in motion will tend to stay in motion, it isn't saying that a potency which is being actualized will tend to continue being actualized. Even if it were suggested that the principle *entails* this claim, the point is that that isn't what the law of inertia itself, as understood in modern physics, is *saying*. Indeed, modern physics has defined itself in part in terms of its eschewal, for purposes of physics, of such metaphysical notions as act and potency, final causality, and the like. So, it is not that Newtonian mechanics falsifies the principle of causality, but rather that it simply makes no use of it.

Third, having said that, there is also a sense in which the Newtonian principle implicitly *affirms* at least an aspect of the Scholastic principle it is usually taken to have displaced. For insofar as modern physics characterizes uniform motion as a "state," it treats it thereby as the *absence* of change. And Newton's law holds that external forces *are* required to move a thing out of this "state" and thus to bring about a change. But then the Newtonian principle hardly conflicts with the Scholastic claim that "motion" -- that is to say, change -- requires something to cause the change. The disagreement is at most over whether a particular phenomenon *counts* as a true change or "motion" in the relevant sense, not over whether it would require a mover or changer if it *did* so count.

Fourth, if Newton is closer to the Aristotelians than is often supposed, so too are the Aristotelians (or at least Aristotle and Aquinas) closer to Newton than is often supposed. As James Weisheipl (1985) has shown, the idea that Aristotle and Aquinas held that no object can continue its local motion unless some mover is continuously conjoined to it is something of an urban legend. To be sure, this was the view of Averroes and of some Scholastics, but not of Aristotle himself or of St. Thomas. On the contrary, their view was that a body will of itself tend to move toward its natural place by virtue of its form. That which generates the object and thus imparts its form to it can be said thereby to impart motion to it, but neither this generator nor anything else need remain conjoined to the object as a mover after this generation occurs. (To be sure, the scientific details of their analysis -- such as the supposition that the natural place of heavy objects is the center of the earth, and that projectile motions differ essentially from natural motions -- are obsolete. The point is that there is nothing in the Scholastic position that entails the crude "conjoined mover" model of causality often attributed to it.)

Finally and most importantly, though, there is the point made in the previous section that physics simply does not give anything like an exhaustive description of nature in the first place, but abstracts from it everything that cannot be "mathematicized" (to use Martin's expression). This, as just indicated, includes the notions of act and potency, and thus causation as the Scholastic understands it. Newton's laws of motion reflect this tendency, insofar as they provide a mathematical description of motion suitable for predictive purposes without bothering about the origins of motion or the intrinsic nature of that which moves. Indeed, that is arguably the whole point of the principle of inertia. As Weisheipl writes:

Rather than proving the principle, the mechanical and mathematical science of nature *assumes* it... [and] the mathematical
sciences must assume it, if they are to remain mathematical...

The basis for the principle of inertia lies... in the nature of
mathematical abstraction. The mathematician must equate: a
single quantity is of no use to him. In order to equate quantities he must assume the basic irrelevance or nullity of other
factors, otherwise there can be no certainty in his equation.
The factors which the mathematician considers irrelevant are...
motion, rest, constancy, and unaltered directivity; it is only the
change of these factors which has quantitative value. Thus for
the physicist it is not motion and its continuation which need
to be explained but change and cessation of motion -- for only
these have equational value...

In the early part of the seventeenth century physicists tried to
find a physical cause to explain the movement [of the heavenly
bodies]; Newton merely disregarded the question and looked
for two quantities which could be equated. In Newtonian physics there is no question of a cause, but only of differential equations which are consistent and useful in describing phenomena...

[T]he nature of mathematical abstraction... must leave out of
consideration the qualitative and causal content of nature...
[S]ince mathematical physics abstracts from all these factors, it
can say nothing about them; it can neither affirm nor deny
their reality... (1985, pp. 42 and 47-48; Cf. Wallace 1956, pp. 163-
64)

Hence it is not merely that Newtonian mechanics *does* not refute the principle of causality, but that it *could* not -- any more than
(to make use once again of analogies appealed to earlier) the drunk
who stays under the lamppost can say anything one way or another
about what lies elsewhere, or any more than the student who takes
only courses he knows he will do well in can say anything one way or
the other about the subject matter of other courses, or any more than
metal detectors can tell us anything one way or the other about the
existence of wood, stone, and water. Objections to the principle of
causality based on Newton's First Law therefore do not even rise to

the level of being well-formulated. Of course, it is perfectly reasonable to ask how the two principles *are* related given that they are not in conflict (a question I pursue in the articles cited above). But the Scholastic is within his rights to insist that however the principle of inertia is interpreted, it must be made compatible with the principle of causality, which captures deeper levels of reality than physics does or can.

2.3.2.4 Objections from quantum mechanics

The same must be said in response to objections to the principle of causality that appeal to quantum mechanics. There are at least three objections of this sort (Cf. Pruss 2006, chapter 8). The first is that the non-deterministic character of quantum systems is incompatible with the principle of causality. The second is that the Bell inequalities show that there are correlations without a causal explanation. The third is that quantum field theories show that particles can come into existence and go out of existence at random.

As to the objection from indeterminism, it is sometimes pointed out in response that the de Broglie-Bohm hidden variable interpretation provides a way of seeing quantum systems as deterministic (see e.g. Bunge 2007, pp. 346-51). But from a Scholastic point of view it is a mistake to suppose in the first place that causality entails determinism, though this may seem to follow from Leibnizian rationalist versions of PSR. As W. Norris Clarke points out (2001, p. 181), PSR in its rationalist version seems to regard an effect as something that can be deduced from its cause. It looks *forward* from causes to their effects. The Thomist, however, looks *backward* from effects to causes. On a Thomistic construal of PSR, for a cause to be *sufficient* to explain its effect it is not *necessary* that it cause it. It need only make the effect intelligible. (Cf. Smart and Haldane 2003, pp. 125-26) And that condition is satisfied on a non-deterministic interpretation of quantum mechanics. As Robert Koons writes:

> According to the Copenhagen version of quantum mechanics, every transition of a system has causal antecedents: the preceding quantum wave state, in the case of Schrödinger evolution,

or the preceding quantum wave state plus the observation, in the case of wave packet collapse. (2000, p. 114)

As to the objection from the Bell inequalities, it is sometimes suggested that one could respond to it by denying that causal influences never travel faster than light (Koons 2000, p. 114), or by allowing for either backward causation, or an absolute reference frame, or positing a law to the effect that the correlations in question take place (Pruss 2006, pp. 166 and 169). As to the objection that particles can come into or go out of existence at random in a quantum vacuum, Alexander Pruss suggests that here too one might propose a hidden variable theory, or, alternatively, propose that the system described by the laws of quantum field theory is what causes the events in question, albeit indeterministically (2006, pp. 169-70; Cf. Craig and Smith 1993, pp. 143-44). And of course, in response to any objection raised from quantum theory, one could opt for an instrumentalist interpretation of the theory.

Of course, all such proposals raise questions, though the interpretation of quantum mechanics is a notoriously vexed issue in any event. But that brings us to the deeper point, which is the one made above in response to the objection from Newton's law of inertia. As Weisheipl wrote, "the nature of mathematical abstraction... must leave out of consideration the qualitative and causal content of nature... [S]ince mathematical physics abstracts from all these factors, it can say nothing about them; it can neither affirm nor deny their reality" (1985, p. 48). This is as true of quantum mechanics as it is of Newtonian mechanics. What we have is what Martin calls a "partial consideration" of material reality by way of "mathematicization." As Russell acknowledges, physics leaves "the intrinsic character" of what it describes in terms of mathematical structure "completely unknown" (1985, p. 13).

Hence, that quantum theory fails to assign a cause to a phenomenon simply does not entail that there isn't one, since the theory does not capture every aspect of the phenomena it describes in the first place. The absence of something in a representation of nature is not the same thing as a representation of its absence from nature. Its absence from the representation does not even make it *likely* that it is absent from nature, if we already know independently that the representation would leave it out even if it is there. If an artist repre-sents a scene he is looking at in a black and white line drawing, the fact that there is no color in the drawing does not show that there is no color in the scene itself. The colorlessness of the image is an arti-fact of the artist's method, not of the phenomenon represented. Sim-ilarly, the "mathematicization" to which physics confines itself *al-ready* by its nature leaves out potency, finality, and any other notions essential to causality as the Scholastic metaphysician understands it. It is the *method* that drains causality out of the world, with quantum mechanics being something like a limiting case. The four-dimensional block universe interpretation of relativity is another limiting case, entailing as it does an essentially Parmenidean picture of the world from which change, and thus real potency, are absent. In both cases we have physical theories which tell us, not whether causality exists in the world itself, but what sort of representation of the world we get when we consistently abstract from causal notions. To draw philosophical conclusions about causality from such theories is to mistake abstractions for concrete realities. (Cf. Maritain 1995, Chapter IV; Rizzi 2004, Chapter 6)

As with the objection to the principle of causality from inertia, then, the objection from quantum mechanics is not even well-formulated. Before we can draw any philosophical lessons from ei-ther, we first have to situate them within the context of a sound met-aphysics. But the Scholastic argues that any sound metaphysics must include the principle of causality. Hence, whatever we are going to get out of quantum mechanics when correctly interpreted, it is *not* going to be a rejection of the principle of causality.

It is worth adding that there is even a sense in which quantum mechanics, if it has any implications for causality at all, if anything points *toward* rather than away from the Scholastic position. To see how, consider once more the analogy of the artist's black and white line drawing. Again, the drawing by itself does not give us evidence that there is no color in the scene represented, since we know that the artist's exclusive use of black and white materials would never capture the color even if it is there. However, his use of those mate-rials could indicate that there *is* color in the scene represented, in the following way. We are familiar with line drawings which represent a contour by depicting it in black ink. The contour of a face, for example, might be portrayed by a set of black lines, as in a comic book. In what is called a "color hold," however, some contours in a finished piece of artwork are not represented in black ink, but only in the color that will be added to the black and white line drawing. The black and white line art might leave off the contour of one side of an object, for example, with the contour of that side being represented by the color that will be added to the line art. If one sees only the unfinished line art itself, from which the color is absent, one will not see this particular contour. He will accordingly not see that part of the object represented. He might, however, be able to infer from the contours that have been rendered in black that the rest of the object -- the part that the colored artwork will portray -- must be present in the scene represented. For instance, he might infer from the presence in the line art of several straight lines and shadows that what is being represented is a cube, and deduce where the edges of the cube that are not drawn in black ink would go. The viewer could mentally "fill in" what is missing from the artwork, and what the finished, colored artwork would have represented.

Now I have suggested that quantum mechanics and physical theories in general are like the black and white artwork, and physical theory together with a sound metaphysics is like the black and white artwork once it is colored. And there is a sense in which quantum theory might be understood as analogous to a piece of black and white artwork to which a "color hold" is going to be added -- a piece of artwork whose lines do not represent, but nevertheless suggest, at least partially, the presence of causality in the reality that is being represented. In particular, as Werner Heisenberg suggested, quantum theory points to something like the Scholastic notion of potency. (Cf. Smith 2005; Wallace 1997) Regarding the "statistical expectations" quantum theory associates with the behavior of an atom, Heisenberg wrote:

> One might perhaps call it an objective tendency or possibility, a "potentia" in the sense of Aristotelian philosophy. In fact, I believe that the language actually used by physicists when they speak about atomic events produces in their minds similar notions as the concept "potentia." So the physicists have gradually become accustomed to considering the electronic orbits, etc.,

not as reality but rather as a kind of "potentia." (2007, pp. 154-5)

And again:

The probability wave of Bohr, Kramers, Slater... was a quantitative version of the old concept of "potentia" in Aristotelian philosophy. It introduced something standing in the middle between the idea of an event and the actual event, a strange kind of physical reality just in the middle between possibility and reality. (p. 15)

And yet again:

The probability function combines objective and subjective elements. It contains statements about possibilities or better tendencies ("potentia" in Aristotelian philosophy), and these statements are completely objective, they do not depend on any observer; and it contains statements about our knowledge of the system, which of course are subjective in so far as they may be different for different observers. (p. 27)

Discussing, more generally, the relationship between matter and energy in modern physics, Heisenberg says:

If we compare this situation with the Aristotelian concepts of matter and form, we can say that the matter of Aristotle, which is mere "potentia," should be compared to our concept of energy, which gets into "actuality" by means of the form, when the elementary particle is created. (p. 134)

As we will see in the next chapter, the Aristotelian notion of prime matter is the notion of pure potency for the reception of form, where form corresponds to actuality. We might say that insofar as quantum theory points in the direction of pure potency or prime matter, and -- in its indeterminism, in the Bell inequalities, and in the notion of particles popping into existence in a quantum vacuum -- portrays the actualization of potency without portraying something doing the actualizing, it approximates the notion of potency without act. (Cf. Grove 2008) The four-dimensional block universe interpretation of relativity theory, meanwhile, approximates the notion of act without potency. Now, since efficient causation involves the actualization of potency, any description which leaves out one or the other is going to leave out causation. In the case of the Parmenidean block universe, what is left out is any potency needing to be actualized; in the case of quantum theory, what is left out is anything to actualize the potency. In both cases what is missing is missing, not because it is absent from reality, but because it is bound to be absent from a consistently mathematicized description of reality.

2.3.2.5 Scotus on self-motion

The principle that *whatever is in motion is put in motion by another* (sometimes called the principle of motion) was cited above as an alternative formulation of, or at least an implication of, the principle of causality. For motion or change is the actualization of potency, and what I characterized as the fundamental formulation of the principle of causality states that *nothing can be reduced from potentiality to actuality, except by something in a state of actuality*. But "Duns Scotus distinguishes the principle of causality from that of motion," and while he accepts the former he rejects the latter (Effler 1962, p. 44; Cf. King 1994; King 2003, pp. 46-48; Rota 2012). As Allan Wolter writes:

> Scotus... effectively challenged the so-called metaphysical principle "Whatever is moved is moved by another"... Among other instances of "self-movement" Scotus singles out the human will's ability to determine itself. As an active potency, the will is formally distinct from, but really identical with, the soul substance, and is either the exclusive or at least the principal efficient cause of its own volition. This volition... is an immanent action that falls under the Aristotelian category of quality, and resides in the soul as subject. When the will makes a positive decision, and thus elicits a voluntary act of either nolition or volition, therefore, it is determining itself, and hence one can correctly say the soul "moves itself" from a state of indeterminacy to a positive state or decision. (Wolter 1986, p. 36)

Henry of Ghent before Scotus, and Suarez after him, were Scholastics who expressed somewhat similar views (though they did not deny that the principle of motion applied in other contexts).

Now Thomists don't deny that there are things (such as animals) which can in a loose sense be said to move themselves. But on analysis, in their view, such "self-motion" really involves the movement of one part of a thing by another. For, they argue, since a potency *qua* potency is merely potential rather than actual, it can't do anything, including actualize itself. Hence something already actual has to be what actualizes it. But Scotus rejects this line of argument. Where self-motion is concerned, he frames his analysis not in terms of *causes* but in terms of the more general notion of *principles*, a "principle" in the relevant sense being that from which something in some way proceeds. A cause is one kind of principle, but there are others, such as a thing's form and matter, or its actualities and potencies. Scotus thus speaks of something's proceeding from a principle as "principiation." And in principiation, he holds, what is principiated need not always be distinct from what does the principiating. Suppose that a thing has a form F which actively principiates a further form G, and that it also has a passive potency to receive G. To take an illustration from medieval physics (now outdated, of course), consider a material object's having the form *heaviness* and its passive potency for receiving the form *falling*, and suppose that the form *heaviness* actively principiates the form *falling*. We can think of the object as a self-mover insofar as its passive potency for falling is actualized by its active principiation (by virtue of its being heavy) of the form *falling*. The will can be said to move itself in a similar way.

For the Thomist, however, this simply blurs the distinction between *a thing's proper accidents flowing from its form* (see chapter 4), and *an effect's being generated by an efficient cause* (Weisheipl 1985, pp. 117-18). Motion qua the actualization of potency is an instance of the latter, but Scotus's account concerns the former. For Aquinas, though a material thing's substantial form is indeed the "principle" by which it moves in the ways it characteristically does (such as a heavy object's tendency to fall), the *cause* of its motion is whatever generated the thing and thus imparted to it its substantial form. It is this cause of the material thing, rather than the thing itself or its form, that is the "mover." Regarding the will, for Aquinas it is moved by itself, not directly, but only insofar as it moves the intellect to take counsel regarding the best means to a given end, where the intellect in turn moves the will (Cf. Wippel 2000, pp. 448-51).

2.3.3 Arguments for the principle

2.3.3.1 Appeals to self-evidence

While Scholastic and other defenders of the principle of causality are naturally in agreement that the objections raised against it fail, they disagree about whether the principle can be or needs to be given a positive defense, and if so, how that defense should proceed. (See De Raeymaeker 1954, pp. 259-61 for a useful brief overview of some opinions on the subject.) Concerning one of the less fundamental formulations of PC, one author argues:

> [T]he Principle of Causality: Whatever begins to be must have a reason for its existence outside itself... is really self-evident in its own right, for the two concepts, "to begin to be," and "to be without a cause," are evidently contradictory. For that which begins to be must first have been in a state of potentiality, and... potentiality cannot become actual without the intervention of some already actual being. (McCormick 1940, p. 141)

Of course, that "potentiality cannot become actual without the intervention of some already actual being" is itself the fundamental formulation of PC. And a critic of PC might deny that *this* formulation is self-evident, for he might suggest that it is at least possible in principle that a potential can become actual without the intervention of something already actual.

However, this is not as powerful an objection as it might at first appear. For its force surely rests on considerations like those associated with Hume, and I have argued that Hume's position has little or no merit. If doubts about the self-evidence of PC are based on Humean considerations, or on any of the other objections considered above, and if the responses to those objections that I have put forward are sound, then the doubts in question are simply not well founded. (Suppose someone claimed to doubt that it is self-evident that round squares are impossible, and gave as his reason the consideration that we could always change the meaning of the word "square" so that it came to refer to circles. If it were explained to him that he was committing a very crude fallacy of confusing the word we use for a thing for the thing itself, and he understood and agreed with the explanation, it would be irrational for him to continue to doubt that it is self-evident that round squares are impossible, if that had been his only reason for doubting it.)

2.3.3.2 Empirical arguments

All the same, many writers have held that more can be said in defense of the claim that a potency can be actualized only by something already actual. One suggestion is that the reality of at least individual instances of causation is something we know from experience both of the external world and of our own actions (Bittle 1939, pp. 345-48). Mumford and Anjum have recently defended this position at some length (Mumford and Anjum 2011, chapter 9; Cf. Mumford 2013, pp. 19-21).

Hume, of course, holds that all we ever actually perceive is that an event of type A is always followed by a later, contiguous event of type B, and that experience of this "constant conjunction" does not amount to experience of causation. We experience the relata but not the causal relation itself. The Scholastic would deny, however, that causation is essentially a relation between temporally separated events. In the paradigmatic cases, causes and their effects are *simultaneous*. Stock examples would include a bowling ball and the impression it makes in the cushion it is resting on, or a bird and the bending it causes in the branch it alights upon. So while the suggestion that we do not observe any causal relation might be plausible where causes and effects are temporally separated, that condition simply doesn't hold in every case of causation. (More on the simultaneity of causes and effects below.)

The Humean might object that our interpretation even of cases of simultaneous causes and effects involves the bringing to bear of knowledge of past regularities -- for instance, of bowling balls being regularly associated with impressions in pillows. We are still not perceiving causation itself but reading it into what we perceive on the basis of constant conjunction. But Mumford and Anjum suggest that this cannot be said of perception of what is going on within ourselves. To experience a feeling of pressure on one's skin, for example, just is to experience being affected in a certain way. It is not to *infer* that one is being affected. Similarly, to be aware of intentionally raising one's arm just is to experience causing it to go up, rather than to infer that one has caused it to go up. We thus seem to perceive ourselves both as patients and as agents, as passively being affected and actively producing effects. (Mumford and Anjum seem to think the former sort of case is at least somewhat less compelling than the latter sort insofar as what affects us is external to us. But it is easy to think of examples where this is not the case. For instance, to feel the pain of an ingrown toenail is to experience being affected by something not external to you. To push one's tongue into the roof of one's mouth involves experiencing both being affected by something that is not external to you and being the cause of that effect.)

To be sure, Hume famously argues that even our experience of agency involves an inference based on constant conjunction. But as Mumford and Anjum point out, this assumes an implausible account of agency, on which all intentional bodily movements are preceded by willings or volitions understood as distinct events. We're supposed to imagine, for example, a conscious willing to raise one's arm followed by the arm's going up, where the "constant conjunction" between separate events of these sorts is what leads us to think that the former caused the latter. But most action is simply not like that. Driving a car, riding a bike, playing football, and walking down the street all involve a large number of intentional actions that are not individually preceded by volitions. (For example, when walking one almost never thinks: "I now will to move my right foot. I now will to move my left foot. I now will to move my right foot again." One just walks.) Moreover, the actions could not be preceded temporally by the volitions that cause them, otherwise there would be no reason why an action should follow at one time after the volition rather than another, nor any way to account for the fact that one could change one's mind or forget about a volition between the time the volition occurs and the later time at which the action occurs. In fact the willing that causes an action and the action itself are simultaneous, and the latter exists only as long as the former does. One might, after all, change one's mind in the course of making a bodily movement, and not complete it.

Nor are the volition and action merely simultaneous. They are, Mumford and Anjum argue, tightly integrated, as cases of proprioception illustrate. When you lift a heavy object, for example, you might adjust your efforts several times in the course of the action as you take account of the fact that the object is not as heavy or light as you thought it was, feel it slipping from your grasp or ready to fall over, and so forth. You might redouble your efforts or instead give up in the course of carrying out the action. There is a kind of feedback mechanism by which the character of the willing and the character of the action alter each other. The volition and the action simply do not comprise neatly demarcated units which we infer to be causally related via constant conjunction. We just perceive an action *as* something we cause.

Perhaps it is on the basis of this experience that we apply the notion of causation to events taking place outside of us, where we do not experience causation "from within" as it were. But such an application will not be ungrounded, since we do have experience of causation in our own case. And we might add to the considerations raised by Mumford and Anjum the point that it is not merely the fact that these external causes and effects are simultaneous that leads us to attribute to them the causality we perceive in ourselves. Like our actions, they too sometimes exhibit integration of the sort manifest in a feedback mechanism whereby the cause's activity is altered in the course of producing the effect. (Consider, for example, the way a cushion to some extent holds the bowling ball up and keeps it from making contact with the floor under it even as the ball causes the cushion partially to give way.) Even if it were granted that we infer causality, rather than perceive it, in the case of events external to us -- and not all critics of Hume would concede this (Cf. Ducasse 1965; Cartwright 1993) -- the inference is grounded in much more than mere constant conjunction.

A Humean might for all this insist that, even if experiences of the sort cited by Mumford and Anjum are indeed experiences of causation -- rather than of mere constant conjunction, into which we read causation, in a separate act as it were -- perhaps the experiences are not veridical, but akin to hallucinations or illusions. Maybe they are systematically in error. But the burden of proof is on the Humean to show why we should take such a suggestion seriously. The Humean approach to causality is, after all, by no means just a straightforward reading of the facts. As we have seen over the course of two chapters, it rests on several dubious and certainly challengeable metaphysical and epistemological assumptions. There is no reason to presume *it*, rather than the Scholastic position (which, unlike Hume's, accords with common sense and everyday experience), innocent until proven guilty.

Now this much by itself might seem to support at most the conclusion that there is *some* genuine causation in the world -- that is to say, that there are indeed some actualized potencies that are actualized by something already actual -- while PC, of course, makes the stronger claim that *any* actualized potencies *must* be actualized by something already actual. But the next step in an empirical argument for PC would be to argue that the principle, "even if taken as a mere inductive generalisation, seems as secure as any truth rooted in experience" (Craig 2002b, p. 92; Cf. Craig 1993a, pp. 60-61). Of course, alleged counterexamples are sometimes put forward, but I have argued in earlier sections that none of the purported counterexamples is genuine. In general, we do in fact find causes when we look for them, and when we don't find them (e.g. when investigating an unsolved murder) we have reason to think they are nevertheless there and would be found if only we had all the pertinent evidence and the time and resources for a more thorough investigation. Not only is this just what we would expect if PC is true, but it is not at all what we should expect if it were false. As W. Norris Clarke points out, if PC were false, "then nothing at all would be required to produce anything at all: an elephant, or a hotel could appear suddenly on your front lawn out of nowhere" and "it should be the easiest thing in the world for them to be popping up all the time" (Clarke 2001, p. 182). But of course this is not the way the world actually works.

The best explanation of why the world works in just the way it does is that there is something in the very nature of potency that requires actualization by something already actual -- that is, the best explanation is that PC is true. Put another way, Putnam's "miracle argument" for scientific realism applies to PC as well, insofar as the facts that we tend to find causes for things that come into being, and that things do not regularly pop into existence without any evident cause, would be miraculous if PC were false.

2.3.3.3 Arguments from PNC

But Scholastics typically regard the principle of causality as more certain than even a well founded inductive generalization or argument to the best explanation. The reason, for those who do not regard PC as self-evident, is that they regard it as derivable from even more secure premises. One approach taken by Scholastic writers is to argue that PC can be derived from the *principle of non-contradiction* (PNC).

Henri Renard sees such an argument as implicit in Aquinas's First Way (Renard 1946, pp. 121-22). Aquinas writes:

> Now whatever is in motion is put in motion by another, for nothing can be in motion except it is in potentiality to that towards which it is in motion; whereas a thing moves inasmuch as it is in act. For motion is nothing else than the reduction of something from potentiality to actuality. But nothing can be reduced from potentiality to actuality, except by something in a state of actuality... Now it is not possible that the same thing should be at once in actuality and potentiality in the same respect, but only in different respects... It is therefore impossible that in the same respect and in the same way a thing should be both mover and moved, i.e. that it should move itself. Therefore, whatever is in motion must be put in motion by another. (*Summa theologiae* I.2.3)

Now if something moves or changes something only insofar as it is actual, but is moved or changed only insofar as it is potential, and nothing can be actual and potential in the same respect at the same time, then nothing can move or change itself in the same respect at the same time. To suppose it does is to suppose it is actual and potential in the same respect at the same time, which is a contradiction. Hence Renard's reading of Aquinas.

An apparent problem with this as an argument for PC, though, is that the critic of PC might argue that he need not maintain that a potency can actualize itself. He might say that it can be actualized without being actualized either by another thing *or* by itself (Rowe 1998, pp. 73-75). As Hume objects:

But this reasoning is plainly inconclusive, because it supposes that in our denial of a cause we still grant what we expressly deny, viz., that there must be a cause, which therefore is taken to be the object itself; and that, no doubt, is an evident contradiction. But to say that any thing is produced, or to express myself more properly, comes into existence, without a cause, is not to affirm, that 'tis itself its own cause; but on the contrary in excluding all external causes, excludes a fortiori the thing itself, which is created. An object that exists absolutely without any cause certainly is not its own cause, and when you assert that the one follows from the other, you suppose the very point in question... (*A Treatise of Human Nature*, Book I, Part III, Section III)

Nor will it do to object that in this case, the critic of PC is saying that a potency is actualized by nothing, but that nothing cannot actualize anything since *ex nihilo nihil fit*. For the critic of PC can say that he is not saying that a thing can be caused by nothing rather than by another thing or by itself -- as if he were treating nothing as an unusual kind of cause -- but rather that it lacks any cause at all (Rowe 1998, pp. 75-76). As Hume continues:

It is sufficient only to observe that when we exclude all causes we really do exclude them, and neither suppose nothing nor the object itself to be the causes of the existence, and consequently can draw no argument from the absurdity of these suppositions to prove the absurdity of that exclusion. If everything must have a cause, it follows that upon the exclusion of other causes we must accept of the object itself or of nothing as causes. But it is the very point in question, whether everything must have a cause or not, and therefore, according to all just reasoning, it ought never to be taken for granted. (Ibid.)

It should be emphasized that Hume's objections do not apply to Aquinas himself, since he does not explicitly try to derive PC from PNC, nor does he accuse the critic of PC of claiming that a thing can be caused by nothing. In the passage in question, Aquinas's concern appears to be more with arguing against the claim that a potency can actualize itself than with arguing against the claim that it could be actualized without anything at all doing the actualizing (though of course he would also deny that this is possible). He just does not seem to be trying in that passage to address objections of the sort that would later be raised by Hume.

Some Thomists explicitly reject attempts to argue from PNC to PC. Clarke, for instance, says of PC:

> [T]his is an insight into the *dynamic intelligibility* of being... not into a logical impossibility, governed by the static Principle of Non-Contradiction. It would indeed be a logical contradiction to say, "Being is non-being"; but not "Being *comes from* non-being"... There is no strictly and purely logical proof of the need for an efficient cause. (Clarke 2001, p. 182)

However, we should not be too quick to dismiss the argument from PNC to PC on the basis of the objections raised by Clarke and Hume. Consider, first, that it would be a mistake to suppose that PC, in its fundamental formulation anyway, is concerned solely with the dynamic order of things. (Cf. Phillips 1950b, pp. 237-38) For as we have seen, as Scholastic metaphysicians have developed the theory of act and potency, it is concerned not only with the problem of change but also with the problem of multiplicity. For the Scholastic, each distinct member of a class of things has an essence distinct from its act of existence, and the essence and act of existence are related as potency to act. (We'll address this issue in chapter 4.) This is as true in a static order as in a dynamic one. Hence for a thing to exist at all, even for an instant, is for its potency for existence to be actualized at that instant.

Consider, second, that Hume's objections are not aimed precisely at what we have called the fundamental formulation of PC, viz. that an actualized potency is always actualized by something already actual. He is evidently thinking, as Parmenides would, in terms of something going from sheer non-being to being rather than from potency to act; and of course he is also thinking of causes and effects as temporally separated, rather than thinking (as the Scholastic would) of the immediate cause of an effect being simultaneous with it. Now if we think of causation as essentially a matter of there first being a moment when a thing in no way has being, and then a later moment when it has being, then it is indeed hard to see any outright contradiction in the idea that this transition might lack a cause. But for the

Scholastic that is the wrong way to characterize the situation. We should think instead of a thing's potency for existence (which is not *nothing* even if it is not actual) being actualized at any particular instant it exists (and not merely by a temporally precedent cause).

Now seen in this light it may not seem so clear that denying PC does not involve a contradiction. For if the critic of PC is saying that a thing's potential for existence can be actualized at a given instant without there being anything that does the actualizing, does that not entail that he is saying that the thing is at that instant both potential and actual with respect to its existence? And is that not a contradiction?

But that inference too would be too quick. For of course, the Scholastic himself says that a thing is at any instant both potential and actual. There is no contradiction here, because a thing is potential and actual *in different respects*. It is in potency with respect to its essence, but in act with respect to its existence. Now the critic of PC, it seems, can appeal to this very difference in order to defend himself against the charge of contradiction. He can say that a thing's potency for existence can at any instant be actualized without a cause in the sense that its essence is conjoined to an act of existence but without anything at that instant doing the conjoining. It is not that the thing itself is causing this, or that something other than the thing itself is causing it, or that "nothing" (considered as an eccentric kind of cause) is causing it. There is no cause of any sort; it is just the case, as a brute fact, that the essence and act of existence are conjoined at that instant. While this suggestion may be objectionable for other reasons, it does not (so the critic of PC might argue) involve a *contradiction*.

2.3.3.4 Arguments from PSR

So the argument from PNC to PC appears to fail. However, a more popular approach among Scholastic writers to demonstrating PC is to appeal to the principle of sufficient reason. (Cf. Gardeil 1967, pp. 227-28; Phillips 1950, pp. 235-37; Renard 1946, p. 125-27) PSR states that "everything is intelligible" (Garrigou-Lagrange 1939, p. 181), and that "there is a sufficient reason or adequate necessary objective explanation for the being of whatever is and for all attributes of any being" (Wuellner 1956b, p. 15). But if PC were false -- if the actualization of a potency, the existence of a contingent thing, or something's changing or coming into being could lack a cause -- then these phenomena would not be intelligible, would lack a sufficient reason or adequate explanation. Hence if PSR is true, PC must be true. PC is an application of PSR to things that are mixtures of act and potency and essence and existence, and which therefore -- unlike God, who as pure actuality and subsistent being itself has the sufficient reason or adequate explanation for his existence within himself -- require an explanation by reference to something outside them.

Here two key issues must be addressed. First, is PSR the sort of principle to which an Aristotelian-Scholastic philosopher can or should appeal? Second, is PSR true? Let us address these in turn.

Some twentieth-century Thomists have expressed the concern that appeals to PSR in the work of modern Scholastic philosophers reflects an uncritical and potentially dangerous adoption of assumptions deriving from the rationalism of thinkers like Leibniz and Wolff. (Cf. Gilson 1952a, pp. 112-21; Gilson 1952b; Gurr 1956; Gurr 1959; Owens 1955; Sweeney, Carroll, and Furlong 1996, pp. 252-55) This suggestion reflects the more general view held by Etienne Gilson and writers influenced by him to the effect that modern inheritors of the Scholastic tradition have too often lapsed into a rationalist "essentialism" and thereby moved away from the "existentialism" one finds in Aquinas. The idea is that whereas the rationalist tries to ground metaphysics in an abstract order of essences considered as concepts or essentially mental items, any serious form of Thomism must follow Aquinas in grounding metaphysics in the knowledge of concrete existents that we acquire through the senses. Otherwise Scholastic thought will be open to the same Humean and Kantian objections raised against rationalist metaphysics, to the effect that it reflects only the way the mind *conceptualizes* reality, but not reality as it is in itself.

Certainly it cannot be emphasized too strongly that Scholastic metaphysics does not share rationalism's epistemological foundations. It is not grounded in a doctrine of innate ideas, nor in mere "conceptual analysis." But it would be a mistake to suppose that adoption of the label "principle of sufficient reason," or even a reference to reality's being intelligible in the formulation of the principle, entails a tacit commitment to a rationalist epistemology. For one thing, while PSR is typically formulated in terms of intelligibility or explanation -- which are epistemological or logical, rather than metaphysical, notions -- it need not be so formulated. As Jacques Maritain notes, PSR can be formulated as the principle that "whatever is, has that whereby it is" (1939, p. 99). This makes no explicit or implicit reference to the intellect's operations -- as talk of intelligibility and explanation do -- but it has the generality of the more usual formulations of PSR, which PC lacks. Actualizations of potency, contingent things, and changes and beginnings of existence have that whereby they are, namely their causes; and that which is uncaused insofar as it is pure actuality or subsistent being itself also has that whereby it is, namely its own nature.

For another thing, even if PSR is formulated in terms of the intelligibility of things or their having an explanation, this cannot be regarded as *per se* objectionable from a Thomistic point of view. The reason is that on the Scholastic doctrine of the transcendentals, being is convertible with truth. (Cf. Bittle 1939, Part II; Feser 2009, pp. 31-36; Gardeil 1967, Chapter 4; Koren 1960, Chapter 2; Renard 1946, Section IV) A transcendental notion is one which is above every genus, common to all things and thus not restricted to any category or individual. *Being* is a transcendental insofar as everything real, whether a substance, an accident, or whatever, is a being of some sort or other. *Truth* is also a transcendental insofar as everything real is truly the thing it is. (Consider how "true" is often used in the sense of "real" or "genuine.") Being and truth are *convertible* in the sense that they are the same thing considered under different aspects. Being is reality considered in itself, truth is reality considered in its relation to an intellect which grasps it. In other words, truth is just being considered as intelligible. Now if every being is in this sense true -- and that this is Aquinas's own view is uncontroversial -- then it follows that every being is intelligible. And that is just what PSR says. (Cf. Gardeil 1967, pp. 139-42; Maritain 1939, pp. 97-105)

It seems hard to deny, then, that a version of PSR is at least *implicit* in Thomism, even if it was not made explicit until after Scholastic writers were moved by the work of rationalists like Leibniz to take the principle on board. What must be given no less emphasis, however, is that the Scholastic metaphysician is not and need not be committed to everything associated with the rationalist version of PSR, which is the version that is typically in view in contemporary debate about the subject (Clarke 2001, pp. 2023; Gardeil 1967, pp. 139-42). For instance, in the contemporary debate, propositions are often regarded as among the things which require an explanation given PSR, and logical entailment is often regarded as the mode by which one proposition explains another. But as Peter Weigel writes:

> Aquinas's explanatory model focuses on finding due account for the existence and ontological character of contingently-existing substances. That is, his interest is in the explanation of concrete extant objects and their arrangements... The demands of his model are thus notably different in scope from what in Leibniz is the *principle of sufficient reason*, in which the phenomena to be explained include propositions. As Leibniz presents the principle, every fact and every true proposition -- at least every contingent proposition -- must have an explanation. What is sufficient reason furthermore assures the truth of what it explains... Hence Leibniz's rendition has a logical cast to it, whereas Aquinas is not fishing for reasons for every logically contingent proposition. For Aquinas, to say X explains or accounts for Y is not to say it necessary [sic] entails it (when Aquinas is talking about real-world causation). Aquinas thus in his model cautiously keeps in view the explanation of the existence of objects, not reasons for literally everything. Aquinas thinks truth and falsity always accrue to individual beliefs in minds. Propositions for him are thus beings of reason and do not exist as disembodied *abstracta*, so they are not things out there to be explained in the manner real beings are. (Weigel 2008, pp. 128-29)

This point is crucial for understanding why some objections to the rationalist construal of PSR do not apply to PSR as understood by Scholastic writers. For example, one well-known objection to PSR asks us to consider the proposition comprising the conjunction of all true contingent propositions. Since each of its component conjuncts is contingent, this big proposition is contingent. In that case, the explanation of this big proposition cannot be a necessary proposition, for whatever is entailed by a necessary proposition is itself necessary. But neither can its explanation be a contingent proposition. For if it were, then that contingent proposition would itself be one conjunct among others in the big conjunction of contingent propositions. That would mean that the big conjunctive proposition explains itself. But the PSR tells us that no contingent proposition can explain itself. So, the big conjunctive proposition cannot have an explanation. But in that case there is something without an explanation, and PSR is false. (Cf. Ross 1969, pp. 295-304; Rowe 1997; Rowe 1998; Van Inwagen 1983, pp. 202-4; and the critical discussions in Gerson 1987 and Pruss 2009, pp. 50-58) From a Scholastic point of view this sort of argument is a non-starter, since on the Scholastic understanding of PSR, propositions are not among the things requiring explanation in the first place, and explanation does not require logical entailment.

Furthermore, the rationalist application of PSR tends to go hand in hand with an appeal to the notion of possible worlds and the conception of modality associated with it in modern philosophy. What is possible, it is thought, is what obtains in at least one possible world. What is contingent and thus requires an explanation outside itself is what holds in some possible worlds but not others. What is necessary and thus self-explanatory is what holds in every possible world. Recent discussions of PSR thus inevitably bring to bear the arcana of the large contemporary literature on modality and possible worlds. From a Scholastic point of view, this is all misguided. (Cf. chapter 4.) Possibility, contingency, and necessity are grounded, not in the Leibnizian notion of possible worlds, but in the Aristotelian theory of act and potency. Whereas the rationalist tends to collapse all possibility into what the Scholastic calls logical or objective potency -- possibility *qua* object of thought, where for many a contemporary metaphysician this is determined by "conceiving" what a thing might be like in different possible worlds -- for the Scholastic, what is possible for a thing is a function of its real or subjective potencies, which are grounded in the various ways in which it is in act or actual. That a thing is contingent is due to its having an essence distinct from its act of existence, where the former is in potency relative to the latter. That which is absolutely necessary is so because it is purely actual or devoid of potentiality, and has no essence distinct from its act of existence. While there might be some utility in grounding a notion of possible worlds in this approach, the approach is not itself grounded in any theory of possible worlds, and the notion of possible worlds is not essential to the use Scholastics make of notions like possibility, contingency, and necessity. Hence neither is it essential to their conception of explanation or their use of PSR.

Let us turn to the question of whether PSR, as the Scholastic metaphysician understands it, is true. We have already noted that objections to PSR that assume that a sufficient reason for something must logically entail it misfire, since the defender of PSR need not make that assumption. Nor is the assumption plausible in any case. As Alexander Pruss notes, "[s]cientific causal explanations, in general, simply do not give conditions that *entail* the explanandum" (2009, p. 52). This is obviously true in the case of statistical explanations, but it is also true of non-statistical scientific explanations. For example, when we explain the elliptical orbits of the planets by reference to the gravitational influence of the sun, we don't mean that the existence of this gravitational influence strictly *entails* that the planets will move in elliptical orbits, since they could still fail to do so if there were some interfering gravitational influences. (Cf. the discussion in the previous chapter of "finks," "masks," and the like.) What PSR requires is that an explanans make an explanandum intelligible, and there is no reason to think that that requires logical entailment.

Other common objections to PSR are variations on those directed against PC (e.g. Humean objections to the effect that it is conceivable that something might come into being without any explanation), and they fail for the reasons already considered. Objections that appeal to quantum mechanics are even less plausible when directed against PSR than when directed against PC. For whether or not we want to say that eccentric quantum phenomena have a *cause*, they certainly have an *explanation*, since they presuppose and are made intelligible by the laws of quantum mechanics (Pruss 2009, p. 58; Smart and Haldane 2003, pp. 125-26).

Are there good positive arguments for PSR? One important argument is a variation on the empirical argument for PC. Considered as an inductive generalization, PSR is as well-supported as any other. For one thing, we tend to find explanations when we look for them, and even when we don't we tend to have reason to think there is an explanation but just one to which, for whatever reason (e.g. missing evidence), we don't have access. For another thing, the world simply doesn't behave the way we would expect it to if PSR were false (Pruss 2009, p. 32). Events without any evident explanation would surely be occurring constantly and the world would simply not have the intelligibility that makes science and everyday common sense as successful as they are. This would be a miracle if PSR were not true.

As with PC, though, Scholastic philosophers take PSR to be more certain than a mere empirical hypothesis can be. Indeed, like PC it is often regarded as *self-evident*. This does not entail that it is universally assented to, or that it can be known to be true from an analysis of the concepts or the terms in which it is formulated. (Cf. Klubertanz 1963, pp. 154 and 158) The idea is rather that, as Garrigou-Lagrange writes, "though it cannot be directly demonstrated, it can be indirectly demonstrated by the indirect method of proof known as *reductio ad absurdum*" (1939, p. 181). Garrigou-Lagrange's way of trying to show this is to argue that to deny PSR entails denying PNC as well -- though this strategy does not seem more promising than the attempt to derive PC from PNC.

However, there are ways of carrying out a *reductio* other than by arguing that to deny PSR entails directly denying PNC itself. One can argue that anyone who denies PSR would, if he is consistent, also have to deny other things he would not deny or even could not coherently deny. This amounts to an application to the defense of PSR of the method of retorsion which, as we saw in chapter 1, can be applied in a critique of the Eleatic and Heraclitean positions vis-à-vis change and permanence. One way in which this might go is suggested by some remarks from Pruss, who was in turn developing a point made by Robert Koons (Pruss 2009, p. 28; Koons 2000, p. 110). Denying PSR, Pruss notes, entails radical skepticism about perception. For if PSR is false, there might be no reason whatsoever for our having the perceptual experiences we have. In particular, there might be no connection at all between our perceptual experiences and the external objects and events we suppose cause them. Nor would we have any grounds for claiming that such a radical disconnect between our perceptions and external reality is improbable. For objective probabilities depend on the objective tendencies of things, and if PSR is false then events might occur in a way that has nothing to do with any objective tendencies of things. Hence one cannot consistently deny PSR and be justified in trusting the evidence of sensory perception, nor the empirical science grounded in perception. (Notice that one could give this sort of argument not only for PSR but directly for PC itself, as Koons does.)

Of course a determined critic of PSR could just bite the bullet and accept perceptual skepticism, but I think the Pruss/Koons line of argument could be pushed even further than they push it. Consider that whenever we accept a claim we take to be rationally justified, we suppose not only that we have a reason for accepting it (in the sense of a rational justification) but also that this reason is the reason *why* we accept it (in the sense of being the cause or explanation of our accepting it). We suppose that it is *because* the rational considerations in favor of the claim are good ones that we are moved to assent to the claim. We also suppose that our cognitive faculties track truth and standards of rational argumentation, rather than leading us to embrace conclusions in a way that has no connection to truth or logic. But if PSR is false, we could have no reason for thinking that any of this is really the case. For all we know, what moves or causes us to assent to a claim might have absolutely nothing to do with the deliverances of our cognitive faculties, and our cognitive faculties themselves might in turn have the deliverances they do in a way that has nothing to do with truth or standards of logic. We might believe what we do for no reason whatsoever, and yet it might also falsely *seem*, once again for no reason whatsoever, that we do believe what we do on good rational grounds. Now this would apply to any grounds we might have for doubting PSR as much as it does to any other conclusion we might draw. Hence to doubt or deny PSR undercuts any grounds we could have for doubting or denying PSR. The rejection of PSR is self-undermining. Even the critic of PSR willing to embrace perceptual skepticism and retreat into a redoubt of *a priori* knowledge will find no shelter there. To reject PSR is to undermine the possibility of *any* rational inquiry.

There is arguably another way in which science in particular implicitly presupposes PSR. Some philosophers have taken the view that there can be genuine explanations, including scientific explanations, even if PSR is false. One finds such a view in J. L. Mackie (1982, pp. 84-87) and Bertrand Russell (Russell and Copleston 1964, pp. 168-78). The idea is that we can explain at least some phenomena in terms of laws of nature, those laws in terms of more fundamental laws, and perhaps these in tern of some most fundamental level of laws. The most fundamental laws would, however, lack any explanation. That the world is governed by them would just be an unintelligible "brute fact."

But it is far from clear that this is coherent. Suppose I told you that the fact that a certain book has not fallen to the ground is explained by the fact that it is resting on a certain shelf, but that the fact that the shelf itself has not fallen to the ground has no explanation at all but is an unintelligible brute fact. Have I really explained the position of the book? It is hard to see how. For the shelf has in itself no tendency to stay aloft -- it is, by hypothesis, just a brute fact that it does so. But if it has no such tendency, it cannot impart such a tendency to the book. The "explanation" the shelf provides in such a case would be completely illusory. (Nor would it help to impute to the book some such tendency, if the having of the tendency is *itself* just an unintelligible brute fact. The illusion will just have been relocated, not eliminated.)

By the same token, it is no good to say: "The operation of law of nature C is explained by the operation of law of nature B, and the operation of B by the operation of law of nature A, but the operation of A has no explanation whatsoever and is just an unintelligible brute fact." The appearance of having "explained" C and B seems completely illusory if A is a brute fact, because if there is neither anything about A itself that can explain A's own operation nor anything beyond A that can explain it, then A has nothing to impart to B or C that could possibly explain their operation. The notion of an explanatory nomological regress terminating in a brute fact seems, when carefully examined, as incoherent the notion of an effect being produced by an instrument that is not the instrument of anything. (A series of ever more fundamental "laws of nature" is in this regard like a series of what Scholastic writers call instrumental causes ordered *per se*. See below.)

So, PSR not only gives general support to PC, but provides an especially powerful defense against science-based objections to PC in particular, such as Russell's objection and objections from inertia and quantum mechanics. All rational inquiry, and scientific inquiry in particular, presupposes PSR. But PSR entails PC. Therefore PC cannot coherently be denied in the name of science. It must instead be regarded as part of the metaphysical framework within which all scientific results must be interpreted.

2.4 Causal series

2.4.1 Simultaneity

I have noted several times that for Scholastic metaphysicians, the immediate cause of an effect is simultaneous with it (rather than, as Hume would have it, temporally prior to it). Cause and effect are not two events, but two elements of one event. The basic idea is that to cause is just to produce an effect, and it makes no sense to think of a cause producing without its effect being produced, or an effect being produced without its cause producing it. As Clarke puts it, "the cutting-of-the-orange-by-the-knife must be identical with the-orange-being-cut; otherwise the knife is not cutting anything at the moment of its cutting, nor is the orange being cut by anything at the later moment of its being cut" (2001, p. 191). (Cf. Aristotle, *Physics*, Book VII, Chapter 2; McInerny 2004, pp. 254-5; Smith and Kendzierski 1961, p. 93)

It is important to emphasize, however, that *simultaneous* does not entail *instantaneous*. An event is of course spread out through time. The point is that a cause's producing its effect is part of the same one event in which the effect is being produced, however long this event lasts. Once again to quote Clarke, "it indeed takes me time to push a chair across the room; but there is no time at all between my pushing the chair and the chair being pushed" (2001, p. 192; Cf. Mumford and Anjum 2011, pp. 109 and 111-12).

Mumford and Anjum have recently defended the simultaneity of causes and effects at some length (2011, Chapter 5; Cf. Huemer and Kovitz 2003). As they note, the standard Humean examples used to support the claim that a cause and its effect are essentially temporally separated are not convincing. For instance, to say that the motion of billiard ball A caused the later motion of billiard ball B is not quite

right, for A's motion could have been stopped before A had any causal influence on B, and B's motion may or may not continue regardless
of the continued presence of A. It is only at the point of impact that
there is really any causation going on vis-à-vis A and B. But ball A's
impacting B and B's being impacted by A are not temporally separated. They are just the same event. As we saw earlier, it is not quite
right either to speak of *the throwing of a brick* causing *the breaking of
glass*. It is rather the brick's pushing into the glass that is the immediate cause and the glass's giving way that is the effect, and these
(unlike *the throwing of the brick* and *the breaking of the glass*) are not
temporally separated but rather parts of one and the same event. Of
course, the motion of billiard ball A and the throwing of the brick are
causally relevant, and there is a perfectly legitimate sense in which
we can speak of them as causes of the effects in question. But what
they are not are the *immediate* causes of these effects, and *immediate*
causes are always simultaneous with their effects.

But, it might be objected, would this not make all the causes
and effects in a causal chain simultaneous, which would have the absurd implication that there are no causal chains extended through
time? No. For one thing, remember that "simultaneous" does not
entail "instantaneous." The single event in which a cause generates
its effect can take place over the course of seconds, minutes, even
hours or much longer. (Think of a potter molding a vase, a cube of
sugar dissolving in water, or a heater warming a room.) For another,
as Mumford and Anjum note, we must "[distinguish] causal episodes
that are a part of a single process from causal processes that are ena-
bled by powers instantiated in earlier causal processes" (2011, p. 125).
Consider, to borrow their example: a cube of sugar being dissolved in
tea, followed ten minutes later by the tea being drunk and tasting
pleasant to the drinker, which is then followed in turn by the tea's
being converted into energy after it reaches the stomach. Each of
these three events is a causal process, but they are not themselves related causally *in the sense* in which causation occurs *within* each event.
That is to say, the sugar dissolving in the tea is one causal process,
but it does not in turn cause the drinking of the tea. Rather, it results
in a set of conditions which ten minutes later play a role in the separate causal process of the tea's being drunk. Nor does the drinking of
the tea cause the conversion of the tea into energy. Rather, it is one

causal process which sets up the conditions for the other (even if in this case there is a partial temporal overlap between the two processes). What we don't have is one process causing another which causes another *in the sense* in which (say) the water and molecular structure of the sugar cube cause dissolution. In that latter process the cause and effect are simultaneous. But since the tea's dissolving is not in the same sense a cause of the drinking of the tea, there is no question of simultaneity and thus no question of this long series of events (sugar dissolving, tea being drunk, tea converted to energy) collapsing into one big simultaneous causal event.

But, it might still be objected: Hasn't Einstein refuted the claim that causes and effects are simultaneous, insofar as special relativity holds that whether two spatially separated events are simultaneous is relative to the observer's frame of reference? No, because the view we've been considering is precisely that an effect and its immediate cause are part of the *same* event rather than distinct events, and the examples we've been appealing to involve causes and effects occupying the *same* spatial location rather than separate locations. So, relativity is irrelevant. (Cf. Mumford and Anjum 2011, p. 121)

2.4.2 Per se versus per accidens

Aquinas, Scotus, and other Scholastics distinguish between series of efficient causes ordered *per se* or essentially, and series ordered *per accidens* or accidentally. Scotus identifies three key differences between the two sorts of causal series:

> *Per se* or essentially ordered causes differ from accidentally ordered causes in three respects. The first difference is that in essentially ordered causes, the second depends upon the first precisely in its act of causation. In accidentally ordered causes this is not the case, although the second may depend upon the first for its existence or in some other way. Thus a son depends upon his father for existence but is not dependent upon him in exercising his own causality, since he can act just as well whether his father be living or dead. The second difference is that in essentially ordered causes the causality is of another nature and order, inasmuch as the higher cause is more perfect.

Such is not the case, however, with accidentally ordered caus-es... The third difference is that all *per se* and essentially or-dered causes are simultaneously required to cause the effect, for otherwise some causality essential to the effect would be wanting. In accidentally ordered causes this is not so, because there is no need of simultaneity in causing inasmuch as each possesses independently of the others the perfection of causali-ty with regard to its own effect. (1987, pp. 40-41; Cf. Cross 1999, p. 16-18 and Cross 2005, pp. 21-26)

Let's examine each of these differences in turn. First, what is meant by saying that in an essentially ordered series of causes but not in an accidentally ordered series, "the second depends upon the first precisely in its act of causation"? Consider the stock example of a hand which moves a stick which in turn moves a stone. The stick causes the stone to move, but not under its own power. It moves the stone only insofar as it is being used by the hand to move it. The hand (or, more properly, the person whose hand it is) is what Scho-lastics would call the *principal* cause of the stone's motion, with the stick being the *instrumental* cause. The stick has power to move the stone in only a derivative or "secondary" way, and in that sense "de-pends upon the first [i.e. the hand] precisely in its act of causation." That sort of dependence is the defining feature of an essentially or-dered series of causes. There is an essential connection between the members of the series qua members insofar as the members lower down in the series have their causal power, for as long as the series exists, only insofar as they derive it from a member higher up.

Accidentally ordered series are not like this. Scotus's illustra-tion, a father who begets a son who in turn begets a son of his own, is another stock example. Though the son exists only because his fa-ther begat him, once he exists he is capable of begetting his own son whether or not his father is still around. Contrast this with the stick, which would be unable to move the stone if the hand were no longer around. Unlike the stick, the son has "built in" power to produce an-other member of the series in question. He begets his own son inde-pendently of his own father, rather than functioning as a mere in-strument in the begetting of his son. In that sense the relationship between the members of the series is accidental or non-essential.

The second difference between essentially ordered and accidentally ordered series, Scotus tells us, is that "in essentially ordered causes the causality is of another nature and order, inasmuch as the higher cause is more perfect." The stick in our example has power to move the stone, but not inherently; whereas the hand (or rather, the person whose hand it is) does, in a sense, have the inherent power to move other things, by virtue of which it imparts power to the stick. (When you pick up a stick so as to move a stone with it, no one has to pick you up in turn and move the stick through you.) In that sense the mover of the stick has causal power of "another nature and order" than the stick, and of a "more perfect" sort. Principal or underived causality, in other words, is of a higher and more perfect sort than instrumental or merely derivative causality. In accidentally ordered series, by contrast, the members -- such as the fathers and sons in our example -- have casual power of the same sort. The son's power to beget sons of his own is no more derivative in the relevant sense than his father's was.

The third difference is that the causes and effects in an essentially ordered series are simultaneous, but need not be in an accidentally ordered series. The stick pushes the stone only when and insofar as the hand pushes the stick. (Recall that "simultaneous" does not entail "instantaneous." The process may extend over a considerable period of time.) By contrast, the son's begetting of his own son may occur long after his own father is dead, in a distinct and temporally separated event. This difference follows from the others insofar as the later members of an essentially ordered series cannot operate without the continued presence of the earlier member from which they derive their causal power, whereas the later members in an accidentally ordered series do not require the continued presence of any earlier member.

Though there are causal series of both kinds in the world, the essentially ordered kind is more fundamental insofar as each stage in an accidentally ordered series is going to involve various series of causes ordered *per se* or essentially. For example, at the crucial stages in the series of fathers begetting sons, an egg's being fertilized is simultaneous with and dependent on a sperm cell's doing the fertilizing; the actions that result in the fertilization are going to involve various essentially ordered bodily movements; and so on.

The standard Scholastic view is that accidentally ordered series of causes can in principle extend backward to infinity, but essentially ordered series cannot. Since each member of an accidentally ordered series has its causal power inherently rather than derivatively, there is no need to trace any member's action back to the activity of a first member; again, when the son begets a son of his own, it is he who does the begetting, not his father who does so using him as an instrument. Hence such a series need not have a beginning. By contrast, Aquinas holds, "in efficient causes it is impossible to proceed to infinity *per se* – thus, there cannot be an infinite number of causes that are *per se* required for a certain effect; for instance, that a stone be moved by a stick, the stick by the hand, and so on to infinity" (*Summa Theologiae* I.46.2). He sets out the reasons in the *Summa Contra Gentiles*:

> In an ordered series of movers and things moved (this is a series in which one is moved by another according to an order), it is necessarily the fact that, when the first mover is removed or ceases to move, no other mover will move or be moved. For the first mover is the cause of motion for all the others. But, if there are movers and things moved following an order to infinity, there will be no first mover, but all would be as intermediate movers. Therefore, none of the others will be able to be moved, and thus nothing in the world will be moved...

> That which moves as an instrumental cause cannot move unless there be a principal moving cause. But, if we proceed to infinity among movers and things moved, all movers will be as instrumental causes, because they will be moved movers and there will be nothing as a principal mover. Therefore, nothing will be moved. (I.13.14-15)

The basic idea, then, is that since the later members of a causal series ordered *per se* have no causal power on their own but derive their power entirely from a cause which does have such power inherently -- a cause which, as it were, uses the others as instruments -- there is no sense to be made of such a series having no such first member. If a first member who is the source of the causal power of the others did not exist, the series as a whole simply would not exist, as the movement of the stone and the stick cannot occur in the absence of the hand. In other words, a series without such a first member would be like an instrument that is not the instrument of anything. "But even the unlearned perceive how ridiculous it is to suppose that instruments are moved, unless they are set in motion by some principal agent" (Aquinas, *Compendium of Theology* I.3).

Barry Miller (1982; 1992, Chapter 6) has suggested that the logical form of an explanation which makes appeal to a necessarily terminating regress of causes would be something like:

A is being caused to G by [B inasmuch as it is being caused to G by (C inasmuch as it is being caused to G by {M})]

Given its form, however many iterations of "___ inasmuch as it is being caused to G by ___" we might want to add to this sentence so as to describe a yet longer series, the sentence cannot actually be completed in a way that would leave open the possibility of there being an *infinite* number of such iterations. The only way to complete it will be at some point to insert a term like M (or whatever), which names a first member. In the case at hand, if we substitute "move" for G, "the stone" for A, "the stick" for B, "the hand" for C, and "the person" for M, we have a sentence expressing an explanation of the stone's motion of just the sort represented by our example of a causal series ordered *per se*.

As all of this indicates, what is meant by a "first" cause in this context is not merely "the cause that comes before the second, third, fourth, etc." or "the one which happens to be at the head of the queue." Rather, a "first cause" is one having *underived* causal power, in contrast to those which have their causal power in only a derivative or "secondary" way. As some commentators have pointed out, even if there could in some sense be an infinite regress of essentially ordered causes, there would still have to a source of causal power outside the series to impart causal power to the whole (Brown 1969; Wippel 2000, p. 423). Otherwise, as A. D. Sertillanges puts it, you might as well say "that a brush can paint by itself, provided it has a very long handle" (quoted in Garrigou-Lagrange 1939, p. 265). Even an infinitely long paint brush handle could not move itself, since the wood out of which it is made has no "built in" power of movement. The length of the handle is irrelevant. By the same token, even an infinitely long series of instrumental causes could not exhibit any causality at all unless there were something beyond the series whose instruments they were. (Cf. Suarez 2004, pp. 72-73)

In this light, some objections sometimes raised against the idea that an essentially ordered series of causes must have a first member can be seen to miss the point. It is no good, for instance, to point to infinite mathematical series as counterexamples, because these do not involve instrumental and principal causes. Scholastic writers do not in any event rule out all infinite series as such. They allow not only for infinite mathematical series, but, as has been noted, generally agree that a series of accidentally ordered causes extending backward in time (which also do not involve instrumental and principal causes) could in principle lack a beginning. Hence it also simply misses the point to raise the objection that there are cosmological models favoring a universe, or at least a "multiverse," without a beginning. (Though Bonaventure was one Scholastic who did argue against the possibility of such an infinite temporal regress, on the basis of what is today commonly referred to as the *kalām* cosmological argument.)

It is also sometimes thought that the key reason an infinite regress of essentially ordered causes is supposed to be impossible has to do with their simultaneity. Ockham, who was critical of Scotus's arguments on this subject (Ockham 1990, pp. 115-25; Cf. Adams 1987, pp. 772-84, and Wood 1990), supposed this. The objection might then be raised that the argument rests on the controversial Aristotelian view that an actually infinitely large collection is impossible. But in fact neither infinity nor simultaneity *per se* is what is doing the work in the argument. (Cf. Brown 1969, pp. 226-29) Again, the key point is that in an essentially ordered series, all the members other than the principal cause have only instrumental or derivative causal power. Thus they would have no causal efficacy at all unless there was something outside the series of instrumental causes that imparted to them their efficacy. As we have seen, this would remain true even if the series were infinite. It would also remain true if the members were somehow not all simultaneous. Suppose for the sake of argument that a "time gate" of the sort described in science fiction stories (like Robert Heinlein's story "By His Bootstraps") were possible. Suppose further that here in 2014 you take a stick and put it halfway through the time gate, while the other half comes out in 3014 and pushes a stone. The motion of the stone and the motion of the hand are not simultaneous – they are separated by 1000 years – but we still have a causal series ordered *per se* insofar as the former motion depends essentially on the latter motion.

It is also sometimes objected that the argument for a first member of an essentially ordered series begs the question, insofar as characterizing other causes as instrumental itself presupposes that there is such a first member. But there is no begging of the question. To characterize something as an instrumental cause is merely to say that it derives its causal power from something else. There is nothing in that characterization that *presupposes* that a series of such causes cannot regress to infinity or that there must be some cause which has underived causal power (Brown 1969, pp. 222-23). Even the skeptic can perfectly well understand the idea that a stick cannot move the stone under its own power, whether or not he goes on to agree that a regress of such moved movers must terminate in a first member.

Needless to say, the notion that an essentially ordered series of causes must terminate in a first member plays a crucial role in Scholastic arguments in natural theology. (Cf. Feser 2009, Chapter 3; Feser 2011) When Scholastic writers characterize God as the First Cause, they do not mean that God is one cause alongside the others, but the one who happens to stand at the head of the queue. What they mean is that as pure actuality he has absolutely underived causal power whereas all other things have their causal power in only a derivative way, with God being the source from which they ultimately derive it. Scholastic writers thus distinguish the *primary causality* which can belong only to that which is pure actuality from the *secondary causality* possessed by everything else. (The dispute between occasionalists, concurrentists, and mere conservationists vis-à-vis divine causality has to do with whether and to what extent secondary causes are true causes. Cf. Freddoso 1988, 1991, 1994, and 2002)

2.5 The principle of proportionate causality

The *principle of proportionate causality* (PPC) states that "effects must needs be proportionate to their causes and principles" (*Summa Theologiae* I-II.63.3) such that "whatever perfection exists in an effect must be found in the effective cause" (*Summa Theologiae* I.4.2). For a thing cannot give what it does not have. More precisely, whatever is in an effect must be in its *total* cause in *some* way or other, whether *formally, virtually*, or *eminently*. A simple example will illustrate the idea. Suppose I give you a twenty dollar bill. Your having it is the effect. One way in which I could cause you to have it is by virtue of having a twenty dollar bill in my wallet and handing it to you. I have the "form" of *possessing a twenty dollar bill* and I cause you to have the same form. That would be a case of what is in the effect being in the cause "formally." But it might be that I do not have a twenty dollar bill on hand ready to give you, but I do have at least twenty dollars in the bank, and I can wire the money from my account to yours so that you can withdraw it from an ATM. In that case what is in the effect was in the total cause -- me plus my bank account, etc. -- "virtually" rather than formally. Or it might be that I do not have even twenty dollars in my account, but I do somehow have access to a U.S. Federal Reserve Bank printing press and can get a genuine twenty dollar bill printed off for you on demand. In that case what is in the effect is in the total cause -- me, the printing press, etc. -- "eminently." For while in this case I don't have an actual twenty dollar bill or even twenty dollars in the bank, I would have something even more fundamental, causally speaking, namely the power to *make* twenty dollar bills.

PPC follows straightforwardly from PC and PSR. If there were some aspect of an effect that didn't come from its total cause, then that would involve a potency that was actualized without anything doing the actualizing, which would violate PC. It would be an aspect of the effect that lacked any explanation, which would violate PSR. Yet it is sometimes claimed that PPC is easily refuted. Consider Descartes' dictum in the Third Meditation that "there must be at least as much reality in the efficient and total cause as in the effect of that cause" (Descartes 1985, p. 28). This variation on PPC, sometimes labeled the "Causal Adequacy Principle" by commentators (Cottingham 1986, p. 49), is the version of the principle best-known to contemporary philosophers. John Cottingham characterizes it as "seem[ing] to imply a kind of 'heirloom' view of causation" insofar as it regards properties as passed down from causes to effects, and he suggests that it is open to counterexamples (1986, p. 50). For instance, "helium has properties which were not present in the hydrogen from which it was formed by fusion" and "a sponge cake... has many prop-erties -- e.g. its characteristic sponginess -- which were simply not present in any of the material ingredients (the eggs, flour, butter)" (p. 51).

There are several problems with this sort of objection, though. First of all, Cottingham's examples, by his own admission, concern only the material causes (as opposed to the formal, final, and efficient causes) of the effects in question. Here he follows Gassendi, who thought Descartes' principle was plausible at most in the case of material causes. Yet the PPC, even as formulated by Descartes, is not concerned merely with the material factors involved in an effect's production. It says that whatever is in an effect can in some way be found in its *total* cause, not in the material factors alone. It is quite absurd, then, to qualify the PPC in a way its defenders would reject, attack the qualified version, and then pretend that one has struck a blow against the PPC itself! This seems a clear example of a straw man fallacy.

Second, to attribute an "heirloom" view of causation to defenders of the PPC is also to attack a straw man, and indeed to attribute to them a thesis they sometimes explicitly reject. As one Scholastic author writes:

> The mediaeval scholastics embodied this truth in the formula: *Nemo dat quod non habet* -- a formula which we must not interpret in the more restricted and literal sense of the words *giving* and *having*, lest we be met with the obvious objection that it is by no means necessary for a boy to have a black eye himself in order to give one to his neighbour! (Coffey 1970, p. 60)

And Aquinas writes:

> Again, it is laughable to say that a body does not act because an accident does not pass from subject to subject. For a hot body is not said to give off heat in this sense, that numerically the same heat which is in the heating body passes over into the heated body. Rather, by the power of the heat which is in the heating body, a numerically different heat is made actual in the heated body, a heat which was previously in it in potency. For a natu-

ral agent does not hand over its own form to another subject, but it reduces the passive subject from potency to act. (*Summa Contra Gentiles* III.69.28)

The "heirloom" interpretation of PPC essentially supposes that the principle holds that what is in the effect must be in the cause *formally*. But that is not the case. It could be in the total cause *virtually* or *eminently* instead.

Now Cottingham does agree that "the sponginess does not arise *ex nihilo*; it emerges from the complex chemical changes produced by the mixing and the baking" (1986, p. 51). But he thinks this does not help the PPC:

> But this fact simply does not support the conclusion that the sponginess was somehow present in some form in the materials from which it arose. (One may be tempted to say that the sponginess must have been 'potentially' present in the materials, but this seems to defend the Causal Adequacy Principle at the cost of making it trivially true. (1986, p. 51)

As the passage from Aquinas just quoted indicates, the defender of the PPC *would* indeed say that the characteristics that end up in the effect were in it potentially. In my example above, the total cause's having what is in the effect virtually or eminently involved having various active and passive potencies -- for instance, the passive potency of my bank account to have twenty dollars drawn from it, and the active potency of the Federal Reserve Bank printing press to run off a new twenty dollar bill. How does this make the PPC only "trivially true"? No doubt what Cottingham has in mind is a variation of Molière's "dormitive virtue" objection to causal powers. But as we saw in Chapter 1, Molière's objection fails. Explanations in terms of powers may often be only *minimally* informative, but they are not necessarily *non*-informative or trivial.

That the PPC is not trivial is evident from the fact that naturalistic philosophers, who in general would have no truck with Scholastic or Cartesian metaphysics, sometimes implicitly make use of the principle in their own argumentation. For example, Paul Churchland argues that both the individual human being and the human species as a whole have purely material beginnings and develop from these beginnings via purely material processes. The end result, he concludes, must therefore be purely material (2013, pp. 43-44). What this assumes, of course, is that if the total cause is material, so too must the effect be material. The dualist would agree with him about that, but argue that since part of the effect (the human intellect) is not material, neither could the total cause have been purely material. PPC itself is implicitly taken for granted by both sides.

This naturally leads us to the question of evolution, which is also sometimes taken to be a counterexample to PPC. (Cf. Cottingham 1986, pp. 51-52) The idea is that if simpler life forms give rise to more complex ones, then there is something in the effect that was not in the cause. But in fact that is not the case even on the standard naturalistic account of evolution. On that account, every species is essentially just a variation on the same basic genetic material that has existed for billions of years from the moment life began. A new variation arises when there is a mutation in the existing genetic material which produces a trait that is advantageous given the circumstances of a creature's environment. The mutation in turn might be caused by a copying error made during the DNA replication process or by some external factor like radiation or chemical damage. So, it is not that a simpler life form just up and gives rise to a more complex one, full stop. Rather, the existing genetic material, the mutation, and the environmental circumstances work together to generate a new biological variation, where none of these factors by itself would be sufficient to do so. So, even on the standard naturalistic account, evolution respects the principle that a *total* cause must contain what is in its effect in *some* way, whether formally, virtually, or eminently. Indeed, as the physicist Paul Davies has pointed out, to deny that the information contained in a new kind of life form derives from some combination of preexisting factors -- specifically, in part from the organism's environment if not from its genetic inheritance alone -- would contradict the second law of thermodynamics, which tells us that order, and thus information content, tends inevitably to decrease within a closed system (Davies 1999, Chapter 2).

But there is in any event no reason why a Scholastic metaphysician should accept a purely naturalistic understanding of evolution. With evolution as with Newton's principle of inertia, quantum mechanics, and relativity theory, those who purport to draw metaphysical lessons *from* science are in fact reading metaphysical assumptions *into* it. The Scholastic would argue that PPC is something we know to be true on grounds more certain and fundamental than anything empirical science does or can provide. Hence evolution must be interpreted in light of PPC, and if it turns out that this entails a conflict between Scholastic and naturalistic accounts of the metaphysics of evolution, so much the worse for naturalism. (For discussions of the metaphysics of evolution written from the point of view of Scholastic metaphysics, see Clarke 2001, pp. 194-96 and Chapter 15; Donceel 1961; Klubertanz 1953, especially pp. 412-27; Koren 1955; Oderberg 2007, Chapters 8 - 10; Oderberg 2013; and Royce 1961, pp. 337-53.)

3. Substance

3.1 Hylemorphism

3.1.1 Form and matter

Aristotle's four causes are the *formal cause*, the *material cause*, the *efficient cause*, and the *final cause*. Our consideration of the theory of act and potency has led us to the latter two causes. A potency is always a potency *for* some actuality. It points beyond itself to an end or range of ends. Hence to understand a thing's potencies is to understand it in terms of final causality. A potency can be actualized only by what is already actual. Hence to understand a thing's coming into being or changing -- that is to say, its becoming actual in various respects -- is to understand it in terms of efficient causality. A thing's final and efficient causes are *extrinsic* principles of its being, since the ends to which it points and the causes which actualize it are outside of it.

Now the theory of act and potency also leads us naturally to two *intrinsic* principles of a thing's being, namely its material and formal causes -- that is to say, its matter and form (*hylē* and *morphē* in Greek, hence the term "hylemorphism" or "hylomorphism"). There are two fundamental lines of argument for hylemorphism (Cf. Koren 1962, Chapter 2), though Scholastic writers have also put forward a number of secondary arguments (Cf. the readings collected in Part III of Koren 1965). These two primary arguments may be labeled the *argument from change* and the *argument from limitation*, and they are implicit in what was said in chapter 1 in exposition of the general theory of act and potency.

In change, as we have seen, there is both the potency that is to be actualized and the actualization of that potency. Consider the ink in a dry-erase marker. While still in the pen it is actually liquid but it has the potency to dry, on the surface of the marker board, into a particular shape, such as a circular shape. When you use the pen to draw a circle on the board, that potency is actualized. Having dried into that shape, the ink has yet other potencies, such as the potency to be removed from the board by an eraser and in the process to take on the form of dust particles. When you erase the circle and the dried particles of ink fall from the board and/or get stuck in the eraser, those potencies are actualized.

Now, what we have in this scenario is, first of all, a determinable substratum that is the seat of the potencies in question -- namely, the ink. We also have a series of determining patterns that the substratum, the ink, takes on as the various potencies are actualized -- patterns like *being liquid, being dry, being circular,* and *being particle-like.* The determinable substratum of potency is what the Scholastic means by *matter,* and the determining patterns that exist once the potency is actualized is what is meant by *form.* If change is real -- and that it is real is something that has been defended in the preceding chapters -- then matter and form must be real. Matter is, essentially, that which needs actualizing in change; form is, essentially, that which results from the actualization.

Note that *any* determining, actualizing pattern counts as a "form" in this sense -- a form is not merely the shape of a thing, nor always a matter of the spatial configuration of parts (though shape and spatial configuration are kinds of forms). *Being blue, being hot, being soft,* etc. are all forms in the relevant sense. Note also that "matter" is not meant here in the same sense in which it is used in modern science -- though hylemorphism is not in competition with modern science, just as (as we saw in chapter 1) the notion of active potencies or causal powers is not in competition with modern science. To say that opium has the power to induce sleep is not, as we saw, to say anything that conflicts with what chemistry tells us about opium. It is rather to tell us what must as a matter of basic metaphysics be true, whatever the chemical details turn out to be, if opium is to have any causal efficacy at all vis-à-vis sleep. Similarly, whatever chemists tell us about the chemistry of ink, and whatever physicists tell us about the nature of matter more generally, change presupposes "matter" *in the sense of* a determinable substratum of potency. For the purposes of science, that, like the notion of a causal power, is only minimally informative. But it is not non-informative, and it is very significant indeed for understanding the metaphysical framework presupposed by any possible natural science.

The argument from limitation appeals to considerations of the sort raised in chapter 1 when discussing the second of the twenty-four Thomistic theses (to the effect that act is limited only by potency). It was pointed out there that a pattern like *roundness* is of itself universal rather than particular, and *perfect* or exact rather than approximate. Now, the circle you draw on the marker board is round, but only imperfectly or approximately; and it is a particular instance of roundness rather than roundness as such. Hence there must not only be something by virtue of which the thing in question, the circle, is round, but also something by virtue of which it is round in precisely the limited way that it is -- round only to *this degree*, and round in *this particular* point in time and space. And if being round is a way of being *actual*, being round only in these limited ways is (given the second of the twenty-four theses) a way of being *potential*. For insofar as the circle is imperfectly round, it has, you might say, only partially actualized the potency for circularity; and insofar as it is in some particular time and place, it is a potency at *that* time and place, rather than at another, that has been actualized. Now that by virtue of which the circle is actually round to the extent it is just is its *form*; while that by virtue of which it is limited, or remains in potency, in the extent to which it is round is its *matter*.

Hylemorphism is thus the application of the theory of act and potency -- which, as we have seen, is the Scholastic answer to the Eleatic and Heraclitean opposite extremes vis-à-vis the problems of *change versus permanence* and *multiplicity versus unity* -- to the analysis of the *intrinsic* determinants of things, just as the principles of finality and (efficient) causality are applications of the theory of act and potency to the analysis of the *extrinsic* determinants of things. Form is that intrinsic principle by which a thing exhibits whatever permanence, perfection, and identity that it does. It represents, as it were, the Eleatic side of things. The circle drawn on the marker board persists to the extent that it retains its circular form, is perfect to the extent that it approximates that form, and is identical to other circles insofar as it is an instance of the same form they instantiate. Matter, by contrast, is that intrinsic principle by which a thing exhibits the changeability, imperfection, and diversity that it does. It represents the Heraclitean side of things. The circle drawn on the marker board is impermanent insofar as its matter can lose its circular form, is imperfect insofar as that matter only approximates the form, and is distinct from other things having the same form insofar as it is one parcel of matter among others which instantiate it.

As with (on the Thomistic view) act and potency in things composed of both, form and matter are really distinct but not separable. Matter in the sense in question is passive and indeterminate, form active and determining. The same bit of matter can take on different forms, and the same form can be received in different bits of matter. Hence they are as really distinct as act and potency. But matter nevertheless always has *some* form or other. If the ink is not in a liquid form, it is in a dry, circular form, and if not that then in the form of particles. And if the particles are broken down further so that the ink is in no sense still present, then the form of the chemical constituents of the ink would remain. If matter lacked *all* form it would be nothing but the pure potency for receiving form; and if it were purely potency, it would in no way be actual and thus not exist at all. Similarly, for the Scholastic qua Aristotelian (even if not for the Platonist) the forms of purely material things always exist in some matter or other. If circularity exists in mind-independent reality but not in ink marks, that will be because it exists in a steel hoop, or a ceramic plate, or a plastic Frisbee, or some other bit of matter.

However, just as act can exist without potency even if potency cannot exist without act, so too can *some* forms exist without matter even though matter can never exist without form. For the Scholastic, the intellect is essentially immaterial (Aquinas, *Summa Theologiae* I.75.2; Aquinas, *Summa Contra Gentiles* II.49-51; Ross 1992; Oderberg 2007, Chapter 10; Feser 2013a). A purely intellectual substance -- which is what an angel is on the Scholastic view -- would have a form of a sort, but without matter. As this indicates, the distinction between form and matter is not the *same* distinction as that between act and potency, but a special case of that distinction. Everything composed of form and matter is thereby composed of act and potency, but not everything composed of act and potency is composed of form and matter. A purely intellectual but non-divine substance would, qua something less than pure actuality, need to be actualized at least vis-à-vis its existence, and thus have potency. It would thus be a compound of act and potency but not a compound of form and matter.

3.1.2 Substantial form versus accidental form

With the distinction between form and matter in hand, Scholastic philosophers go on to draw a crucial further distinction between a *substantial form* and an *accidental form*. It is usefully approached by way of yet another distinction, viz. the Aristotelian distinction between natural objects on the one hand and everyday artifacts and accidental arrangements on the other. Aristotle sets the theme in the *Physics*:

> Some things exist by nature, others are due to other causes. Natural objects include animals and their parts, plants and simple bodies like earth, fire, air and water... The obvious difference between all these things and things which are not natural is that each of the natural ones contains within itself a source of change and of stability, in respect of either movement or increase and decrease or alteration. On the other hand, something like a bed or a cloak has no intrinsic impulse for change – at least, they do not under that particular description and to the extent that they are a result of human skill, but they do in so far as and to the extent that they are coincidentally made out of stone or earth or some combination of the two.
>
> The nature of a thing, then, is a certain principle and cause of change and stability in the thing, and it is *directly* present in it – which is to say that it is present in its own right and not coincidentally. (*Physics*, Book II, Part 1, in Aristotle 1996, p. 33)

The basic idea is that a natural object is one whose characteristic behavior – the ways in which it manifests either stability or changes of various sorts – derives from something intrinsic to it. A non-natural object is one which does not have such an intrinsic principle of its characteristic behavior; only the natural objects out of which it is made have such a principle. We can illustrate the distinction with a simple example. A *liana vine* – the kind of vine Tarzan likes to swing on – is a natural object. A *hammock* that Tarzan might construct from living liana vines is a kind of artifact, and not a natural object. The parts of the liana vine have an inherent tendency to function together to allow the liana to exhibit the growth patterns it does, to take in water and nutrients, and so forth. By contrast, the parts of the hammock – the liana vines themselves – have no inherent tendency to function together as a hammock. Rather, they must be arranged by Tarzan to do so, and left to their own devices – that is to say, without pruning, occasional rearrangement, and the like – they will tend to grow the way they otherwise would have had Tarzan not interfered with them, including in ways that will impede their performance as a hammock. Their natural tendency is to be liana-like and not hammock-like; the hammock-like function they perform after Tarzan ties them together is extrinsic or imposed from outside, while the liana-like functions are intrinsic to them.

Now the difference between that which has such an intrinsic principle of operation and that which does not is essentially the difference between something having a substantial form and something having a merely accidental form. Being a liana vine involves having a substantial form, while being a hammock of the sort we're discussing involves instead the imposition of an accidental form on components each of which already has a substantial form, namely the substantial form of a liana vine. A liana vine is, accordingly, a true *substance*, as Scholastic philosophers understand substance. A hammock is not a true substance, precisely because it does not qua hammock have a substantial form -- an *intrinsic* principle by which it operates as it characteristically does -- but only an accidental form. In general, true substances are typically natural objects, whereas (Aquinas tells us, commenting on Aristotle) "some things are not substances, as is clear especially of artificial things" (*Sententia super Metaphysicam* VII.17.1680, in Aquinas 1995, at p. 552). Again:

> Man and wood and stone are natural bodies, but a house or a saw is artificial. And of these the natural bodies seem to be the more properly called substances, since artificial bodies are made out of them. Art works upon materials furnished by nature, giving these, moreover, a merely accidental form, such as a new shape and so forth... (*Sententia super De anima* II.1.218, in Aquinas 1994, at p. 73)

The liana-like tendencies of the vines are paradigm instances of intrinsic or "built in" finality or teleology, and such finality is a mark of the presence of a substantial form. For these tendencies involve an orientation toward certain ends – growth patterns of a certain sort, the taking in of water and nutrients, and so forth – that a liana vine has just by virtue of being a liana vine. By contrast, the hammock-like tendencies of the vines are paradigm instances of extrinsic finality, or teleology imposed "from outside." Those tendencies are not ones that the vines have given their substantial form or nature as vines. They are there only insofar as an artificer has put them there.

But not all accidental forms are the result of artifice. A group of liana vines which has by chance taken on a hammock-like arrangement does not have a substantial form *qua* hammock-like arrangement, any more than a pattern made by a trail of ants that looks vaguely like the word "No" is really the word "No." For while this arrangement is not an artifact (not having been deliberately constructed, as Tarzan's hammock was), the resulting object still does not have an *intrinsic* tendency to function as a hammock. Hence it does not have the substantial form of a hammock (if there were such a thing as the "substantial form of a hammock"), but is a mere accidental arrangement of parts, like a heap of stones that has formed at the bottom of a hill over time as a consequence of erosion. So, though in one sense it obviously occurred "naturally," it is not a "natural" object *in the sense* in which Aristotle contrasts nature with art, since a tendency to work together in a "hammock-like" way is not *inherent* to the parts.

What's true of a hammock (or a hammock-like chance object) made of living liana vines is no less true of a hammock made of dead liana vines, even though the difference between artifacts and natural objects is in this case less dramatic. For while dead vines will not exhibit the growth patterns the living vines will (constantly threatening to upset the hammock-like function Tarzan has imposed on them) they still have no *inherent or built-in* tendency to function as a hammock. Being dead, they have lost the substantial form of liana vines, but they have not taken on the substantial form of a hammock (if, again, there were such a thing). Rather, they have the very same substantial form that other bits of dead liana lying randomly around the forest have – the substantial form of a kind of wood, say. Perhaps this substantial form gives them enough durability to make them useful to put together into the form of a hammock, but that does not mean that they now have a natural "hammock-like" tendency *per se*, only that they have a natural tendency toward a certain degree of durability (which might also make them useful for making lots of things other than hammocks).

What has been said about hammocks is true also of watches, knives, computers, cars, houses, airplanes, telephones, cups, coats, beds, and countless other everyday artifacts. Like the hammock, these objects do not count as natural or as true substances because their specifically watch-like, knife-like, etc. tendencies are extrinsic rather than intrinsic, the result of externally imposed accidental forms rather than substantial forms. To be sure, the distinctively *metallic* tendencies of the parts of the watch or the blade of the knife *will* be instances of intrinsic finality, for these tendencies follow from the nature or substantial form of these components. As Aquinas puts it, "a knife has in itself a principle of downward motion, not insofar as it is a knife, but insofar as it is iron" (*Sententia super Physicam* II.1.142, in Aquinas 1999, at p. 75). But functions like time-telling, meat-cutting, and the like do not follow from the substantial form of the metal parts, and thus are not intrinsic to them.

I have noted that some objects that lack substantial forms, and thus are not "natural" in the technical sense Aristotle uses in the *Physics* – a heap of stones which has gradually formed at the bottom of a hill, a group of liana vines which by chance has grown into a hammock-like arrangement – are not artifacts. But the converse is also true; that is to say, it is possible for something to be a product of "art" or human skill and yet to have a substantial form, and thus to be in the relevant sense "natural." Aquinas says:

> Art is not able to confer a substantial form by its own power... [but] it is nevertheless able to do so by the power of natural agents, as is made clear by the fact that the form of fire is induced in wood through art. (*Scriptum super Sententiis* 2.7.3.1 ad 5, as translated by Michael Rota in Rota 2004, at p. 245)

Fire is something natural, and remains so even if it is generated by human beings rather than (say) lightning. Similarly, water synthesized out of hydrogen and oxygen in a laboratory is in no relevant respect different from water from a river or from the clouds. Dog breeds are also man-made, but a dog of any breed is still a natural object, for its parts have an inherent tendency to function together in a dog-like way (by contrast with a watch, whose parts have no inherent tendency to function in a watch-like way). Of course, fire and water already exist in many places no human being has ever trod, and dogs are variations on a kind of animal (the gray wolf) that already occurs in the wild. But even something which in no way exists apart from human intervention could also count as something having a substantial form, and thus as "natural" in the relevant sense. Eleonore Stump suggests Styrofoam as a possible example (Stump 2003, p. 44).

Stump's rationale is that it seems to be essential to a thing's having a substantial form that it has properties and causal powers that are irreducible to those of its parts. (Cf. Stump 2006 and 2013) Hence water has properties and causal powers that hydrogen and oxygen do not have, whereas the properties and causal powers of an axe seem to amount to nothing over and above the sum of the properties and powers of the axe's wood and metal parts. When water is synthesized out of hydrogen and oxygen, then, what happens is that the matter underlying the hydrogen and oxygen loses the substantial forms of hydrogen and oxygen and takes on a new substantial form, namely that of water. By contrast, when an axe is made out of wood and metal, the matter underlying the wood and the matter underlying the metal do not lose their substantial forms. Rather, while maintaining their substantial forms, they take on a new accidental form, that of being an axe. The making of Styrofoam, Stump suggests, seems to be more like the synthesis of water out of hydrogen and oxygen than it is like the making of an axe. For Styrofoam has properties and causal powers which are irreducible to those of the materials out of which it is made, and which therefore indicate the presence of a substantial form and thus a true substance.

This dovetails with what was said above about intrinsic finality being a mark of the presence of a substantial form. For causal powers or active potencies are, as we have seen, directed toward the production of their typical effects as to an end. For something to have *irreducible* causal powers is thus for it to be *irreducibly* directed toward the production of a certain outcome or range of outcomes as to an end; it is for it to exhibit irreducible teleology. Water, for example, is directed at effects like acting as a solvent for other substances, seeking its own level, freezing at 32 degrees Fahrenheit, etc. This cannot be reduced to the sum of the ends toward which the casual powers of oxygen and hydrogen are directed, since those powers aim at very different effects. Things with merely accidental forms are not like this. A heap of stones which has formed by chance at the bottom of a hill has by virtue of its weight the power to hold down one side of a scale you might put the heap on. It is, you might say, directed toward that sort of effect as to an end. But this amounts to nothing more than the heap's possessing the sum of the causal powers that the parts possess by virtue of their individual weights. It is not irreducible teleology. There is no finality or directedness toward an effect on the part of *the heap* as such; rather, there is just the sum of the finalities exhibited by each stone individually as its causal powers manifest themselves.

The causal powers of artifacts are reducible to the sum of the causal powers of their parts together with the ends imposed externally by their designers and users. A clock has the power to display the time, and is therefore directed to that end. But its having a power directed to that end is reducible to its parts being arranged in such a manner that the hands will move across certain marks on the face of the clock in a regular way, together with the intentions of the designers and users of the clock to interpret these movements as indicative of the time. The finality is extrinsic, imposed from outside by the designers and users, and thus the causal powers of the clock *qua time-telling device* -- as opposed to *qua* collection of bits of metal -- are nothing more than the causal powers of those bits of metal to produce effects upon which the designers and users can *impose* a time-telling interpretation.

To summarize, then: To have a substantial form is to be a "natural" object in Aristotle's sense of something which "contains within itself a source of change and of stability." This in turn involves being intrinsically directed toward certain ends, where this directedness manifests itself through the operation of a thing's causal powers. Hence, that water has an intrinsic tendency to act as a solvent and to freeze and 32 degrees Fahrenheit, that a liana vine has an intrinsic tendency to take in nutrients through its roots and to exhibit certain growth patterns, that a dog has an intrinsic tendency to grow four legs and a tail and to bark, howl, and chew, and that a human being has an intrinsic tendency to grasp abstract concepts, put them together into judgments, and reason from one judgment to another, indicate that water, liana vines, dogs, and human beings have substantial forms. They are, accordingly, substances in the Scholastic sense. As Aristotle says:

> The things which have a nature are those which have the kind of source I have been talking about. Each and every one of them is a substance, since substance is an underlying thing, and only underlying things can have a nature. They are all natural, and so is any property they have in their own right, such as the property fire has of moving upwards. (*Physics*, Book II, Part 1, in Aristotle 1996, p. 34)

Accidental forms, by contrast, merely modify already existing substances and are not associated with any intrinsic directedness to an end. Stones are substances, but being arranged into a heap is a merely accidental form that the stones have taken on, so that a heap is not a true substance. Liana vines are substances, but a chance growth pattern that results in the vines being arranged into something resembling a hammock is a merely accidental form that the vines have taken on, and is not itself a true substance. Even a hammock-like arrangement deliberately imposed on the vines by an artificer does not result in a true substance, for the hammock function is extrinsic rather than reflective of any intrinsic tendency and thus amounts to the having of a merely accidental form. The same is true of at least the most obvious results of human artifice -- houses, beds, clocks, computers, and the like.

The products of human action sometimes have substantial forms and thus count as true substances -- children, new breeds of dog, water synthesized in a lab, and, arguably, novel materials like Styrofoam -- and natural processes sometimes result in objects such as heaps of stones and chance growth patterns that have merely accidental forms and are thus not "natural objects" in Aristotle's technical sense of things having an intrinsic principle of operation. Thus, Aristotle's distinction in the *Physics* between nature and art is best regarded as a loose way of stating a distinction better described as that between things having substantial forms and those having only accidental forms. It is a natural first approximation to the latter distinction insofar as the *paradigmatic* examples of things having substantial forms happen to be objects that exist "naturally" in the sense of apart from human action, and the *paradigmatic* examples of things having merely accidental forms happen to be human artifacts.

3.1.3 Prime matter versus secondary matter

Hylemorphism, Scholastics argue, is necessary if we are to account for the reality of change. The distinction between substantial form and accidental form entails a distinction between two kinds of change. Accidental change involves a substance losing or gaining an accidental form, where the substance itself persists through the change. Substantial change involves the loss of a substantial form and the appearance of a new one, and thus the corruption of one substance and the generation of another. But as we have seen, what loses or takes on a form when a change occurs is matter. Corresponding to the distinctions between substantial and accidental form and substantial and accidental change, then, is a distinction between two kinds of matter: *prime matter* and *secondary matter*.

Secondary matter is matter having some substantial form or other. It is matter that is already water, or stone, or a liana vine, or a dog, or a human being. Its status as a substance is already determined, and what it awaits, as it were, is the reception of various accidental forms. Secondary matter is thus the subject of accidental change. Prime matter is matter lacking any substantial form, and indeed any form at all since accidental form presupposes substantial form. It is matter that is not yet any particular thing or other. It is indeterminate, the pure potency for form. It is the subject of substantial change.

Hylemorphism is also necessary in the Scholastic view if we are to explain limitation. Secondary matter accounts for the ways in which accidental forms are limited in the ways they are -- that is, limited to a particular time and place, and limited in the degree of perfection to which a thing instantiates them -- and prime matter accounts for the ways in which substantial forms are limited in the ways *they* are.

Prime matter, like potency more generally, is a real feature of the world, and must be if it is to do its job of accounting for the possibility of change and limitation. However, that does not entail that it can exist separately from form, any more than potency can exist separately from act. As the pure potency for taking on form, prime matter existing all by itself would be in no way actual and thus nonexistent. In extra-mental reality, then, prime matter can only exist together with substantial form. Our knowledge of it is accordingly indirect, based on inference from what must be the case for substantial change to be possible. To a first approximation we can appeal to analogies, like clay or molten plastic, which are in the ordinary sense amorphous or without determinate shape. Prime matter is like that insofar as it is literally amorphous or without any form whatsoever but, like the clay or plastic, ready to take on some form. Clay and plastic are not *strictly* formless in the relevant sense, however. On the contrary, they each have a number of forms -- those associated with the chemical properties of clay or plastic, along with accidental forms such as a certain color and temperature. When a bit of clay takes on the form of pottery or a bit of plastic takes on the form of a child's toy, this is merely accidental change, the acquisition of an accidental form rather than the generation of a new substance. By contrast, prime matter *as such* lacks not only any shape, but also any color, temperature, weight, chemical properties, or any other feature we commonly attribute to a purportedly amorphous "stuff" of everyday experience.

Again, though, since substances, understood as things having substantial forms in the sense described above, come into being and pass away, and since substantial forms, like accidental ones, are limited in the ways described above, prime matter must exist. There are only two other apparent alternatives to prime matter -- either that some rudimentary kind of secondary matter can do the job prime matter is supposed to do, or that nothing need do it -- and neither alternative survives close analysis. (Cf. Oderberg 2007, pp. 71-76) Let's consider these apparent alternatives in order. One problem with the suggestion that some rudimentary kind of secondary matter can do the job of prime matter is that it seems a non-starter with respect to the argument from limitation. Such secondary matter would have some substantial form or other -- that's why it is *secondary* rather than primary -- and whatever that substantial form is, we need an explanation of why it is limited in just the ways it is. Hence suppose it is suggested that the rudimentary sort of secondary matter in question consists of particles of the form F. What is it that limits F to the spatiotemporal locations these particles happen to be? To appeal to some even more rudimentary sort of secondary matter to answer the question would just raise the same problem over again, while to appeal to prime matter would defeat the whole purpose of positing the rudimentary sort of secondary matter in question.

Then there is the argument from change. For one thing, there is no empirical reason to believe in a rudimentary sort of secondary matter that underlies all substantial changes. As Oderberg points out, "[a]ccording to current physical theory, even quarks can be substantially transformed into other quarks" (2007, p. 64). But then there must be something underlying the substantial change of one quark into another, in which case quarks cannot be the fundamental sort of matter. But even apart from the empirical evidence, the very idea of a rudimentary sort of secondary matter underlying all substantial change is metaphysically fishy. Again, suppose it is suggested that the rudimentary sort of secondary matter in question consists of particles of the form F. Just by virtue of the fact that it is of form F -- rather than form G, or H, or any other form -- we already know that any such particle is limited to the extent of being just the sort of thing it is rather than some other sort of thing. It is limited to being *this* rather than *that*. Its actuality is therefore less than *pure* actuality. But being less than pure actuality, it is simply not the sort of thing that could exist necessarily. It is rather the sort of thing that could at least in principle be generated or corrupted. But in that case there must be something that *underlies* its potency for being generated or corrupted. And once again, to posit some even more rudimentary sort of secondary matter as the substrate of this potential generation or corruption would raise the same problem over again, while to appeal to prime matter would defeat the whole purpose of positing the rudimentary sort of secondary matter in question.

So there is no alternative to prime matter if we are to acknowledge that something must underlie all change and account for the limitation of form. But what if we simply deny that there *is* any underlying principle, that there is anything that persists through change? This would really be to deny *change itself*. For it would in this case not be that there is something that persists while losing one form and taking on another, but rather that a thing is annihilated and another takes its place. For instance, when hydrogen and oxygen are combined to form water, it wouldn't on this view be that the matter that once had the forms of hydrogen and oxygen loses those forms and takes on the form of water, but rather that the hydrogen and oxygen are annihilated and water immediately takes their place.

As Oderberg points out (2007, p. 74), one problem with this suggestion is that it would violate the first law of thermodynamics, according to which energy is neither created nor destroyed. But there are even more fundamental metaphysical problems with it. For instance, if what appears to be change is really the annihilation of one thing and the sudden creation of another, with nothing that continues through the change, then why is there even the *appearance* of continuity? Why is the hydrogen and oxygen always replaced with water rather than with something else -- a bird, a plane, Superman, or nothing at all? With no persisting substrate of change, things would be inherently "loose and separate" in Hume's sense, so that nothing would be more likely to appear after an annihilation than anything else. And yet that is not in fact the way the world works. Each stage of an apparent change evidently *constrains* what might follow, which points to something that *does* persist. But that in turn entails prime matter, for the reasons we've seen.

Furthermore, if, instead of thinking of a tree, a dog, or water as substances composed of a substantial form and prime matter, we regard each as a series of fleeting stages annihilated and created in rapid succession, then each stage itself amounts to an ephemeral substance. Now each stage, though fleeting, is still not nothing. It is actual; in particular, it is actually a fleeting tree stage, or dog stage, or water stage. But that it is not *pure* actuality is evident from the fact that it goes out of existence. If it is actual without being pure actuality, though, then given the theory of act and potency that can only be because it is a mixture of act and potency. But for even a fleeting stage of a tree, a dog, or water to posses potency as well as act is just for there to be matter underlying its form, and thus for there to be just the sort of substrate that the proposal on the table was denying.

And for the reasons given above, that substrate will have to be prime matter.

A related point has to do with the argument from limitation. If we suppose that there are only continuously annihilated and created stages of a tree, a dog, water, etc., then in the case of each stage a form will be limited in the ways described above. For instance, even a fleeting tree stage existing at time t_1 that gives way to ashes at t_2 will involve the limitation of the form of a tree to t_1; and a fleeting circle stage will only approximate perfect circularity. Since having a form even fleetingly is a kind of actuality, this limitation of form entails potency. And for a tree or a circle to possess potency as well as act is for there to be matter underlying its form, where, again, given what was said above this matter will have to be prime matter.

With the distinctions we've been drawing in hand, we have the ingredients for a more precise characterization of the Scholastic position. Hylemorphism maintains that all natural objects -- things whose characteristic operations are grounded in an intrinsic direction toward certain ends -- are composed of *substantial form* and *prime matter*, related to one another as act and potency. A material *substance* is just that which is composed of substantial form and prime matter. Such a substance constitutes the *secondary matter* which is the subject of *accidental forms*. (Immaterial substances also have substantial forms and accidental forms, but by definition these forms will not inhere in *matter*. More on this below.)

3.1.4 Aquinas versus Scotus and Suarez

There is disagreement among Scholastics about the precise nature of substantial form and prime matter. Scotus and Suarez, contrary to Aquinas, held that prime matter could exist apart from form. (Cf. King 2003, pp. 49-50; Hattab 2012) Their reasons are related to their denial of the real distinction between essence and existence (a topic to be addressed in the next chapter). If the essence of prime matter is not distinct from its existence, then it must have existence. Thomists, who insist on the real distinction, would deny the basic presupposition of this sort of argument. In addition, they would argue that if prime matter had any actuality on its own, then any form that informed it would really be an accidental rather than a substantial form. (Cf. Phillips 1950a, pp. 48-49) This would, in effect, reduce substantial change to accidental change, and as was argued above, that sort of position falls apart on analysis.

There is also disagreement about how many substantial forms a thing can have. Scotus holds that a living thing has two substantial forms, viz. the substantial form of a corporeal thing and the substantial form of a living thing. For when a living thing dies, its body remains at least for a time, so that (so the reasoning goes) the substantial form of a living thing must have overlain, as it were, the substantial form of a corporeal thing, with the latter persisting even when the former is removed. (Cf. King 2003, pp. 50-53)

Thomists, by contrast, insist on the *unicity* of substantial form, the thesis that a single substance has only a single substantial form. Prime matter is in potency to being a substance. When prime matter is informed by a substantial form, this potency is actualized, so that the matter is no longer in *potency* to being a substance, but actually *is* a substance. The matter can lose this form and become another substance by taking on a new substantial form -- as it does in substantial change -- but it cannot intelligibly *retain* the first form *while* taking on the second. (Cf. Koren 1962, pp. 49-50) A related point is that if a living thing had a separate substantial form of a corporeal thing, to which the substantial form of a living thing was added, then this latter form would not really be a *substantial* form at all but merely an *accidental* form. A living thing would not be a true substance *qua* living, but only *qua* corporeal. (Cf. Koren 1955, p. 43)

Hence it is one and the same substantial form by virtue of which a living thing is both living and corporeal. Upon death, a living thing's prime matter loses this substantial form and takes on the substantial form of *another* corporeal thing, which merely superficially resembles the living thing that has died. Or rather, it takes on a *number* of substantial forms, becoming an aggregate of new substances, which is precisely why a dead body starts to disintegrate and does not remain the unified material object that existed when the organism was alive -- as one would expect it to if there really was a separate substantial form of corporeality that persisted after death. (Cf. Koren 1955, pp. 43-44)

The dispute over the unicity versus plurality of substantial forms is even more vexed than this lets on. (Cf. Bittle 1941, pp. 305-12; Phillips 1950a, pp. 129-35) The Arabic thinker Avicebron affirmed a plurality of substantial forms in a thing, so that a living thing would have a substantial form of being a substance, another substantial form of being corporeal, yet another substantial form of being alive, and so forth. Bonaventure appears to have taken a view that is somewhat similar if less extreme, though how to interpret him is a matter of controversy (Cullen 2006, pp. 48-49). The view that things have a plurality of substantial forms might seem to be lent plausibility by what modern physics and chemistry tell us about the composition of material things. For instance, if water is H_2O, doesn't that show that in water there is not only the substantial form of water, but also the substantial forms of hydrogen and oxygen? The Thomist position is that this does not follow at all. But this naturally brings us to the dispute between hylemorphism and atomism.

3.1.5 Hylemorphism versus atomism

The ancient atomists held that all change can be accounted for in terms of the arrangement and rearrangement of fundamental particles. A dog, a tree, and water are on this view at bottom all the same thing, namely collections of fundamental particles. They differ only insofar as the arrangements of the particles differ. This entails that the differences between them are really accidental rather than substantial, and that even the most radical changes they undergo -- as when a dog dies, a tree is burned and turned to ash, or water is decomposed into discrete parcels of hydrogen and oxygen -- are really accidental rather than substantial changes. Whereas the hylemorphist would contrast such natural objects with accidental arrangements like a pile of stones which has formed by chance at the bottom of a hill, the atomist maintains that dogs, trees, water, etc. really differ only in degree and not in kind from such accidental arrangements. The arrangement of their parts is far more stable and complex, but no less accidental rather than substantial. Hence, just as it is for the hylomorphist the stones and not the pile that are the true substances, for the atomist it is the fundamental particles, and not the many sorts of arrangements into which they can be put, that are the true substances.

Modern reductive and eliminative materialists would not endorse the crude mechanical model of combination and recombination of basic particles that the ancient atomists had in view, but they are committed to essentially the same picture of the world, e.g. to the view that "there are just fermions and bosons and combinations of them" (Rosenberg 2011, p. 179). If reductionists, they might say that water (for example) is real but really nothing but the oxygen and hydrogen that make it up, that the oxygen and hydrogen in turn are real but really nothing but the particles that make them up, and so forth. If eliminativists, they might say that only particles of a certain sort are real and that the objects composed of these particles do not strictly exist. Either way, they would appeal to modern physics and chemistry in defense of their position.

There are, however, several grave problems with such views. First of all, the appeal to science is a *non sequitur*. The Thomist does not deny that there is a sense in which water (for example) is composed of hydrogen and oxygen, but he would say that the hydrogen and oxygen are in the water only *virtually* rather than *actually*. This is evident from the way water behaves. As David Oderberg writes:

> [I]f the water contained actual hydrogen, we should be able to burn it -- but in fact the opposite is the case. If the water contained actual oxygen, it should boil at -180°C -- but in fact it boils at +100°C (at ground level).

> Of course the response is that the oxygen and hydrogen are bonded in water and so cannot do what they do in the absence of such a bond. But that is precisely the point. The combustibility of hydrogen and the specific boiling point of oxygen are *properties* of those elements in the technical [Scholastic] essentialist sense -- they are accidents that necessarily flow from their very essence. Since the properties are absent in water, we can infer back to the *absence* of the essences from which they necessarily flow. Therefore neither hydrogen nor oxygen is actually present in water. Rather, they are *virtually* present in the water in the sense that some (but not all) of the powers of hydrogen and oxygen are present in the water (though all proper-

ties requiring the elements to be actually present will be gone), and these elements can be *recovered* from the water by electrolysis -- not in the way that biscuits are recovered from a jar, but in the way that the ingredients of a mixture can (sometimes) be reconstituted. (2007, p. 75)

Something similar can be said of the other chemical elements, and of quarks and other particles present in inorganic and organic substances (Oderberg 2007, pp. 70-71 and 75-76; Cf. Hoenen 1955; Koren 1962, pp. 51 and 62). They are present virtually rather than actually, and *cannot* be actually present given that the properties that flow from their essences or substantial forms are not present. (The Scholastic understanding of essence and properties to which Oderberg makes reference will be examined in the next chapter.)

One implication of this is that contrary to deniers of the unicity of substantial form, there is no plurality of substantial forms in natural substances. In water, for example, there is only the substantial form of water, and the substantial forms of hydrogen, oxygen, quarks, etc. are not actually present because hydrogen, oxygen, quarks, etc. themselves are only virtually rather than actually present. In a living thing, water itself, at least insofar as it has been incorporated into the tissues of the living thing, is only virtually rather than actually present. Once again to quote Oderberg:

[S]ubstantial form *permeates* the entirety of the substance that possesses it, not merely horizontally in its parts -- there is as much dogginess in Fido's nose and tail as in Fido as a whole -- but also *vertically*, down to the very chemical elements that constitute Fido's living flesh... [T]he chemical elements exist *virtually* in Fido, not as compounds in their own right but as elements fully harnessed to the operations of the organism in which they exist, via the compounds they constitute and the further compounds the latter constitute, through levels of compounds -- DNA, the proteins coded for by that DNA, the organelles that make up the cells, the organs made up of the cells, and so on. (2007, pp. 70-71; Cf. Wallace 1996, p. 57)

Another implication is that since atoms, quarks, fermions, bosons, and the like -- at least *qua* parts of water, trees, dogs, etc. rather than in a free state -- do not exist actually in these natural objects in the first place but only virtually, it cannot coherently be said that water, trees, dogs, etc. are reducible to or in any other way less real than such particles. Rather, it is the particles that are less real than the natural objects of which they are a part. Of course the atomist or modern reductive or eliminative materialist would dispute this interpretation of the scientific facts, but the point is that science *itself* is not going to decide the issue. The issue is philosophical rather than scientific, a question of which metaphysics provides the best means of interpreting the results of science. The hylemorphist maintains that we have independent reason to think that it is hylemorphism, rather than atomism or any of its modern materialist descendents, that provides the appropriate interpretive framework.

Nor do appeals to the apparent conflict between the conceptual schemes of common sense and science show otherwise. Eddington famously distinguished the table perception reveals to us, which is colored and solid, from the table physics reveals to us, which is mostly empty space occupied by colorless particles (1963, pp. xi-xii). It is not clear whether Eddington himself believed that physics has shown that the commonsense table doesn't really exist, but others have drawn that conclusion. But as Amie Thomasson (following Susan Stebbing) has noted, since physical science doesn't use terms like "solid" in the same sense in which they are used in everyday contexts, and doesn't make use of concepts like "table" at all, it is hard to see exactly how physics *contradicts* anything common sense affirms vis-à-vis tables and the like (Thomasson 2007, pp. 138-44; Cf. Stebbing 1958). Nor does Wilfrid Sellars' (1963) view that the "manifest image" and the "scientific image" each claim to be complete descriptions of the world hold up. As Thomasson points out, in fact the "scientific image" arises *within* the "manifest image." The "manifest image" points to the "scientific image" as something needed in order to explain its deliverances, while the "scientific image" points back to the "manifest image" as that which it is intended to explain. The "scientific image" *supplements*, rather than *competes* with, the "manifest image" (Thomasson 2007, pp. 147-50).

A second problem with atomism and its modern descendents is that they are no closer now than they ever have been to dissolving at least the *fundamental* divisions in nature traditionally affirmed by hylemorphists. These divisions are, first, that between the inorganic and the organic; second, that between merely vegetative forms of life (in the technical Aristotelian sense of "vegetative," which entails having the capacities to take in nutrients, grow, and reproduce) and sensory or animal forms of life; and third, that between these merely sensory or animal forms of life (which include the capacities of vegetative life but add to them sensation, appetite, and locomotion) and rational or human life (which includes the capacities of the vegetative and animal forms of life and adds to them intellect and will). That it is by no means obvious that the powers of the rational form of life can be reduced to those of the merely sensory form is evident not only from the arguments of contemporary thinkers in the Scholastic tradition for the immateriality of the intellect (Ross 1992; Oderberg 2008b; Feser 2013a), but from the well-known difficulties facing attempts by contemporary philosophers of mind to provide a naturalistic account of the propositional attitudes. (Cf. Feser 2006, Chapters 6 and 7, and Feser 2011b) That it is by no means obvious that the powers of the sensory form of life can be reduced to those of the vegetative form is evident from the intractability of the "qualia problem," also much discussed in contemporary philosophy of mind. (Cf. Feser 2006, Chapters 4 and 5) And that the organic in general cannot be reduced to the inorganic is evident from the difficulties facing attempts to provide a naturalistic analysis of the notion of biological function (Feser 2008, pp. 248-57), as well as the absence of any plausible naturalistic account of the origin of life (Davies 1999; Oderberg 2013). (See Koren 1955 for an overview of the traditional Aristotelian position on the irreducibility of these levels; and see Oderberg 2007, Chapters 8 - 10 for a recent defense.) It is worth adding that even the reducibility of chemistry to physics has recently become a matter of controversy. (See van Brakel 2000, Chapter 5, for an overview of the literature.)

Naturally, the atomist or modern reductive or eliminative materialist would dispute these claims, but the point is that it is, even in contemporary philosophy and even among some philosophers otherwise sympathetic to a broadly materialist view of the world, a matter of controversy whether each of the levels of reality in question can be reduced to, or eliminated in favor of, the level of fundamental particles. This is not what one would expect if the victory of atomism and its modern descendents over hylemorphism had been as decisive as it is often assumed to have been.

This brings us to a third problem with atomism and its modern descendents, which is that even those reductionist analyses that seem most obviously correct turn out on closer consideration to be highly problematic. It might seem unproblematic to maintain, for example, that a stone is really nothing but a collection of particles arranged "stone-wise," or even that the stone is unreal and it is only the particles arranged stone-wise that actually exist. But for reasons indicated by Crawford Elder (2004, pp. 50-58), any reduction or elimination of this sort is illusory. For what is it about the specific group of particles in question that makes it the case that they and only they -- and not some subset of these particles, or particles additional to them -- are arranged stone-wise? If we identify them by reference to the stone itself, then the account is circular. But if we leave out any reference to the stone, then there is no other way uniquely to identify them, and in particular no relation that holds between all and only the particles in question by means of which we might identify them. It will not do, for example, to suggest that the particles that are stone-wise arranged are all and only those that cause us to have experiences of the stone. For there are particles causally involved in our experiencing the stone that are not plausibly part of the collection that is stone-wise arranged (e.g. those in the air between the stone and our sense organs), and there are particles that are part of that collection that are not causally involved in our experiencing the stone (e.g. those in the interior of the stone). (Cf. Elder 2011, pp. 118-24)

A related difficulty for atomism is, as James Madden has pointed out, posed by Peter Unger's "problem of the many" (Madden 2013, pp. 232-35; Unger 2006, pp. 366-71. Cf. Geach 1980). If a given stone is really just a collection of particles arranged stone-wise, then the same collection minus several of these particles (from the top of the stone, say) will also be a stone, and a different stone since the collection is a slightly different collection. But that means that we have two stones occupying the same space. Indeed, the same collection minus several different particles (this time from the bottom of the stone, say) will be yet a third stone, which means that we have three stones occupying the same space. Moreover, if there are billions of particles in the original collection then the same collection minus any one of these particles will yield yet another stone. Hence there will be *billions* of distinct stones occupying the same space. But this is absurd. Hence it cannot be correct to say that a stone is just a collection of particles arranged stone-wise.

Of course, an atomist might embrace this purportedly absurd consequence and try to make it plausible; or, alternatively, he could simply deny that stones are real in the first place and maintain that only the particles are real. (Cf. van Inwagen 1990; Merricks 2001) But this brings us to the fourth and deepest problem with atomism and its contemporary variants. Suppose we allow for the sake of argument that human beings, animals, plants, stones, water, and every other object of everyday experience are nothing more than accidental arrangements of atoms or some other basic particles. That would entail that *those* things are not compounds of substantial form and prime matter, but not that *nothing* is such a compound. For what of the basic particles themselves?

The ancient atomists, of course, regarded these basic particles as indivisible and otherwise unchangeable. But it is one thing to *assert* that there are such entities, quite another to make it plausible that there *could* be. The atomist position and its modern variants basically amount to the idea that a kind of secondary matter underlies all change -- secondary matter having just those properties that atoms (or some other sort of fundamental particle) are supposed to have. But we saw above that this sort of view won't work. Again, there is no empirical evidence for particles that are incapable of substantial change -- even quarks can undergo such change. More importantly, there could be no such particles. If a fundamental particle is of such-and-such a form (with its unique causal powers etc.), specifically, rather than some other form, then we have limitation and thus something less than pure actuality. The form is limited to *this* particle, and *that* one, and *that* one, and does not exist where there are no such particles (e.g. in the ancient atomists' void); the particles are also limited to being actually of *this* sort rather than that. But what is limited in its actuality is limited by potency. Hence such fundamental material particles would be compounds of act and potency; and being *fundamental*, there would be no yet more basic substances out of which they could be composed. But for a thing to be fundamental in that sense while being composed of act and potency is just for it to be composed of substantial form and prime matter. Hence even the atoms themselves, or whatever fundamental particles the contemporary inheritors of the atomist idea would put in the place of atoms, would be compounds of substantial form and prime matter.

That there must be such compounds at *some* level of material reality is thus for the Scholastic an unavoidable truth of metaphysics. Whether this or that specific *kind* of thing counts as such a compound -- human beings, animals, plants, stones, water, or what have you -- is a secondary question, one to be dealt with in such disciplines as the philosophy of nature, philosophy of biology, philosophy of chemistry, and the like, rather than general metaphysics. Hence even if it were conceded (as it should *not* be) that the traditional hylemorphic analysis of these objects is mistaken, that would have no tendency to cast doubt on hylemorphism as such.

3.1.6 Anti-reductionism in contemporary analytic metaphysics

Within contemporary analytic philosophy there has been interest in various positions which, like hylemorphism, are anti-reductionist. In particular, several varieties of non-reductive physicalism, property dualism, and emergence have been explored. Even views characterized as brands of "hylomorphism" have gotten renewed attention.

Non-reductive physicalism has been motivated by two main considerations. One is the doctrine of the "anomalism of the mental" defended by Donald Davidson (1980), according to which ascriptions of psychological states are governed by norms of rationality that have "no echo in physical theory" and rule out any law-like correlation between the mental and the physical. The other concerns the "multiple realizability" of the categories of "special sciences" like psychology, economics, and biology (Fodor 1974). The idea here is that there is no smooth one-to-one matchup between propositional attitude types on the one and brain state types on the other; between economic notions like money on the one hand and any particular physical realization of money on the other; between biological phenomena like wings on the one hand and any particular underlying physiological structure on the other; and so forth. Property dualism has been motivated by arguments to the effect that at least some mental properties, such as qualia, cannot be identified with physical properties, given e.g. that someone could know all the physical facts about a human being without knowing what it's like to see colors (Jackson 1982) or that there could in principle be creatures physically identical to us down to the last particle but lacking any conscious experiences (Chalmers 1996). Emergentism, which has been developed in various ways by philosophers and scientists (Cf. Bedau and Humphreys 2008), holds that some physical systems have properties that arise from and depend on more basic properties but are in some sense autonomous from those more basic properties. Here too mental properties are sometimes given as examples, but the characteristic properties of living things and the higher level properties even of inorganic substances like water are also sometimes cited.

Now, typically these sorts of anti-reductionist views at least implicitly agree with reductive and eliminative versions of physicalism in taking basic particles of the sort described by physics to be the fundamental level of reality. In effect, like modern reductionism and eliminativism they take something analogous to ancient atomism as their starting point, and merely differ over whether and in what sense there can exist phenomena over and above this fundament. Even then they often allow that whatever higher-level phenomena exist are at least nomologically supervenient upon the lower-level phenomena. Like their reductionist and eliminativist rivals, contemporary anti-reductionists thus essentially allow that the level of basic particles "wears the trousers," metaphysically speaking. A common objection raised against such views is that irreducible, non-physical, or emergent properties would be epiphenomenal, doing no causal work that is not already being done by the fundamental physical properties. (Cf. for example Jaegwon Kim's influential "causal exclusion argument," in e.g. Kim 1998.) The charge has real bite given what the anti-reductionist views have in common with their rivals, and the epiphenomenalist implications of the views are naturally taken to be good reason to reject them. Yet the problems facing reductionist and eliminativist positions, which motivated the anti-reductionist views in question in the first place, remain. Hence the seemingly intractable character of the "qualia problem," the "problem of mental causation," and similar puzzles endlessly debated in contemporary analytic philosophy.

Such intractability is the mark of an aporia (cf. Boulter 2013), and for the Scholastic metaphysician it points specifically to the falsity of the presuppositions contemporary anti-reductionists and their reductionist and eliminativist rivals have in common. From the point of view of hylemorphism, if reductive and eliminative physicalism are (to borrow an image from Wittgenstein) like the fly trapped in the fly bottle, the anti-reductionist views in question are like the fly which has made its way to the top of an open fly bottle but refuses to exit. Anti-reductionist arguments often recapitulate, in a piecemeal way, themes or implications of hylemorphism. Multiple realizability arguments point to the primacy of form over matter. Davidson's "anomalism of the mental" is essentially a special case of the irreducibility of finality (of which the intentionality of the mental is an instance) to efficient causality. The qualia problem is just what we should expect given the irreducibility of sensory forms of life to merely vegetative forms. Emergentists sometimes affirm that the causal powers of a substance cannot be reduced to an aggregate of the causal powers of its parts. Emergentist Paul Humphreys even affirms something reminiscent of the thesis that the parts are present in the whole only virtually rather than actually. Emergence, he holds, entails a "fusion" of the parts in the whole such that the parts lose some of their causal powers and cease to exist as separate entities (Humphreys 2008). (For sympathetic discussion by Scholastic writers of some of these anti-reductionist views, see e.g. Haldane 1999, Freddoso 2012, and Stump 2013.)

The trouble is that all of this is bound to sound obscurantist if one implicitly accepts the atomist-cum-physicalist assumption that the level of basic particles is metaphysically fundamental. Even the most ambitious emergentist positions implicitly concede this insofar as talk of "emergence" insinuates that anything other than basic particles has somehow to "emerge" in a bottom-up way from the particles. For the hylemorphist this just gets things fundamentally wrong from the outset. The level of basic particles is in no way privileged. The particles are not somehow "more real" than the substances of which they are parts. On the contrary, it is the *substances* that are more real insofar the particles, like every other part, exist only virtually rather than actually in the whole. To make all this intelligible, however, requires the notions of substantial form and prime matter, which in turn requires the entire Scholastic metaphysical apparatus of causal powers, intrinsic finality, the theory of act and potency, and so forth. To borrow another image from Wittgenstein, non-reductive physicalists, property dualists, and emergentists are like someone trying to repair a torn spider web with their fingers. So far they've succeeded only in recovering isolated strands. To complete the job requires undoing the centuries of metaphysical damage that began when Descartes, Hume, and Co. threw out the Scholastic system and began unpacking the radical implications of this revolution.

Now as I noted above, there are contemporary analytic philosophers who put forward views advertised as versions of hylemorphism (e.g. Fine 1999; Fine 2010; Johnston 2006; Rea 2011). For example, Kathrin Koslicki and William Jaworski have put forward versions of hylemorphism on which form is to be understood as *structure,* and matter as the materials or elements that are structured (Koslicki 2008; Jaworski 2011, Chapter 10). Yet this "structural hylemorphism," as David Oderberg (2013b) has labeled it, is not really hylemorphism as that position has traditionally been understood in the Aristotelian-Scholastic tradition. For one thing, as Oderberg points out, "structure" is an essentially quantitative notion, but while the forms of some things (e.g. mathematical entities) are entirely quantitative, not all forms are. So the notion of structure is simply too narrow to capture everything covered by the Scholastics' notion of form. As Oderberg also argues, the structural hylemorphist also faces a difficulty in identifying the elements that are supposed to be structured. In water, for example, is it atoms that are being structured, or is it rather the quarks that are constituents of the atoms that are, or is it perhaps some even more basic particles? The structural relations the atoms in a water molecule bear to one another are different from the structural relations the quarks in a water molecule bear to one another. Hence if we say it is atoms that are the elements being structured, we're talking about a different structure than we would be if we said it is quarks that are being structured. Thus, if what the form of water gives form to is atoms, we have one form, but if it is quarks that the form of water gives form to, then we are (given the assumption that form is structure) really talking about a different form. If the structural hylemorphist tells us that the answer depends on how we think about or "carve up" a water molecule, then this seems to make form a mind-dependent rather than real feature of water -- which it most definitely is not for the Aristotelian-Scholastic hylemorphist.

There are yet other problems. If each of the structures in question -- the structure of the atoms and the structure of the quarks -- is regarded as really present in water (as opposed to merely dependent on our interests), then the resulting position would be at odds with the unicity of substantial form (Oderberg 2013b, pp. 172-173). Furthermore, it is, for the Scholastic, an error to think of the components of a substance as existing prior to the substance itself, waiting to be "structured," as it were; rather, they exist only virtually rather than actually within the substance (Oderberg 2013b, p. 178).

"Structural hylemorphism" thus seems -- like non-reductive materialism, property dualism, and emergentism -- though salutary in its challenge to reductionist and eliminativist physicalism, nevertheless insufficiently radical. Other recent defenders of views presented as versions of "hylemorphism" seem open to the same charge. For example, Michael Rea (2011) worries:

> [T]here is the looming danger of disconnecting our metaphysics of material objects from empirical reality. Where in physics, or chemistry, or biology do we find something answering to the description "something in a material object that actualizes its potential to be a dog [or a hydrogen atom, or a sodium chloride molecule]"?...

> [H]ylomorphism is on the rise in contemporary metaphysics. But none of its contemporary defenders have remedied... [its] inability to identify viable candidates for matter and form in nature, or to characterize them in terms of primitives widely regarded to be intelligible... [I]dentifying matter and form with potency and act, respectively, leaves us with [this] drawback in spades...

Yet such remarks simply beg the question against the Scholastic position, for reasons that should be evident from what has been said already in the course of this book. Though there is nothing in the actual findings of modern science that is at odds with hylemorphism, the tendency of both philosophical naturalists and of scientists when they are wearing their philosophers' hats has been to read an essentially anti-Aristotelian philosophy of nature *into* science and then to read it back *out* again as "confirmation" of the dubiousness of hylemorphism and related doctrines. In particular, nothing that smacks of final causes, substantial forms, or the like is allowed to *count* as "scientific" in the first place. Post-Humean conceptions of causation and an essentially atomist-cum-"mathematicized" conception of matter are simply taken for granted, and what is "empirical" is identified with what science, *as confined within this metaphysical straightjacket*, has to tell us. Naturally, then, we are not going to find "in physics, or chemistry, or biology" so interpreted any reference to act and potency! But this no more shows that act and potency lack a foundation in "empirical reality" than Procrustes' practice of chopping off people's limbs so as to fit them into his bed shows that people don't really have feet.

On the contrary, no empirical reality would be possible in the first place unless act and potency were real features of the world (or so the Scholastic argues). And causal powers, intrinsic finality, substantial form, prime matter, and the rest of Scholastic metaphysics and philosophy of nature are essentially a working out of the theory of act and potency. Recent analytic metaphysicians sympathetic with hylemorphism have, understandably, sought to make the view palatable to their philosophical peers by finding a way to locate it within the box of options already considered acceptable. From the Scholastic point of view, however, the point is to think outside the box.

3.2 Substance versus accidents

3.2.1 The Scholastic theory

A material substance, I have said, is something whose characteristic operations are grounded in an intrinsic principle, by which it is directed toward certain ends definitive of the operations in question -- something having, in short, a substantial form. Thus does the theory of act and potency, by leading us to the distinction between substantial form and prime matter, lead us to the notion of substance.

Other characterizations of substance are common in Scholastic philosophy. Substance is "the *subject*, the substratum, in which accidents inhere"; and it is that which "*exists in itself* and does not need to inhere in another" (Koren 1960, pp. 184-85). For example, the color, length, and weight of a liana vine exist in the liana vine; but the liana vine itself does not in the same sense exist in another thing. Of these two characterizations of substance, the second captures what is metaphysically more fundamental. Since accidents inhere in another, if that in which they inhere itself inhered in yet another, and so on *ad infinitum*, we would have a vicious explanatory regress. (Cf. the notion of an essentially ordered causal series discussed in the previous chapter.) Ending the regress requires positing something which exists *independently, in itself* rather than inhering in another. It is only because substance is that which exists in this independent way that it can be that in which accidents inhere. (Cf. Koren 1960, pp. 184-85; Phillips 1950b, Part II, Chapter VI)

Now, we have seen that change presupposes an underlying basis in prime matter and that prime matter only ever exists in mind-independent reality together with substantial form. Hence what underlies the changing accidents of a thing must be a composite of prime matter and substantial form. We have seen, furthermore, that a substantial form does not presuppose some preexisting compound of substantial form and prime matter, otherwise it wouldn't *be* a substantial form at all but an accidental form. Hence a compound of substantial form and prime matter does not exist in some other thing, the way an accidental form does. So, any compound of substantial form and prime matter is going to count as a substance in the sense of that which exists independently or in itself and can thus support accidents. The hylemorphic notion of substance thus entails the notion of substance as that which exists independently and is a subject of accidents.

However, the converse is not true. Something could be a substance in the sense of being that which exists independently or in itself and can thus support accidents, without being a compound of substantial form and prime matter. For nothing in the former idea rules out the possibility of an *immaterial* substance. Whether such substances actually exist is a question beyond the scope of our discussion, but Scholastic theologians regard angels, understood as disembodied intellects, as immaterial substances. Such a substance would have a form insofar as it has an intrinsic principle by virtue of which it carries out its characteristic operations, but this form would not inhere in matter. That there could be such forms at least in principle is to be expected given that form and matter correspond to act and potency, and, as we have seen, while potency cannot exist without act there is nothing in the idea of act that rules out act existing without potency. (Of course, insofar as an angel would be less than *pure* actuality it would have to possess *some* potency. For Scholastics like Aquinas, an angel, despite being immaterial, is still composed of an essence together with a distinct act of existence, and these are related as potency and act. The relationship between essence and existence will be addressed in the next chapter.)

Though a material substance exists when a substantial form actualizes the potencies in prime matter, the resulting composite is, in a sense, itself in potency relative to its accidents, which actualize it. (Cf. Koren 1960, pp. 180-81) A stone is moved from one spot to another; a tree grows in height and sprouts leaves; a baby born more or less bald grows hair. In each case we have a substance which is in potency relative to certain accidents, and when these potencies are actualized the accidents are acquired.

Now "accident" is here being used more or less to mean an attribute, characteristic, or quality of a thing, what contemporary analytic philosophers commonly refer to as a "property." But some clarifications are in order. First, "accident" as contrasted with substance does not correspond exactly to "accidental form" as contrasted with substantial form. What the two expressions have in common is the notion of something which inheres in another; an accident exists only in a substance, and an accidental form only in that which already has a substantial form. But while having an accidental form involves having an accident, not all accidents involve having a merely accidental form.

That brings us to a second point, which is that Scholastic metaphysicians do not use the term "property" in the same sense in which contemporary analytic philosophers use it. Among accidents, Scholastics distinguish between *contingent accidents* and *proper accidents*, where a "property" is a proper accident *as opposed to* a contingent accident. A proper accident or property is an accident that follows or flows from a thing's nature or substantial form. For example, the capacities for humor and free choice follow from a human being's nature as a rational animal, and are thus properties of human beings as such. A contingent accident is one that does not follow or flow from a thing's nature, and thus may or may not be present in something of that nature. For example, having light skin and having dark skin are merely contingent accidents of human beings, which is why some human beings have light skin and some dark skin. Skin color is *not* a property of human beings as such, in the relevant sense.

The point is by no means merely terminological. "Property" as used by contemporary analytic philosophers not only ignores the distinction between contingent and proper accidents, but leaves out the crucial notion of that which *follows or flows from* a thing's nature. An accident can be proper, and thus flow from a thing's nature, without being actually manifested. Hence a human being who is severely brain damaged may be unable to exercise free choice; a dog may, due to injury or genetic defect, be missing a leg; and so forth. This doesn't entail that these aren't really properties after all, but rather that the manifestation of a thing's properties can be frustrated. Just as water will flow downhill unless prevented (by a dam, say), so too will a thing's properties "flow" from its nature unless prevented. That water does not in fact flow downhill in some particular circumstance doesn't entail that that is not its natural tendency, and that a thing's properties do not in fact manifest themselves in some particular circumstance does not entail that the thing does not have a natural tendency to manifest them.

Accordingly, it is, from a Scholastic point of view, too crude a procedure to ask (as an analytic metaphysician might) whether a thing might exist without a certain "property" (in some "possible world," say) and then deduce from an affirmative answer that the "property" in question isn't "essential" to it -- where the "essence" of a thing is understood to be (say) the bundle of "properties" it possesses in all "possible worlds." For the Scholastic, a property is just one kind of accident, an essence isn't in the first place a collection even of properties or proper accidents, an accident can be a property even if it doesn't always manifest itself, and appeal to possible worlds to determine a thing's essence gets things backwards. But further elucidation of the differences between the Scholastic and contemporary analytic approaches to these matters will have to wait upon our treatment of essence in the next chapter.

3.2.2 The empiricist critique

Now, an accusation traditionally made against Scholastic and other theories of substance is that they amount to a belief in metaphysical pins in an unknowable pincushion -- accidents being the pins and substance being the "something, we know not what" (as Locke would put it) in which they are stuck. Substance, on this interpretation, is a bare, featureless substratum of accidents, the very notion of which seems hopelessly problematic. If the substratum is itself bare or featureless, why couldn't the substrata underlying the accidents of (say) a dog and a stone change places? Yet that would mean that what now has all the accidents of a dog is really a stone, and what has all the accidents of a stone is really a dog. If to avoid this bizarre result we say that there is something about the substratum of a dog which is inherently different from that of a stone, then the substrata in question are not really bare or featureless after all. But in that case how can they perform the job they were supposed to do of *underlying* all the features of a thing? Then there is the epistemological problem of explaining how we could ever know that such a substratum is present if it is only the accidents or "pins" and never the substratum or "pincushion" itself that we observe. (Cf. Loux 2002, 119-23; Oderberg 2007, pp. 21-23)

In light of such problems, Hume and other empiricists put in place of bare substrata a "bundle theory" of substance, on which what we call substances are really just collections of accidents. A lump of gold, for example, is on this view nothing more than the gold's yellowness, malleability, fusibility, weight, etc. "bundled" together. There is nothing to the gold over and above this, no substratum underlying the bundle. Contemporary trope theories of substance are variations on this basic idea.

For the Scholastic, however, the choice between substratum theories of substance and bundle theories is a false one. Scholastics are not in fact committed to the notion of a bare substratum, but neither do they regard bundle theories as a coherent alternative. Theirs is a third position. (Cf. Loux 2002, pp. 123-35) The Scholastic view is that it is (contra the bare substratum theorist) *the gold itself*, rather than a bare substratum, that is the bearer of its accidents; and that (contra the bundle theorist) the accidents *presuppose* the existence of the gold itself, so that the gold cannot intelligibly be constructed out of its accidents. The mistake both of these competing views make is to suppose that there is something more fundamental than the gold, to which it is reducible. The substratum theory strips away all the accidents of the gold and identifies the gold with whatever it is that is left. Since there doesn't seem to *be* anything left, the bundle theorist takes the stripped off accidents and identifies the gold with them instead. But what the gold really is is substance and accidents together. The substratum theorist is like someone who peels away every layer of an onion and thinks that what an onion "really" is is what is left after all the layers are removed. The bundle theorist is like someone who arranges the peeled away layers into a pile and says that *that* is what an onion "really" is. Of course, what an onion really is is what you had before the layers were stripped off. And what a lump of gold really is is what we have before we abstract the accidents of the gold from the substance. As with form and matter, that the substance and accidents of the gold are really distinct doesn't entail that they can exist apart from one another (short of a miracle, anyway; cf. Oderberg 2007, pp. 155-56).

There really is no coherent alternative to this account, and both the substratum theory and the bundle theory themselves implicitly lead, at the end of the day, to something just like it. Take the substratum theory first. As Michael Loux points out (2002, pp. 121-23), it is hard to see how bare substrata could fail to have *some* accidents. Take the accidents of *being a bearer of accidents* and *being the principle by which two or more objects are distinct*. Are these not accidents of bare substrata, indeed essential accidents? If we say they are not, then it is hard to see how bare substrata could do the job they are supposed to do, viz. bearing accidents and being that by virtue of which one thing is distinct from another. But if we say they are, then "bare" substrata are not really bare after all. And if to avoid this result the bare substratum theorist posits lower-level substrata to underlie the essential accidents of purportedly bare higher-level substrata, then the same problem with arise for these lower-level substrata, resulting in a vicious regress. Hence we cannot really make sense of the idea of substances without accidents. (Cf. Hoffman and Rosenkrantz 1994, pp. 48-49; Hoffman and Rosenkrantz 1997, p. 18)

If the bare substratum theorist never really gets rid of accidents, the bundle theorist never really gets rid of substance. Accidents *themselves* become, in effect, substances (Connell 1988, p. 19-22; Oderberg 2012c). The yellowness of a lump of gold, for example, is treated by the bundle theorist as a substance insofar as it is regarded as existing in itself rather than inhering in another thing. The lump of gold is thus essentially treated as an aggregate of substances, viz. its yellowness, malleability, weight, etc. These even have accidents of their own, e.g. the saturation and brightness of the gold's yellowness. But in that case they are exactly like the substances the bundle theorist was supposed to have gotten rid of. To try to avoid this result by making the yellowness itself a bundle of accidents only leads to further problems. Suppose the lump of gold is thrown through the air. Its motion is an accident, but of what? If we say that the motion is not an accident of any of the other accidents, but is entirely separate from them, then how is it that the other accidents move through the air? Why is it not the motion alone that moves, while the yellowness, malleability, etc. stay still? But if we say instead that the motion is an accident of the accidents, then we're back to the ontology of substances and accidents that the bundle theorist was trying to avoid. (Cf. Connell 1988, pp. 21-22)

We've also got further puzzles. For if the gold's yellowness, malleability, weight, etc. each has its own accident of motion, then the lump of gold flying through the air is like a handful of marbles which have been thrown, each with its own motion. Yet they have a *unity* the marbles do not have; they do not scatter the way the marbles do, but stay together as a lump. So of what is the unity an accident? If we say that the unity is not an accident of any of the other accidents, but a separate accident alongside the gold's yellowness, malleability, etc., then we have the same problem we had when we treated motion as entirely separate. The unity itself will be unified (whatever that means) but the yellowness, malleability, etc. will not. If we say that the yellowness, malleability, etc. each have their own unity, then while each will be unified in itself, we would still not have accounted for the unity of *the lump* as a whole. We will also in this case once again essentially have reintroduced the ontology of substance and accidents that we were trying to avoid.

Should we say that it is the bundle of accidents as a whole that bears this accident of unity? But that leads us to the problem of explaining exactly why it is *this* bundle of accidents that is unified rather than some other. Hume says that we treat accidents as a unified bundle when they are related by "contiguity and causation" (*Treatise of Human Nature* Book I, Part I, Section 6). But the accidents of the lump of gold are related by contiguity and causation to those of the air surrounding it, and yet we do not regard the latter as part of the same bundle. (Oderberg 2012c). Nor will it do to say that it is all and only those accidents that cause us to treat them as unified that count as part of the bundle. For there are accidents causally implicated in our knowledge of the lump of gold that we do not treat as part of the bundle -- again, the accidents of the air that mediates the light that travels between the lump and our eyes would be an example -- and there are accidents that are not causally implicated in our knowledge of the lump which we would still consider part of the bundle, such as the accidents of the interior of the lump. (Cf. Elder's critique of reductionist accounts of physical objects, considered above.)

There is also the problem of identifying the accidents themselves. The yellowness of *this* lump of gold is for the bundle theory different from the yellowness of *that* lump, and different again from the yellowness of a certain taxicab. But what makes them different? The only answer seems to be that they belong to different bundles. Yet the bundles themselves are to be identified by reference to the accidents that make them up. Hence the bundle theory seems afflicted by a vicious circularity. (Cf. Lowe 1999a, p. 206; Oderberg 2007, pp. 77-78)

Bundle theories are thus hopeless as an alternative to the Scholastic account of the metaphysics of substance. (See Hoffman and Rosenkrantz 1994, Chapter 3 and Hoffman and Rosenkrantz 1997, pp. 26-42 for further criticism of such theories.) As to the epistemology of substance, since the Scholastic is not committed to bare substrata, the epistemological problems the empiricist would raise against that view do not apply. When you handle a lump of gold, it is *the gold itself* you see and feel, not merely its accidents. It is true that it is by means of its accidents that we perceive the gold, but that does not entail that it is not the gold, but only its accidents, that we perceive. As Oderberg points out (2012c), that would be like saying that since we see and hear things by means of light and vibrations in the air, it is only light and air that we ever really see or hear.

3.2.3 Physics and event ontologies

Bertrand Russell (1954) held that in light of relativity we should regard material objects as analyzable into groups of events, so that events are metaphysically more fundamental than substances. Others have held that quantum mechanics teaches a similar lesson. As several commentators have pointed out, one problem with such claims is that here as in other cases in which physics is said to deliver this or that metaphysical result, there are alternative ways to interpret the scientific theories in question. Neither relativity nor quantum mechanics *by themselves* entail anything about substance (Aune 1985, p. 124; Hoffman and Rosenkrantz 1997, pp. 7-8; Lowe 2002, pp. 233-37). They have to be interpreted in light of a sound metaphysics, and the Scholastic holds that such a metaphysics must include the notion of substance. *Merely* to appeal to physics in response to the Scholastic is therefore to beg the question.

A second problem is that even as interpreted by critics of the notion of substance, relativity and quantum mechanics don't really get rid of substance but just relocate it. For one thing, the entire space-time continuum would on the sort of view in question amount to a single four-dimensional substance, with everything else being an accident of this substance (Lowe 2002, p. 236). For another, event ontologies inherit the problems with bundle theories insofar as they replace substances with bundles of events. For events, like accidents in the bundle theory, are in effect themselves treated as substances, and ordinary objects as aggregates of these eccentric substances. (Cf. Connell 1988, p. 23)

Event ontologies are essentially recapitulations of the Heraclitean position that all is becoming or flux, and they face similar retorsion objections, especially when put forward in the name of science. Science is, after all, an activity carried out by *people* -- people who design and use scientific instruments, make observations, draw inferences, and so forth -- and people are substances of a sort (Hoffman and Rosenkrantz 1997, p. 7; Lowe 1999a, p. 235). Or if they are not, the event ontologist owes us an account of how they can coherently be said to do the things scientists do. If what we call a person is really just a series of events, then since (say) the events of deducing a certain prediction from a theory, making a certain observation, and drawing a conclusion are distinct events, it seems there is no one thing, the person, who carries out these activities, and thus no one who can be said to learn the things scientists are said to know and on the basis of which the event ontologist puts forward his theory. The theory thus seems self-undermining.

Of course the event ontologist might say that there is such a thing as the person who carries out all these activities, and that this person is just the collection of the relevant events. Again, though, the problem is that just as the bundle theorist has no principled way of showing how it is all and only the "right" accidents that make up a bundle, and the atomist has no principled way of showing how it is all and only the "right" particles that make up a physical object, so too does the event ontologist lack any principled way of showing how it is all and only the "right" events that make up a person. But this naturally brings us to the topic of identity.

3.3 Identity

3.3.1 Individuation

It was noted earlier that for the Scholastic, part of the job matter does is to account for how form, which of itself is universal, can be limited to a particular time and place. Naturally, then, matter is in the Scholastic view crucial to understanding how substances are individuated. *This* lump of gold and *that* lump of gold are in one respect the same -- they are both instances of the form of being gold -- but they are different individual lumps by virtue of being associated with different parcels of matter. Matter is the principle of individuation. That, at any rate, is the Aristotelian position as commonly summarized.

However, while that is correct enough as far as it goes, for the Scholastic things are more complicated than this summary lets on. Strictly speaking it is not *prime* matter as such which is the principle of individuation -- for one thing because it is common to all material things and thus can hardly individuate them, and for another because *qua* pure potentiality it is indeterminate and thus not already divided into parcels the distinction between which can ground the distinction between substances (Koren 1960, p. 151; Oderberg 2007, p. 109; Brower 2012, p. 95). Prime matter *qua* the passive potentiality to receive form can bring what is of itself universal down to earth, as it were, but it cannot by itself account for how what results are distinct *individuals* having the form. The matter that is the principle of individuation is, in Aquinas's view, matter as made distinct by *quantity or dimension* -- *designated matter*, matter "marked-off" as it were from other matter (Carlson 2012, p. 168). This is matter considered in terms more determinate than prime matter, but still as abstracted from substantial form.

How to characterize designated matter more precisely -- and in particular, whether to think of the quantity or dimension in question as itself determinate or indeterminate -- is a matter of controversy among Thomists, and even Aquinas himself modified his views over the course of his career. (Cf. Renard 1946, pp. 218-19; Phillips 1950a, Chapter XII; Koren 1960, pp. 150-55; Oderberg 2002 and 2007, pp. 108-17; Wippel 2000, pp. 351-75) But the key points are two. First, whatever else a material object is, it is something having dimension; hence for prime matter to take on the form of a material substance, it must *ipso facto* take on dimension. Second, dimension is of its nature individuating. *This* set of spatial dimensions is essentially different from *that* one, and if we add the further dimension of time (Oderberg 2007, pp. 112f.) we have distinct individual sets of dimensions which can ground the distinction between individual material substances. So it is prime matter *qua* something requiring dimension in order for it to take on form at all -- again, prime matter as designated or marked-off as being *here* rather than *there* -- that individuates one material substance from another.

A possible objection to this account is that for matter to individuate a substance, it has actually to have dimension or be designated or marked-off prior to its being informed by a substantial form;

and yet prior to its being so informed, matter is supposed to have no such features at all, but to be merely in potency toward them. But this is implicitly to confuse formal causality with efficient causality (Renard 1946, pp. 219-20). Prime matter and substantial form are not related the way the clay and the shape of a piece of pottery are related, where the clay already has various determinate features before the potter causes it to take on the shape in question. Rather, as, respectively, the material cause and formal cause of a material substance, prime matter and substantial form only ever operate in tandem. Prime matter, even as marked-off by quantity, only exists insofar as it is informed by a substantial form, though the substantial form itself only exists insofar as it is informing prime matter. There is nothing *per se* suspect about this because the *kinds* of causality involved here are distinct, both from each other and from efficient cause. (Cf. Wippel 2000, p. 364)

E. J. Lowe objects that space-time location suffices to individuate material substances and that matter in Aquinas's sense does no additional work (1999a, pp. 201-202; cf. Lowe 1999b). But matter *does* do work insofar as it is the potency to receive form, and matter must receive form before it can have a space-time location in the first place. (Lowe no doubt misses this point because he somewhat glibly rejects the notion of prime matter as something he can "make no sense of" (1999a, p. 195). But prime matter, though admittedly not something we can know directly via experience, can quite adequately be made sense of in terms of the general metaphysical work it is needed for, as described above.)

While Thomists follow Aquinas's solution to the problem of individuation, followers of Scotus and Suárez do not. (Cf. Metz 1996, pp. 125-32) This is not surprising given their rejection of the Thomistic view that act is limited only by potency -- matter being in the Thomistic view the principle of potency which limits the actuality of form to this or that particular individual. Scotus famously held that what distinguishes one individual thing of a certain nature from another individual thing of that nature is its form of *haecceitas* or "thisness." (Cf. Ingham and Dreyer 2004, pp. 108-16; Noone 2003, pp. 118-21) Hence there is, for example, the human nature had in common by Socrates and Plato, and the "thisness" of Socrates and the "thisness" of Plato which differentiate them as distinct individual substances having that nature. Suárez instead held that it is by virtue of its entire being, rather than by virtue of some part (such as its matter), that a substance is the individual it is. That is to say, each entity is its own principle of individuation (Gracia 1982).

Naturally, differing as they do on the question of the limitation of act by potency, Thomists do not regard the Scotist and Suárezian positions as well motivated. They also regard them as problematic in other ways. For instance, some Thomists would suggest that Suárez's position, insofar as it regards a substance as individuated of itself, inadvertently tends toward nominalism; while Scotus's position, insofar as it regards the principle of individuation as entirely distinct from a thing's nature -- making the natures of the individuals Socrates and Plato of themselves essentially the same universal nature -- inadvertently tends in the direction of an extreme (as opposed to an Aristotelian or moderate) form of realism vis-à-vis universals (Phillips 1950a, pp. 162-63; cf. Renard 1946, pp. 225-26 and Hart 1959, pp. 131-33). But understanding the force of such criticisms requires understanding the Thomistic account of universals, which will be addressed in the next chapter.

A famous implication of Aquinas's account of individuation is that where *immaterial* substances are concerned, there cannot be more than one member of a species, since there is no matter to differentiate one member from another. Hence each angel is the unique member of its own species. (Disembodied human souls would still be individuated, however, by virtue of having been associated with matter *qua* the substantial forms of living human beings. They subsist after death only as incomplete substances. But this subject takes us beyond general metaphysics into the philosophy of human nature. Cf. Oderberg 2007, Chapter 10.)

3.3.2 Persistence

3.3.2.1 Against four-dimensionalism

If designated matter accounts for a substance's *synchronic* identity -- that is to say, for what makes it *this* substance rather than that one at a given moment of time -- more needs to be said to account for its *diachronic* identity or persistence over time. For a material object gains and loses matter over the course of its existence, yet remains the same object. How?

An account of diachronic identity popular in contemporary analytic metaphysics is *temporal parts theory* or *four-dimensionalism*. (See Sider 2001 for an influential book-length defense.) The view is in part inspired by Minkowski's interpretation of special relativity, according to which a persisting material object is to be conceived of as a four-dimensional space-time "worm." Just as a material object has spatial parts at any particular moment of time, we ought, on the four-dimensionalist view, to think of each stage or segment of the "worm" as a *temporal* part of the object. A persisting material object is to be thought of as a collection of these temporal parts.

As its defenders sometimes acknowledge, this view is not in fact strictly required by special relativity, for Minkowski space-time can be interpreted in a way that makes no use of the notion of temporal parts (Sider 2001, pp. 79-87). Furthermore, when physicists make use of concepts like that of a space-time "worm," they are typically *presupposing* the notion of a persisting material object, and thus cannot coherently be said to have provided an *analysis* of that notion (Oderberg 2009b, p. 58).

But temporal parts theorists argue that their position provides the best solution to the standard puzzles of identity (Sider 2001, Chapter 1). Suppose you weigh 250 pounds on January 1, 2014 but go on a diet and by January 1, 2015 weigh only 150 pounds. Obviously, by Leibniz's Law, the same thing cannot weigh both 250 pounds and 150 pounds. So how can you be the same person in 2015 as the person who weighed 250 pounds in 2014? The answer, says the four-dimensionalist, is that it was two different things that had the two different weights. In particular, it was the January 1, 2014 temporal part that weighed 250 pounds, and the January 1, 2015 temporal part that weighed 150 pounds. Since these are different parts, we don't violate Leibniz's Law by holding that the same thing can have different weights. But since what you are is a collection of temporal parts that includes these particular parts, there is still a *sense* in which you have both weights, just as there is a *sense* in which you might be both red (if you have red hair) and not red (since the other parts of your body are not red). In both cases it is a matter of different *parts* of a thing having the different attributes.

Or consider a lump of clay out of which a sculptor makes a statue. After the statue is made the lump and the statue seem to be the same object. Yet how *can* they be the same object given that the lump has existed for a longer time than the statue? Four-dimensionalism answers that they are not identical full stop. Rather, what we have here is a series of temporal parts that begins whenever the lump of clay began and extends beyond the point at which it was molded into a statue. All of these parts are parts of the lump, but only the later, post-statue parts are parts of the statue. The series of lump parts is like a road, and the series of statue parts is like a particular section of the road.

Then there is the famous puzzle of the Ship of Theseus. Suppose the planks of a certain ship are gradually removed and replaced, and that eventually none of the original planks that made up the ship is still present. Now suppose that the old planks, which have been stored somewhere after removal, are once again assembled into a ship. Which of the resulting ships is identical with the original ship? Should we say that the first ship is identical with the original, because it is the one that was left after the gradual series of plank replacements? Or should we say that the second ship is the one identical with the original, because it is the one with all the original planks?

Four-dimensionalist Theodore Sider suggests that this puzzle is best approached via temporal parts theory together with the *principle of unrestricted mereological composition*, according to which any collection of objects, even an eccentric one (such as the collection made up of your left shoe, a ham sandwich, and the moon) counts as an object which has the other objects as parts (Sider 2001, p. 7). Now each of the planks in the Ship of Theseus example can be seen as a collection of temporal parts making up its own space-time "worm." The temporal parts of the original ship coincide with some of the temporal parts of the original planks. The temporal parts of the ship that results after the replacement of the planks does not correspond to any of the temporal parts of the original planks. The temporal parts of the ship that is made out of the stored collection of old planks coincides with some of the other, later temporal parts of the original planks. What we have, then, are complicated sets of collections of space-time "worms," interrelated in a manner somewhat like a criss-crossing set of roads, with some roads coming together to share a certain stretch before diverging, some coming back to converge again while others do not, and so forth. And that description captures all there is to capture about the metaphysical facts. Whether we want to count *this* later collection of space-time "worms" or *that* one as identical to the original ship depends on our concept of a ship, and may have no determinate answer.

Various objections might be raised again the four-dimensionalist position, but from the Scholastic point of view there are two in particular that are especially crucial. The first is that the very notion of temporal parts is in various ways seriously problematic. For one thing, the notion is supposedly justified in part by analogy with the spatial parts of an object, but there are various disanalogies between space and time. To take just one example, an object cannot be in two places at the same time, but can be at two times at the same place. The temporal parts theorist can get around this problem by holding that it is, strictly speaking, only the spatial parts of an object that cannot be in two places at the same time, and then maintaining that in the same way no temporal part of an object can be at two times at the same place. This restores the analogy between space and time, but the problem is that in order to restore it the temporal parts theorist has had to *postulate* temporal parts. And as Oderberg argues (1993, pp. 98-103), the temporal parts theorist has to do the same thing in order to get around other disanalogies between space and time. But then, it is not that the idea of temporal parts *follows* from an analogy between space and time, but rather that it is being *presupposed* in order to *construct* an analogy. The supposed justification of temporal parts theory by reference to the analogy with spatial parts is therefore bogus.

For another thing, the four-dimensionalist will have to regard temporal parts as instantaneous entities; for if they have duration, their persistence will have to be explained, and persistence was the very thing temporal parts theory was supposed to be an explanation of. Yet as Oderberg objects (2009b, pp. 58-59), if temporal parts are instantaneous or without duration, how can they add up to something with duration? Then there is the problem that, as Lowe argues (1999a, pp. 114-18), the temporal parts analysis seems viciously circular. Just as a spatial "cross-section" or geometrical "slice" of a material object cannot be individuated except by reference to the object of which it is a cross-section or slice, so too a temporal "cross-section" or "slice" of a material object (if we allow for the sake of argument that such a notion can be made sense of at all) cannot be made sense of except by reference to the object of which it *is* a cross-section or slice. And in that case we cannot coherently *analyze* the notion of a persisting material object in terms of its temporal parts.

Hence, like attempts to analyze a material substance in terms of atoms, or bundles of accidents, or events, the attempt to analyze it in terms of temporal parts inevitably fails. In all four cases, the sorts of entities in terms of which the analysis is to be carried out are metaphysically less fundamental than the sort of entity which is to be analyzed, so that the purported analysis is incoherent.

The second problem with four-dimensionalism on which the Scholastic is bound to put special emphasis is that the theory denies the reality of *change* (Oderberg 2004 and 2009b). For one thing, what the temporal parts analysis leaves us with seems to be, not a single thing that persists through change, but rather a series of ephemeral things, one after the other being created and annihilated. The four-dimensionalist may reply that this would only be true if we assume a *presentist* view of time, on which the present moment alone exists, whereas four-dimensionalism is more naturally understood in terms of an *eternalist* view according to which every moment of time is equally real. On this interpretation, the entire space-time "worm" with all its stages or parts exists "all at once," as it were, as a four-dimensional block. But this is only to fall from the Heraclitean frying pan into the Parmenidean fire. That is to say, whereas the presentist interpretation of temporal parts theory leads to the denial that there is a changing *thing*, the eternalist interpretation leads to the denial that there is a *changing* thing.

The four-dimensionalist view is, after all, that time is analogous to space. Yet the fact that the different *spatial* parts of a single object have incompatible accidents at a particular moment of time does not entail change. For instance, that a person's hair is red while his hands are not does not entail change. But then how can the fact that the different *temporal* parts of a single object have incompatible accidents entail change, if temporal parts are supposed to be analogous to spatial parts? Your weighing 250 pounds on January 1, 2014 and 150 pounds on January 1, 2015 will amount to merely your 2014 temporal *part* weighing 250 pounds while your 2015 *part* weighs 150 pounds. Why is this a case of *change* any more than your hair's being red while your hand is not amounts to change -- if, again, temporal parts are like spatial parts (Oderberg 2004, pp. 706-7)?

Sider claims that we do sometimes speak of differences between spatial parts in terms of change; we might say, for example, that a certain road changes in the sense that it *becomes bumpier* the further along one travels down it (2001, p. 216). A difference between temporal parts can, he suggests, be understood as involving change in the same way. But this merely equivocates on the word "change," as is obvious from the sentence: "That road *hadn't changed* at all; it still *became bumpier* the further along it I traveled." This sentence is, of course, not self-contradictory, because when it is said that the road "became bumpier" what is meant is that while one (spatial) part of it is not bumpy, another (spatial) part of it is bumpy; while when it is said that the road "hadn't changed," what is in question is not a difference in its (spatial) parts but rather the fact that it still, at a later point in time, had a feature that it possessed at an earlier point in time.

We might call the road's still becoming bumpier an instance of "change" in the *spatial* sense, while the sense in which the road hadn't changed is a case of the absence of change in the *temporal* sense. Now, the objection on the table is essentially that four-dimensionalism fails to capture change in the *temporal* sense insofar as it models temporal parts on spatial parts. Sider's response is to illustrate how change is to be understood in light of four-dimensionalism by appealing to an example of "change" in the *spatial* sense rather than in the temporal sense. Far from *answering* the objection, then, Sider's response only *reinforces* it.

Yet as we saw in chapter 1, the reality of change in the ordinary, temporal sense cannot coherently be denied. As Richard Healey has argued (2002), it certainly cannot coherently be denied in the name of special relativity or any other physical theory. For physical theory rests on the empirical evidence of observation and experiment, which involves scientists having certain experiences. This is in turn a matter of an event of formulating a prediction being followed by the event of performing an observation to test the prediction; of moving from a state of ignorance to a state of knowledge; and so forth. But all of this involves change. Hence if there is no change, then there is no such thing as having the experiences which provide the empirical evidence for any scientific theory in the name of which someone might take the position that there is no such thing as change. Such a position is what Healey (following Barrett 1999) calls "empirically incoherent."

Now Healey goes on to note that those who would deny change in the name of physical theory are essentially treating it the way Galileo, Locke, and other early moderns treated color, viz. as a secondary quality. Just as, for the Lockean, color is just the tendency of an object to produce in us sensations that do not resemble anything really there in the object itself, so too do those who would deny change in the name of physical theory essentially treat it as an aspect of experience that does not correspond to the objective physical reality that causes the experience. Yet if such a picture is to avoid empirical incoherence, it "cannot establish this experience as wholly *illusory*" (Healey 2002, p. 312), for if the scientist's experience of change is wholly illusory then so too is the evidential base of the theory that leads him to deny that it is wholly illusory. Even if, for the sake of argument, we allow that one can coherently *relocate* change from the external world to the internal world of the observer, we nevertheless cannot coherently *deny* change altogether.

Nor can "change" in Sider's spatialized sense of the term do the job needed. Suppose at some time *t* I hold in my left hand a piece of paper on which are written the sentences "All men are mortal" and "Socrates is a man," and in my right hand a piece of paper on which is written "Socrates is mortal." There is, we can allow for the sake of argument, a spatial "change" in sentences from left to right. But of course, it would be absurd to suggest that this "change" involves anything like an inference. Nor is the point affected if we add conscious subjects to the picture. Suppose at *t* Fred is standing to the left thinking "All men are mortal and Socrates is a man," while Bob is standing to the right thinking "Socrates is mortal." Again, there is a spatial "change" from left to right, and again, it would nevertheless be absurd to suggest that the change involves an inference. Now if we think instead of a temporal part of Fred at t^1 thinking "All men are mortal and Socrates is a man" and a temporal part of Fred at t^2 thinking "Socrates is mortal," and the "change" from Fred at t^1 to Fred at t^2 as a case of "change" in Sider's spatialized sense, then *this* "change" too will no more count as an inference than the "change" from Fred to Bob did.

By the same token, a spatialized "change" from a temporal part of Fred at t^1 formulating a prediction to a temporal part of Fred at t^2 performing an experimental test would no more count as testing a scientific theory than the previous example counted as an inference. Thus the cognitive tasks presupposed in any scientific theorizing -- or philosophical theorizing for that matter -- simply cannot be made sense of on a four-dimensionalist picture. The view is self-undermining.

3.3.2.2 Identity as primitive

What view would the Scholastic put in place of four-dimensionalism? As Oderberg argues, it is a mistake to look for any sort of *reductive* account of identity over time in the first place, for identity is *primitive* or *basic* (1993, pp. 143-6 and Chapter 7; 2007, pp. 117-20). That does not mean that we cannot say anything more than that a thing's identity is primitive. What we can and should say is that a material substance's identity is determined by its *substantial form*, which grounds its characteristic properties, powers, operations, and the like. But a substantial form is in turn instantiated in matter, and it is the form of a particular individual substance precisely because it informs a particular parcel of designated matter. This is not a *reductionist* analysis, because the form and matter are ultimately intelligible only by reference to the substance of which they are parts. The analysis is *holistic*, which is why, despite our being able to say more about identity over time than that it is primitive, identity nevertheless remains primitive.

It is because a thing's substantial form determines its identity that it remains the same substance over time despite the loss and acquisition of matter. In the usual case this loss and acquisition is gradual. (The death and resurrection of a human being, which involves a person's substantial form or soul subsisting after death and thus entirely separated from matter -- but later once again informing its matter -- is an unusual case. Again, though, this raises special issues in the philosophy of human nature which go beyond general metaphysics. See Oderberg 2005; Oderberg 2007, Chapter 10; and Oderberg 2012d.) It is no surprise, then, that spatio-temporal continuity might seem to be the key to identity over time, as it has historically to many philosophers. However, as Oderberg puts it, such continuity is a *symptom* of identity rather than the *ground* of identity (1993, p. 175). That is why it is both pervasive and yet not without counter-examples (e.g. a thing's being dismantled and reassembled).

How would such a view of identity approach the well-known puzzles of identity referred to above? The first thing to note is that the so-called "problem of temporary intrinsics," of which "puzzles" like that of how the same thing can weigh both 250 pounds and 150 pounds at different times are illustrations, is bogus. There can seem to be a violation of the Principle of Non-Contradiction or of Leibniz's Law here only if we formulate these principles tendentiously. For Aristotle, after all, PNC holds that a thing cannot both have and lack a certain attribute *at the same time and in the same respect*. Leibniz's Law can be formulated with a similar qualification. It is only if we formulate the principles without this qualification that "puzzles" like the one about your different weights can arise. But as Oderberg writes, "why would anyone want to affirm [such a formulation] unless they had not thought carefully about the Law of Non-contradiction in the first place, or they wanted something to puzzle about for the sake of it?" (2009b, p. 62).

Crucial to understanding how a Scholastic metaphysician like Aquinas would approach the other two examples -- that of the statue and that of the Ship of Theseus -- is, as Christopher Brown notes (2005, Chapter 6), that these both involve paradigmatic artifacts having merely accidental rather than substantial forms. If a statue were a true substance, it would certainly be puzzling how it is related to the lump of clay, another substance. But it is not. That the lump of clay takes on the shape of a man, a horse, or whatever the statue is a statue of, is no more significant metaphysically than the fact that it might take on a flattened shape if you dropped it on the ground or a cigar-like shape if you rolled it between your hands. Like these other shapes, the shape of the statue is merely an accidental form the acquisition of which doesn't amount to a substantial change (Brown 2005, pp. 160-2; Oderberg 2007, pp. 169-70).

Something similar can be said about the Ship of Theseus. *Being a ship* is merely an accidental rather than substantial form. The true substances in the example would be the planks, or rather (if we think of *being a plank* as itself a kind of accidental form) the wood that has been given the shape of planks. Hence when the wood that made up the original ship loses the accidental form of a ship -- as it does when a sufficient number of its original planks have been removed -- the original ship goes out of existence. Thus neither of the later ships -- the one that resulted from the gradual replacement of planks and the one made from the old planks gathered together again -- is identical with the original ship. They are both replacements of the original. (Cf. Brown 2005, 144-50; Oderberg 2007, p. 114)

Of course, what counts as a number of lost planks "sufficient" for the ship going out of existence is a tricky question. But that is only to be expected given that artifacts -- in the sense of man-made objects having merely accidental forms (as opposed to man-made objects with substantial forms, such as dog breeds or water synthesized in a lab) -- have identity conditions as vague as the purposes to which we put them.

4. Essence and existence

4.1 Essentialism

4.1.1 The reality of essence

The *essence* of a thing is its nature, that whereby it is *what* it is. It is what we grasp intellectually when we identify a thing's *genus* and *specific difference*. To take a stock example, consider the traditional Aristotelian definition of a human being as a rational animal. (Whether this definition is correct or not is irrelevant for present purposes.) The definition gives *animal* as the genus under which human beings fall and *rationality* as that which differentiates human beings as the species they are within that genus (hence "specific difference"). If the definition is correct it gives us the essence of a human being.

In the previous chapter, a material thing's substantial form was characterized as its nature. The point was to emphasize that that by virtue of which a material substance carries out its distinctive activities is something immanent to it rather than either imposed by artifice or the result of accidental circumstances. In a broader sense, however, the essence or nature of a stone, tree, dog, or other material substance includes both its form and its matter, since matter is essential to the operations such things carry out by virtue of their substantial forms. The essence or nature of an immaterial substance, however, would be identical to its form.

That we describe things *as if* they have essences is obvious. It is also obvious that the essences of some things are at least in part the product of convention. What makes something a carburetor or a can opener, for example, is determined by the purposes for which we make such artifacts. The question is whether the essences of at least some things, and in particular of natural objects or substances in the

Scholastic sense, are real or mind-independent as opposed to merely being the product of convention. *Essentialism* is the thesis that there are such real essences. (Readers of Etienne Gilson should not confuse this with the "essentialism" of which he was famously critical. Gilson's target was the rationalist tendency to try to read off reality from essences considered in the abstract, as objects of thought. To this he contrasted the "existentialism" of Aquinas, for whom knowledge of real concrete existents must come through experience. There is nothing in essentialism as I am defining it that entails rationalism of this sort, and Aquinas was clearly as much an "essentialist" in my sense as he was an "existentialist" in Gilson's sense. For a useful discussion of Gilson's views, see White 2009, Chapter 4.)

Can it be proven that natural objects have real, mind-independent essences or natures? One way to approach this question would be to follow Aristotle's view, expressed in Book II of the *Physics*, that it would be absurd to try to prove that things have natures. The idea is not that it is *doubtful* that things have natures or essences, but rather that it is *obvious* that they do -- indeed, that the belief that things have essences is more obviously correct than any argument that can be given for or against it. As with Hume's challenge to the principle of causality or empiricist challenges to the notion of substance, it is (so the Scholastic would argue) only by making highly controversial and indeed dubious philosophical assumptions that the reality of essence could seriously be doubted.

Since there *are* those who doubt it, though, more needs to be said. To begin with, it is worth noting that Putnam's "no miracles" argument for scientific realism, which we've had reason to refer to before, can be adapted to present purposes as well. The world is just the way we would expect it to be if things really had essences. In particular, things exhibit the *unity* we would expect them to if they had real essences, in two respects (Oderberg 2007, pp. 44-47). For one thing, they are related to one another in a way that exhibits unity. This oak tree, that one, and the other one are united in a way they are not united to stones, dogs, or people; this polar bear, that one, and the other one are united to one another in a similar way; this sample of copper, that one, and a third one are so united as well; and so on. These groups of things manifest common causal powers and other properties in just the way we would expect if there were a common real essence or nature they all instantiated, but which would be mysterious -- a "miracle," as Putnam might say -- if their being grouped together was merely a matter of human convention. For another thing, each individual thing exhibits a unity of its own. An oak, a polar bar, and a sample of copper will each behave over time in a uniform and predictable manner, exhibiting characteristic properties and patterns of operation, persisting despite changes in superficial features, and having parts that function in an integrated way. This too is just what we would expect if each of these things had a real essence or nature, and would be mysterious if what we thought of as their essences were merely a matter of human convention.

Of course, whether certain natural objects really should be grouped into the same class or not, and whether a given object really exhibits a substantial or only accidental unity, might sometimes be difficult questions to settle. Precisely *what* a thing's essence is is by no means always easy to determine. But these considerations by themselves do not cast doubt on the reality of essence. Common caricatures aside, no serious essentialist believes that the natures of things can always be discovered easily -- from the armchair as it were, or from everyday experience. What is at issue at the moment is in any case not *what* the essences of various things are or whether we can always discover them, but whether they are nevertheless *there* even if we cannot always discover what they are. And the point is that the unity and order of things would be mystifying if essence were not a pervasive feature of mind-independent reality.

That much is evident from common sense. But both the practice and results of modern science reinforce the point. As to the practice, the "new essentialist" philosophers of science discussed in chapter 1 have (as the name implies) argued that physical science is in the business of discovering essences as well as causal powers, insofar as the powers science aims to uncover are powers things have *essentially*. As Nancy Cartwright emphasizes (1992, 1999, Chapter 4), a serious problem with the Humean idea that science merely establishes regularities on the basis of observation is that the sorts of regularities the hard sciences tend to uncover are rarely observed, and in fact are in ordinary circumstances impossible to observe. Beginning students of physics quickly become acquainted with idealizations like the notion of a frictionless surface, and with the fact that laws like

Newton's law of gravitation strictly speaking describe the behavior of bodies only in the circumstance where no interfering forces are acting on them, a circumstance which never actually holds. Moreover, physicists do not in fact embrace a regularity as a law of nature only after many trials, after the fashion of popular presentations of inductive reasoning. Rather, they draw their conclusions from a few highly specialized experiments conducted under artificial conditions.

None of this is consistent with the idea that science is concerned with cataloguing observed regularities. But it is consistent, in Cartwright's view, with the Aristotelian picture of science as in the business of uncovering the hidden natures of things. Actual experimental practice indicates that what physicists are really looking for are the powers a thing will manifest when interfering conditions are removed, and the fact that a few experiments, or even a single controlled experiment, are taken to establish the results in question indicates that these powers are taken to reflect a nature that is universal to things of that type. Writes Cartwright: "Modern experimental physics looks at the world under precisely controlled or highly contrived circumstance; and in the best of cases, one look is enough. That, I claim, is just how one looks for natures..." (1999, p. 102).

We also noted in Chapter 1 that Brian Ellis (2001, 2002) argues that essences are necessary in order to ground laws of nature. (Cf. Ross 2008, pp. 144-6) And as Ellis also notes, the actual results of modern science (let alone the practice or method) support the claim that there are *natural kinds*, each with its own essence:

> Every distinct type of chemical substance would appear to be an example of a natural kind, since the known kinds of chemical substances all exist independently of human knowledge and understanding, and the distinctions between them are all real and absolute. Of course, we could not have discovered the differences between the kinds of chemical substances without much scientific investigation. But these differences were not invented by us, or chosen pragmatically to impose order on an otherwise amorphous mass of data. There is no continuous spectrum of chemical variety that we had somehow to categorize. The chemical world is just not like that. On the contrary, it gives every appearance of being a world made up of sub-

stances of chemically discrete kinds, each with its own distinctive chemical properties. To suppose otherwise is to make nonsense of the whole history of chemistry since Antoine Lavoisier. (Ellis 2009, p.59)

To be sure, while Ellis finds ample grist for the essentialist mill in physics and chemistry, he would not extend essentialism to biological kinds. In this he differs from Scholastic thinkers, including contemporary ones (Koren 1955; Oderberg 2007, Chapters 8 and 9, and 2013a). Now, determining exactly *which* kinds found in nature have true essences and what they are -- like the related question of which of the things we find in nature have irreducible causal powers and count as true substances -- would take us beyond general metaphysics and into more specific philosophical sub-disciplines such as the philosophy of nature, philosophical psychology, philosophy of biology, philosophy of chemistry, and the like, not to mention the relevant special sciences. What cannot plausibly be denied is that science reinforces the judgment that there are *some* real essences to be found in nature.

Metaphysical considerations make the reality of essence unavoidable in any case. For the arguments of the last three chapters are indirect arguments for the reality of essence. If a thing really has a substantial form, if by virtue of that substantial form it really has irreducible causal powers, if these powers really are directed at the generation of certain effects as to a final cause, and so forth, then it hard to see how it could intelligibly be denied that it has an essence. What could it mean to say that a thing has an intrinsic principle of operation, that its operations are intrinsically ordered to certain ends, etc., but that there is no mind-independent fact of the matter about what kind of thing it is?

There is also a retorsion argument, defended recently by Crawford Elder, against the view that all essences are conventional (Elder 2004, Chapter 1; cf. Rea 2002, Chapter 7). The conventionalist (e.g. Sidelle 1989) holds that a thing's essence, that whereby it is what it is, is a product of our ways of thinking, our linguistic habits, and so forth. It is, in short, *mind-dependent*. But for the consistent conventionalist this would have to be as true of the human mind itself (whether we identify the mind with the brain or think of it as something immaterial) as it is of everything else. That is to say, what makes the mind what *it* is would have to mind-dependent -- our ways of thinking, linguistic conventions, etc. But for something to be mind-dependent entails that it *presupposes*, and is thus *posterior to* (ontologically if not temporally), the existence of the mind. The mind will be *prior to* that which depends upon it, to that which exists only relative to its ways of thinking and linguistic habits. Hence the consistent conventionalist will have to say that the mind is both prior to itself and posterior to itself. But this is incoherent.

So, we cannot coherently take a conventionalist view about our *own* essence, or at least about the essence of our minds. That there is at least *one* real essence, *our* essence, cannot be denied. And Elder's point can be supplemented as follows. The arguments for conventionalism would, if they had any force at all, apply to us just as much as to anything else. Yet we know they are wrong when applied to us. What reason can we have, then, to take them seriously when applied to other things?

4.1.2 Anti-essentialism

That naturally brings us to the various anti-essentialist arguments that have been put forward in modern philosophy. (Cf. Oderberg 2007, Chapter 2) Especially influential in contemporary analytic philosophy have been the objections raised by W. V. Quine. Quine asks us to consider a person who is both a mathematician and a cyclist. Now a mathematician is, we may suppose, necessarily good at arithmetic, while a cyclist is not; whereas a cyclist is necessarily bipedal though a mathematician is not. So what do we say of our hypothetical cyclist mathematician? Is he both necessarily bipedal and not necessarily bipedal, and necessarily good at arithmetic and not necessarily good at it? This purported paradox ought in Quine's view to lead us to be suspicious of notions like necessity, essence, and the like (Quine 1960, p. 199). However, the paradox is bogus (Plantinga 1974, pp. 23-26; Oderberg 2007, pp. 27-29). The appearance of paradox arises from giving the relevant propositions a *de re* reading; for instance, if I say of cyclists that they are necessarily bipedal and of mathematicians that they are not necessarily bipedal, then I will end up ascribing inconsistent properties to the cyclist mathematician.

But the appearance of paradox disappears when we give the relevant propositions a *de dicto* reading. If I say that it is necessarily true that if someone is a cyclist then he is bipedal and that it is not necessarily true that if someone is a mathematician then he is bipedal, I am not committing myself to any ascription of inconsistent attributes when I say of a person who is both a cyclist and a mathematician that he is bipedal.

Another well-known example from Quine calls attention to alleged puzzles posed by propositions like the following (Quine 1960, pp. 197-99; Quine 1980c):

(1) 9 is necessarily greater than 7.

(2) The number of planets is 9.

(3) The number of planets is necessarily greater than 7.

(1) and (2) are true (or at least, (2) is true if we count Pluto as a planet), but (3) is false, since there could have been fewer than seven planets. In Quine's view this puzzle too casts doubt on notions like necessity. But once again the supposed paradox is bogus, and may be resolved in various ways. For instance, if we take (2) to be asserting the existential claim that *there are nine planets*, then (3) doesn't follow; or if instead we read (2) and (3) as propositions about the *actual* number of plants, then (3) will follow from (1) and (2) but won't be false (Oderberg 2007, pp. 29-30; cf. Plantinga 1974, pp. 222-51).

Then there is Quine's famous view (put forward in 1980b and elsewhere) to the effect that any proposition may be either held on to or abandoned if we are willing to make changes elsewhere in our system of beliefs. Logical and mathematical truths seem necessary, on this view, only because abandoning them would have such a radical effect on the overall system. But in principle, on this view, they might be abandoned too, and thus are not really necessary. That the angles of a triangle necessarily add up to 180° might seem an example of a truth that once seemed necessary but was later shown to be false in light of non-Euclidean geometry.

But that it remains true within *Euclidean* geometry that the angles of a triangle necessarily add up to 180° should be a clue that there is something wrong with such claims. As Oderberg points out

(2007, pp. 26-27), there is no reason to interpret non-Euclidean geometry as having cast doubt on the necessity of propositions like the
one in question. One could hold that the term "triangle" has simply
become ambiguous after the discovery of non-Euclidean geometry --
that it could be meant in the original sense of "closed, three-sided,
rectilinear figure in Euclidean space" or in the newer sense of
"closed, three-sided, rectilinear figure in non-Euclidean space" -- and
that as long as we are clear that in the claim that *the angles of a triangle add up to 180°* "triangle" is meant in the first sense, the claim is as
necessary as it ever was. Alternatively, we could say that the discovery of non-Euclidean geometry revealed that Euclidean triangles are
merely a species of triangle, but what we knew to be necessarily true
of triangles of that species is still necessarily true, even if we now
know that there are other sorts of triangle of which it is not true. Either way we don't have a case in which a purportedly necessary truth
turns out not to be necessary. In any event, even if we had such a
case, that wouldn't show that there are no necessary truths or essences, but only that when we thought we knew the essence of a
thing we were mistaken. But that does not disprove essentialism,
which does not claim in the first place that our judgments about essences are infallible.

Quine also suggests that our tendency to group things into natural kinds is a product of natural selection (1969, p. 133), and Robert
Nozick holds that it cannot plausibly be thought that evolution has
given us a faculty for discovering necessary truths (2001, p. 122). Yet
to say that we have merely been molded by natural selection to attribute essences to things and have no reason to think these essences
have any mind-independent reality is to adopt a Darwinian variant of
conventionalism, and a thoroughgoing conventionalism remains self-
defeating for the reasons considered above, whether or not it is put
forward on Darwinian grounds (Oderberg 2007, pp. 44-45). And there
is another self-refutation problem facing those, like Quine and
Nozick, who would cast doubt on necessity in general. If we have no
reason to believe that what we regard as necessary truths of logic and
mathematics actually reflect mind-independent reality, then we have
no reason to regard any of our philosophical or scientific arguments
as formally valid, and thus no reason to regard them as giving us true
conclusions. But that includes the arguments of those who cast

doubt on necessity on philosophical or scientific grounds. (Cf. Nagel 1997, Chapter 4)

Karl Popper was another twentieth-century critic of essentialism, but his remarks are essentially directed at a straw man, and are certainly irrelevant to the Scholastic understanding of essentialism. For example, according to Popper, "Aristotle held with Plato that we possess a faculty, intellectual intuition, by which we can visualize essences and find out which definition is the correct one," and that the deliverances of this faculty are "unerringly and indubitably true" (1962, pp. 15 and 292). Of course, different people's intuitions may conflict, and when they do "the essentialist is reduced to complete helplessness" (p. 292). But this is a ludicrous caricature of Plato and Aristotle, and has no force against the Scholastic either. Note first that we have to distinguish the question of *whether* things have essences and the question of *what*, specifically, the essence of some particular thing is. Now we have so far looked at several arguments for the claim that things have essences, and none of these arguments has appealed to a special faculty of "intellectual intuition" and none of them has involved "visualizing" anything. It has been claimed that the reality of essence is unavoidable, but this claim has been backed by arguments, which like all arguments are open to critical evaluation. The claim has not been supported by appeal to some "unerring and indubitable" faculty.

When it comes to the question of what, specifically, the essence of some particular material thing is, the Scholastic holds that this must be determined empirically. To be sure, there are general metaphysical principles that the Scholastic thinks must guide us in our study of the essences of things, such as the theory of act and potency, hylemorphism, the principle of causality, the principle of finality, and so forth. But like the reality of essence in general, these principles have been argued for rather than defended by appeal to a purportedly unerring faculty of intellectual intuition. And knowing the essence *itself* requires sensory experience. To know the essence of water, or stone, or a tree, or a dog, or a human being, you have to study the causal powers and other properties of these things, which can only be known empirically. To know them in detail requires scientific investigation. Naturally such investigation is fallible and its results are thus subject, in good Popperian fashion, to criticism and revision. There is, again, simply no appeal to the "unerringly and indubitably true" deliverances of a special "faculty" of "intellectual intuition."

Popper also characterizes essentialism as committed to "*the doctrine that science aims at ultimate explanation*; that is to say, an explanation which (essentially, or by its very nature) cannot be further explained" and alleges that belief in essences is "obscurantist" and "does not help us in any way and indeed is likely to hamper us" (1968, p. 105). To this he opposes the view that "we may seek to probe deeper and deeper into the structure of our world or, as we might say, into properties of the world that are more and more essential, or of greater and greater depth" (1979, p. 196). But there are many problems with this criticism. First of all, even if it were true that a belief in essences "hampered" us by somehow discouraging us from pursuing inquiry as deeply as we otherwise might, that wouldn't show that there are no such things as essences -- as Popper himself basically concedes (1968, p. 105). So if (as I have tried to show) there are compelling arguments for essentialism, then we are simply stuck with it and had better find a way around the bad consequences alleged by Popper -- again, if it were true that there are such bad consequences.

But it is not true. For one thing, as Oderberg argues (2007, pp. 32-34), the historical record just doesn't support Popper's allegation that belief in essences is likely to hamper scientific progress. ("New essentialist" philosophers of science like Cartwright and Ellis would, for reasons we've considered, also no doubt find Popper's allegation dubious.) For another thing, it simply isn't true that attributing an essence to something by itself entails closing off inquiry. To say, for example, that it is essential to water that it is composed of hydrogen and oxygen in no way entails that we shouldn't bother looking into exactly how hydrogen and oxygen are combined in water, or investigating the nature of hydrogen and oxygen themselves, or asking any number of other questions about water and its constituents. But it should also be pointed out that it is as dogmatic to rule out the possibility that there are ultimate explanations as it is to close off investigation prematurely. And for reasons examined in chapter 2, if ultimate explanations are not to be found at *some* level of reality, then there could not be any explanations at all. (Cf. Oderberg 2007, pp. 34-38)

Finally there is Popper's "anti-essentialist exhortation" to the effect that *what must be taken seriously are questions of fact*" rather than *"problems about words and their meanings"* (1992, pp. 15-16). This may (or may not) be well-taken as a criticism of the view of earlier generations of analytic philosophers that philosophical problems could largely or entirely be solved via the analysis of language. But, early modern caricatures notwithstanding, it is irrelevant to Scholastic essentialism, which is very much concerned with the essences of things themselves rather than the ways we talk about them.

Wittgenstein's famous remarks about games and "family re-semblances" (1968, s. 66ff.) are often thought to pose a challenge to essentialism. There is (so the argument goes) no one feature or set of features that is common to all and only games, but merely a set of overlapping similarities like those exhibited by members of a family. The similarities may lead us to assume there must be some one attribute had by all the things to which we apply the word "game," but that is an illusion. And in general (so the argument continues) it is overlapping similarities of this sort that lead us to attribute essences to things, where often there is in fact no single common set of attributes. "Grammar" (in the technical Wittgensteinian sense) tells us what things are (1968, ss. 371 and 373), and it does not point us in the direction the essentialist supposes it does.

As is sometimes pointed out in response, it is not clear that Wittgenstein was correct to hold that there is no set of features all games have in common. A deeper point is that games are not natural kinds but human artifacts -- inheriting all the variability of the purposes to which human artifacts are put -- so that it is hardly surprising that it would be difficult to find in them a common set of features. (Cf. the discussion of substantial versus accidental forms in the preceding chapter.) The Wittgensteinian claim would be harder to defend using a natural kind as an example. (Cf. Oderberg 2007, pp. 38-43) In any event, the Scholastic would not agree in the first place with the background assumption that it is to "grammar" that we must look to resolve (or dissolve) metaphysical problems, nor with the Wittgensteinian supposition that there is such a thing as "ordinary language" hermetically sealed off from the philosophical use of language and to which the latter must answer (Oderberg 2007, pp. 41-43). For the Thomist these usages are related by *analogy* in a sense to be discussed below.

Wittgenstein's example raises the issue of *vagueness*, which anti-essentialists often raise as an objection to essentialism whether or not they are Wittgensteinians. The idea is that especially in the biological context, the boundaries between kinds are sometimes ill-defined (as in the case of transitional forms), and there seems to be no fact of the matter about whether a given thing falls on one side of the boundary rather than the other. How could this be the case if these things really had essences? Now this sort of objection doesn't undermine essentialism *per se*, since some essentialists (such as Ellis) do not extend their essentialism to biology in the first place, but confine it to areas like physics and biology, where it is harder to defend the claim that boundaries between kinds are vague. But the Scholastic metaphysician is an essentialist about biological kinds and thus needs to say more. (Cf. Oderberg 2007, pp. 224-34)

The first point to make is that though it might seem at first glance plausible to hold that a transitional form lacks an essence, on more careful consideration the proposal doesn't really make sense. Every organism, including those characterized as transitional, has characteristic properties, causal powers, patterns of activity, and the like, which differ from those of other things. It is not somehow less intelligible than other things or more random in its behavior. What can it mean, then, to say that there is no fact of the matter about what it is? Second, we must not let the tail wag the metaphysical dog. Most kinds even in biology are *not* vague. The anti-essentialist would have us judge the vast majority of cases by reference to the exceptional ones. The vague kinds seem not to have essences (so the reasoning goes), therefore nothing has an essence. But why not reason instead that since the vast majority of kinds clearly have essences, the apparently vague kinds must have them too, appearances notwithstanding? Indeed, we couldn't judge some cases to be vague in the first place unless we had non-vague cases to compare them to. So why evaluate the latter in light of the former rather than the other way around?

The vagueness in question, then, is really *epistemic* rather than metaphysical. If it is not clear to us exactly what kind a thing belongs to, that is a fact about our *knowledge* of the thing rather than a fact about the thing itself. And that everything has an essence simply does not entail that we always know or even could know what its essence is. Where we are not sure whether a thing falls into kind *A* or kind *B*, further investigation may reveal that it is after all one of these rather than the other, or it may show instead that it belongs to some third, heretofore unknown kind *C* (Oderberg 2007, pp. 230-34). Even if investigation yielded no clear answer, though, that wouldn't show that there is no fact of the matter, and we know on independent metaphysical grounds that there must be. For the anti-essentialist to make of vagueness a serious objection to essentialism, he would have to show that if things have essences we should always be able clearly to determine what they are. But why should we suppose that?

Naturally, empiricism raises questions about *how* we can know essences when we do know them. The empiricist challenge to essentialism is best answered in the context of the Scholastic approach to universals.

4.1.3 Moderate realism

Though Ockham famously took a nominalist (or at least conceptualist) approach to the problem of universals, the standard Scholastic position has been realist. An essence is something that can be *common* to many particulars. The essence of water is something the water in Lake Michigan shares with the water coming out of your tap and the water frozen in the ice caps of Mars; the essence of being a dog is something Rover shares with Spot and Fido; and so forth.

For the Scholastic, realism is unavoidable if we are to make sense of the world and our knowledge of it, for reasons that go back to Plato's "one over many" argument. Universals like *triangularity, redness, humanness,* etc. are not reducible to any particular triangle, red thing, or human being, nor even to any collection of triangles, red things, or human beings. For any particular triangle, red thing, or human being, or even the whole collection of these things, could go out of existence, and yet triangularity, redness, and humanness could come to be instantiated once again. They also could be, and often are, instantiated even when no human mind is aware of this fact. Hence triangularity, redness, humanness, and other universals must in some way be real features of the world rather than mere inventions of the human mind or artifacts of language.

Not only ordinary language and everyday knowledge, but both the *a priori* and the *a posteriori* sciences presuppose realism about universals. Two and two make four *universally, modus ponens* is a valid form of inference *universally*, and affirming the consequent is invalid *universally* -- not only on every other Tuesday or in the Western hemisphere alone. Since these are necessary truths, the universals they presuppose cannot be sheer inventions of the human mind. The laws and classifications of empirical science, being general or universal in their application, also necessarily make reference to universals, and science is in the business of discovering mind-independent facts. Hence to accept the results of science is to accept that there are universals that are not merely the invention of the human mind.

Nominalist and conceptualist attempts to avoid realism face notorious problems. The nominalist who says that there is no such thing as *redness* but only the general term "red," which we apply to different things because they resemble one another, faces a vicious regress problem (Russell 1988, Chapter 9). For *resemblance* is itself a universal. A Stop sign resembles a fire truck, which is why we call them both "red"; grass resembles the Incredible Hulk's skin, which is why we call them both "green"; and so on. What we have, then, are multiple instances of one and the same universal, *resemblance*. The nominalist might seek to avoid this difficulty by saying that we only call these examples cases of "resemblance" because *they* resemble each other, without specifying the respect in which they resemble each other. But then the problem just crops up again at a higher level. These various cases of resemblance resemble other various cases of resemblance, so that we have a higher-order resemblance, which itself will be a universal. And if the nominalist tries to avoid *this* universal by once again applying his original strategy, he will be just faced with the same problem again at yet a higher level, *ad infinitum.* Then there is the fact that a general term like "red" is *itself* a universal. You utter the word "red," I utter the word "red," Barack Obama utters the word "red," and these are all obviously particular utterances of the *same* one word, which in some way exists over and above our various utterances of it. For the nominalist purportedly to eschew universals in favor of general terms is really just to invoke the very thing he is supposed to be denying.

A conceptualist like Locke regards universal essences as entirely the product of the human mind. *"[T]he boundaries of the species, whereby men sort them, are made by men*; since the essences of the species, distinguished by different names, are ... of man's making" (*An Essay Concerning Human Understanding* 3.6.37; Cf. Feser 2007, pp. 56-66). But this sort of view is incoherent, and for reasons that also undermine the nominalist view that universals are mere artifacts of language. If we say that our concepts and general terms reflect nothing extra-mental or extra-linguistic, then we shall have to provide an account of how they are formed in a way that makes no reference to mind-independent and language-independent universal essences. But this is not possible. Locke would of course appeal to an empiricist theory of ideas, perhaps along with a corpuscularian account of how external objects cause changes in the sense organs in such a way as to generate ideas. A contemporary nominalist or conceptualist might add considerations from evolutionary psychology, Marxian economics, postmodernist cultural criticism, or the like. But such accounts will necessarily appeal to various universals -- for example, to *ideas, corpuscles, Darwinian selective pressures, genetic mutations, class interests, social trends*, etc. -- and to standards of valid reasoning which are also universal. All these universals will have to pre-exist the minds and languages whose concepts and general terms the theories that make reference to them are intended to explain. Hence such views either have to admit that there are universals that are not the product of the human mind or artifacts of language -- which defeats the whole point of defending them -- or they will have to say that the relevant universals are both the *products of* human thought and language and *pre-exist* human thought and language -- which is incoherent.

Of course, much more could be said about the problem of universals -- including much more in favor of realism and against its rivals. (Cf. Armstrong 1989; Jubien 1997, Chapter 3; Moreland 2001; Lowe 2002, Chapter 19) What needs to be emphasized in the context of a discussion of essentialism is that the Scholastic does not advocate a *Platonic* or "extreme" version of realism, but rather an Aristotelian or "moderate" version (Bittle 1936, Chapters XIII-XIV; Phillips 1950b, Part I, Chapters VIII-XI; Coffey 1958, Chapters IX-XII; Peterson 1999; Oderberg 2007, pp. 81-85). For a Scholastic like Aquinas, essences do not exist in a Platonic "third realm" but only as either *immanent* to the particular things whose essences they are, or as *abstracted* by an intellect. The essence of being a dog exists immanent to Fido, Rover, and Spot; the essence of being a human being exists immanent to Socrates, Plato, and Barack Obama; and so forth. These essences exist in an individuated way insofar as Fido's matter sets him off from Rover, Socrates' matter sets him off from Plato, and so on. The essences are universal *qua* abstracted from the particular individuals by an intellect which knows them. But considered absolutely, in themselves, they are neither individual nor universal. As Robert Pasnau and Christopher Shields explain Aquinas's position:

> If the nature had individuality built into it, then it wouldn't apply to *all* individuals. If the nature had commonness built into it, then it wouldn't apply to *any* individual. The solution is to say that when we conceive of *humanity* (for example), the content of that thought is neither individual nor common. (2004, p. 75)

The moderate realist position is thus the middle ground between unacceptable extremes. To regard natures or essences as having individuality *per se* or "built into them" would be to deny that there is any true universality in the world -- an essentially nominalist or conceptualist position, neither of which, as I've argued, can be correct. But to regard natures or essences as having universality *per se* or "built into them" would entail that they couldn't truly exist in individual particular things, but only as Platonic Forms. *Humanness* wouldn't really be in Socrates at all, nor *dogginess* in Fido, nor *treeness* in a tree. Neither Socrates, nor Fido, nor a tree would be a true substance, any more than a shadow or a reflection in a mirror is a true substance. For like these things they would lack any *intrinsic* principle of operation and the independence characteristic of substances. They would just *be* shadows, reflections, or emanations of a sort -- which is, of course, exactly how they are treated in the Platonic tradition. (Cf. Oderberg 2007, pp. 84-85)

Moderate realism is *moderate*, then, insofar as it involves no commitment to the metaphysical and epistemological baggage of Platonism. There are, for the moderate realist, no such things as mind-independent abstract objects. As Oderberg writes, "nothing abstract exists without abstraction. And abstraction is an *intellectual* process by which we recognize what is literally shared by a multiplicity of particular things." (2007, p. 83) This process begins with sensory experience; there is no appeal to "intellectual intuition," innate ideas, Platonic recollection, or the like. Moderate realism is *realist* insofar as, unlike Lockean conceptualism, it takes essences really to exist in individual things themselves, so that even though the essences are universal only as abstracted by the intellect, the conceptual product of this abstractive activity has a foundation in mind-independent reality. And so too, contra nominalism, do the words that signify the resulting concepts.

Now, to return to the empiricist critique of essentialism, while this is not the place for a full-scale treatment of Scholastic epistemology, enough can be said to show that the classical empiricist position -- whether deployed in criticism of essentialism, or substance, or the principle of causality, or anything else -- is hopeless. Berkeley, Hume, and almost certainly Locke were committed to *imagism*, the thesis that every concept is essentially a kind of mental image (or what Scholastics would call a "phantasm"). But imagism has been refuted about as conclusively as a philosophical theory can be (Bittle 1950, pp. 24-28; Crane 2003, pp. 13-20; Feser 2007, pp. 41-46; Feser 2013a). Concepts are *abstract and universal* in a way no image can be. The concept *triangle* applies to every triangle without exception, but any mental image we can form of a triangle will always be of an isosceles, scalene, or equilateral triangle, a right, acute, or obtuse triangle, a black, red, or green triangle, etc. The concept *man* applies to every man without exception, but any mental image we can form of a man will always be of a tall man or a short one, a man with hair or a bald man, a fat man or a skinny man, etc. There will always be various concrete and particular features in a mental image that the concept leaves out. Concepts are also *determinate* in a way no mental image can be. There is nothing in the mental image of a triangle by itself that determines that what it represents is a particular triangle, or triangles in general, or a dunce cap, or a piece of pizza, etc The concept *triangle*, by contrast, determinately represents triangles. To borrow a famous example from Descartes, there is no clear difference between a mental image of a chiliagon (a polygon having 1,000 sides) and a mental image of a myriagon (which has 10,000 sides), but the concepts *chiliagon* and *myriagon* are clearly and distinctly different. We also have many concepts (like *logical consistency, law, abstraction, economics, certainty*, etc.) that are so abstract that no mental image at all (except images of the written or spoken words they are merely contingently associated with) corresponds to them.

There is no way the classical empiricist can coherently deny that we have such universal and determinate concepts. In order to deny that we really have a determinate and universal concept like *triangle*, you first have determinately to grasp what it would be to have such a concept and what it would be for it to be universal, and then go on to deny that we have it. The very act of *denying* it thus *deploys* it. In order to argue for the plausibility of such a denial, you have to make use of valid forms of inference which are themselves determinate and universal. (See Ross 1992; Ross 2008, Chapter 6; and Feser 2013a for detailed discussion of these issues.)

Collapsing conceptual thought into imagination, classical empiricism thus has a demonstrably false account of our intellectual capacities. (Notice that this criticism does not beg the question at issue, since a non-essentialist could agree that the empiricist account of concepts is false.) The empiricist account of perceptual experience is also gravely deficient. Experiences are taken to be reducible to aggregates of Humean impressions, sense data, or the like -- patches of color, sounds of this or that pitch, feelings of warmth or coolness, etc. Notoriously, the very possibility of constructing the notion of a mind-independent material substance and coming to know that such substances even *exist* (never mind knowing their essences) becomes problematic on this picture. Yet the notion of a sense datum or Humean impression is itself highly dubious, an *abstraction from* an actual experience. When you read a book it is a book that you are perceiving, not a whitish rectangular expanse, a feeling of smoothness, a sound as of paper crinkling, etc. These "impressions" or "sense data" are not more basic than the experience as a whole, any more than a foot or a kidney is more basic than the organism of which they are parts. Organisms are more basic than their organs, and the latter have to be understood in light of the former rather than the other way around. "Sense data" and the like are related to ordinary experiences in the same way. (Cf. Wilfrid Sellars' famous critique (1956) of the "myth of the given.")

If our knowledge of essences seems problematic given empiricism, then, that is hardly surprising, since almost *all* of our knowledge is problematic given empiricism. Yet it would be a mistake to think that rejecting empiricism entails embracing rationalism (or, for that matter, Kantianism, which from a Scholastic point of view combines rather than transcends the errors of empiricism and rationalism). With the rationalist, the Scholastic insists on a difference in kind between intellect on the one hand and sensation and imagination on the other. But the Scholastic agrees with the empiricist that our concepts must be derived from experience and are not innate. Through *abstraction* from sensory experience the intellect can arrive at the universal concepts that the rationalist rightly affirms but wrongly supposes must be innate, and the empiricist wrongly denies because he rightly sees that they are not innate.

Of course, much more would have to be said fully to defend a Scholastic approach to epistemology, which would take us well beyond general metaphysics. (Cf. Bittle 1936; Coffey 1958a and 1958b; Van Steenberghen 1949; Wilhelmsen 1956; O'Callaghan 2003; McInerny 2007; Ross 2008, Chapter 5) Suffice it for present purposes to say that if the empiricist insists that our concepts and knowledge must derive from experience, the Scholastic agrees. *That* much by itself poses no problem for essentialism. What poses a problem is the specific *way* the empiricist would develop this common epistemological commitment. Yet the empiricist's way of developing it casts doubt not only on our knowledge of essences, but also our knowledge of substance, causality, and the external world in general; and the empiricist account of intellect and perceptual experience is problematic even apart from these difficulties. The Scholastic position, meanwhile, has none of these problems. Hence the empiricist really hasn't a leg to stand on in criticizing Scholastic essentialism on empirical grounds.

4.1.4 Essence and properties

From a Scholastic point of view, much contemporary discussion of essentialism, pro as well as con, reflects a misunderstanding of the relationship between the *essence* of a thing and its *properties*. Part of the problem is terminological. Contemporary analytic philosophers tend to use the term "property" to refer more or less indiscriminately to any characteristic, feature, or attribute of a thing. As we saw in the previous chapter, for the Scholastic a "property" is not just any characteristic but only a "proper accident" of a thing -- something *proper* to it in the sense of belonging to it given its essence or nature -- as opposed to a "contingent accident."

It might seem that this difference is merely terminological, and that the distinction in question here is the same as the distinction analytic philosophers commonly draw between "essential properties" and "accidental properties." But that is not the case. For contemporary analytic philosophers also typically characterize the essence of a thing as itself a property or set of properties, namely the property or properties the thing cannot exist without. "Essential properties" are thus, on this usage, those properties that make up the set or cluster which comprise the essence. But this is simply *not at all* what the Scholastic metaphysician has in mind, and the difference with contemporary analytic views is absolutely crucial.

The essence of a thing, as Scholastics understand it, is *not* a property or cluster of properties. It is rather that *from which* a thing's properties *flow*, that which *explains* its properties. Consider again the traditional Aristotelian definition of man as a *rational animal*, which if correct gives the essence of man. (And again, for present purposes it does not matter whether or not one accepts this definition. It is being used as an illustration.) Given this essence, human beings have properties like the capacity for perceptual experience, the capacity for locomotion or self movement, the ability to form concepts, the ability to reason from one judgment to another in a logical way, and so forth. But *rational animality* itself is not the set or cluster of these properties. Neither is *animality* the set or cluster of properties like the capacity for perceptual experience, the capacity for locomotion, etc.; nor *rationality* the set or cluster of properties like the ability to form concepts, the ability to reason from one judgment to another in a logical way, etc. *Animality* is rather that *by virtue of which* an animal has the properties in question, *rationality* that *by virtue of which* a rational being has its distinctive properties, and *rational animality* that *by virtue of which* rational animals, specifically, have theirs.

Rational animality is an essence defining a *species* (in the traditional logical sense rather than the modern biological sense). *Animality* is the *genus* under which this particular species falls, and *rationality* is its *specific difference* or that which distinguishes the species from others in the same genus. ("Definition" here is meant in the sense of what Scholastics call a *real definition* or description of the nature of *a thing itself* -- as opposed to a *nominal definition*, which merely gives the sense of a word we use to talk *about* things.) Species, genus, and specific difference are what Aristotle would call *predicables*, since like properties they can be truly predicated of a substance. But metaphysically they have a different status than properties have. As Oderberg puts it, "whereas genus, species, and difference are *constitutive* predicables, accidents and properties are *characterizing* predicables" (2007, p. 160).

The essence of a thing *must* be distinct from its properties, for several reasons. One reason is that treating an essence as a set of properties is as problematic as treating a substance as a cluster of accidents. Oderberg calls this the "unity problem" (2011a; cf. 2007, pp. 156-62). If an essence is a set of properties, then what is it that makes it the case that all and only the properties that make up a certain kind of thing's essence occur together in that kind of thing? It might seem that this could be explained by appealing to laws of nature: it is just a law that all and only such-and-such properties are always found together in things of this kind. But it should be obvious from what was said about laws of nature in earlier chapters why the Scholastic metaphysician will regard this as a non-starter. Laws are just a shorthand description of the way a thing operates given its essence. Laws therefore *presuppose* essences and can hardly coherently be appealed to in order to *explain* essences.

As Oderberg argues (2011a), there are several other problems with such a proposal. For instance, suppose (to use his example) that electrons are defined as *elementary particles carrying a unit negative electrical charge*, and that we posit a law connecting the properties be-

ing an elementary particle and *carrying a unit negative electrical charge.* The problem is that there *is* no such law, since there are elementary particles without a unit negative electrical charge and non-elementary particles with a unit negative electrical charge. Nor will it help to add that such a law obtains only in the case of electrons, since why these properties occur together in electrons is what the appeal to the law is supposed to be *explaining.*

So, a thing's essence must be distinct from its properties as the ground of their unity, just as a substance must be distinct from the accidents that it grounds. Indeed, where substances are concerned, to talk about a substance and its essence is really to talk about the same thing considered from different points of view. "By 'essence' we indicate *what* a reality is, whereas by 'substance' we indicate the *mode of being* of this reality" (Koren 1960, p. 186). As this indicates -- and as is indicated also by the fact that we can describe the essence of man as *rational animality* even though *rationality* and *animality* aren't properties -- an essence *qua* that from which properties flow is *not* to be understood as a "bare substratum," any more than a substance is a bare substratum (for reasons considered in the previous chapter).

A second reason for distinguishing a thing's essence from its properties is to make sense of how we actually come to know the natures of things. Contrary to the usual caricatures, the Scholastic essentialist in no way supposes that determining the essence of a thing is in general an easy matter, something that can be done from the armchair by consulting intuitions, the dictionary, or superficial observational evidence. Often what we suppose to be parts of the essence of a thing turn out merely to be its properties. Hence at one time it might have seemed that the essence of gold was to be a metal that is yellow, malleable, fusible, etc. But it turns out that yellowness, malleability, fusibility, etc. are really only properties of gold, which flow from its essence of being a metal whose atomic constituents have atomic number 79. Scientific investigation was required in order to determine this. Still, the older description of gold's essence, while superficial, was hardly wrongheaded. It was on to something even if it didn't go deep enough. The distinction between essence and properties makes sense of both these facts -- the fact that determining a thing's nature is often very difficult, and the fact that a relatively superficial understanding of it can nevertheless point us in the right direction. What are available to a relatively superficial investigation and point to something deeper are the *properties* of a thing; that to which they point, and the determination of which is much more difficult, is the *essence* of a thing.

A third reason we need to distinguish the essence of a thing from its properties is to make sense of the distinction between *normal* and *defective* instances of a kind. One needn't be a Scholastic to see that the latter distinction is needed. As Philippa Foot (following Michael Thompson) notes, living things can only adequately be described in terms of what Thompson calls "Aristotelian categoricals" of a form such as *S's are F*, where *S* refers to a species and *F* to something predicated of the species (Foot 2001, Chapter 2; Thompson 1995). To cite Foot's examples, "Rabbits are herbivores," "Cats are four-legged," and "Human beings have 32 teeth" would be instances of this general form. Such propositions cannot be adequately represented as either existential or universal propositions, as these are typically understood by modern logicians. "Cats are four-legged," for instance, is not saying "There is at least one cat that is four-legged"; it is obviously meant instead as a statement about cats in general. But neither is it saying "For everything that is a cat, it is four-legged," since the occasional cat may be missing a leg due to injury or genetic defect. Aristotelian categoricals convey a *norm*. If a particular *S* happens not to be *F* – if, for example, a particular cat is missing a leg – that does not show that *S's* are not *F* after all, but rather that this particular *S* is a *defective* instance of an *S*.

The distinction between essence and properties makes sense of the distinction between normal and defective instances. A thing's properties flow or follow from its essence, but like water held back by a dam, the flow might, as it were, be blocked if the thing is damaged in some way. Given its essence, a cat has four legs, but this property might not manifest itself in a particular cat if the cat is genetically or otherwise damaged. Its lack of four legs does not mean that being four-legged is not after all a property of the cat -- it *is* a property of the cat, indeed an "essential property" (to speak redundantly) insofar as four-leggedness flows from the essence of the cat. Its lack of four legs just makes it a defective cat, and precisely *because* four-leggedness is one of its properties. Similarly, every human being without exception is a rational animal, even if some human beings (e.g. those with severe brain damage) cannot exercise the powers that flow or follow from their rationality.

Immature instances of a kind can be understood in a similar way. That human beings have 32 teeth is not falsified by the fact that a newborn human baby has no teeth. Having 32 teeth is as much a property of a newborn human being as it is of an adult human being or a very old human being whose teeth have fallen out. If damage to an instance of a kind (as in the case of the human being who has lost his teeth) is like a dam which blocks the flow of a thing's properties, immaturity (as in the case of the newborn who hasn't yet grown teeth) is, we might say, comparable to the failure of an underground flow of water to reach the surface yet. Similarly, newborn and unborn human beings are, like adult human beings, rational animals, even though the properties that flow from their rationality haven't yet manifested themselves.

What exactly is it for properties to "flow" from an essence (as it is traditionally put)? Oderberg (2011a) suggests that it is a matter of properties being *caused by* and *originating from* the essence, where the causation in question is *formal* causation. Just as a triangle has various properties (e.g. angles adding up to 180°) by virtue of its form, so too do substances in general have the properties they have by virtue of their essences acting as formal causes, even if in material substances the formal causation has a complementary material cause (e.g. a genetic one in the case of living things). Both the causal and originating elements need in Oderberg's view to be specified as aspects of "flow," since not all origination is causation (e.g. water can originate from a well without being caused to exist by it) and not all causation is origination (since the immediate cause of a thing need not be its ultimate source). "Flow" as used by Scholastics captures the idea that the essence of a thing is *both* the formal cause and origin of its properties.

As all of this indicates, it is *through* a thing's properties that we know its essence, but acquiring such knowledge is not always a straightforward matter. It may require considerable scientific investigation, as determining the essence of gold or water from their properties did. Too hasty a consideration of a thing's accidents may lead to mistaken judgments about which of them are properties, and thus to mistaken judgments about the essence of the thing. Even what might seem in the face of much observational evidence to be a property may turn out not to be, as in the case of whiteness and swans. And what actually is a property might not always be manifest, as in the case of damaged or immature members of a kind.

There are general principles that can guide us. For example, in the case of a living thing, if a certain accident is very widespread in living things of the kind in question and is absent only in cases where the thing is damaged and/or where the absence is associated with what on independent grounds we can judge to be dysfunction, then we have good reason to judge that the accident in question is a *proper* accident or property and thus flows from the thing's essence. Thus we are *not* reduced to the circular reasoning of saying that such-and-such really are properties because normal members of the kind have them, and those members of the kind are the normal ones because they have such-and-such properties. It would be ridiculous to allege that only circular reasoning could lead us to say that having eyeballs (for example) is a genuine property of human beings rather than merely a contingent accident. For having eyeballs is almost universal to human beings, human beings who lack eyeballs are severely impaired in their various basic activities, and the absence of eyeballs is typically the result of fairly easily specifiable damage of a physical or genetic sort. (Cf. Oderberg 2007, pp. 160-62; 2011a) Still, this shows that judgments about essence are fallible and may require much empirical investigation for their justification -- a fact acknowledged by Scholastic essentialists, if not by the straw men attacked by Popper and others.

4.1.5 Modality

For the Scholastic, what is possible, impossible, or necessary is grounded in what is *real* (Oderberg 2007, pp. 125-30; Ross 2008, Chapters 1-3; Ross 2012). Reality contains both *being-in-act* and *being-in-potency*, and these kinds of being are further specified in terms of the four causes. In the world of material reality, there is prime matter, which is the pure potency for the reception of the forms of material things; there is substantial form, which actualizes the potencies of prime matter resulting in a substance with various specific properties and powers; there are the various efficient causes of matter taking on new forms; and there are the specific outcomes or ranges of outcomes to which these causes point as to a final cause. Prime matter, since *qua* pure potency it is indifferent to what form it might receive, of itself makes any material thing possible. But that prime matter is actually informed only by certain specific substantial forms, that these forms impart only certain specific efficient causal powers to the things that have them, and that these powers are directed toward the generation only of certain specific outcomes, puts significant constraints what might happen in the material world. What material things will always do given their formal, material, efficient, and final causes is what is necessary in the world of material things; what they haven't done but will do given that they are acted upon in certain ways is what is possible in the material world; and what they will never do given their formal, material, efficient, and final causes is what is impossible in the material world. (These are *metaphysical* constraints, not merely nomological ones, given that laws themselves are grounded in the essences of things.)

Or at least, that is what is necessary, possible, and impossible in the material world *considered by itself*. Natural theology is beyond the scope of this book, but if we consider also God's relationship to the world as its creating and sustaining cause, the range of possibilities radically increases. Unlike things which are mixtures of potentiality and actuality, God as pure actuality has unlimited causal power. There are in the divine intellect concepts of non-actual things (unicorns, phoenixes, golden mountains, etc.) as well as actual ones. Factoring this in, the range of what is possible in the material world includes any way that prime matter would have been actualized so as to take on the forms of the non-actual things of which God has a concept in his intellect, had he chosen so to actualize it. There are also those things that might happen in the material world as it actually is if God causes a miracle to occur. If we also add to the picture angels understood as immaterial intellects, then what is possible, necessary, or impossible will also include what follows from angels having the natures they do.

Whether we consider just the material world or the material world together with the angelic world and the divine source of both worlds, modality is grounded in concrete reality, whether purely actual or a mixture of act and potency. This includes intellects -- human, angelic, and divine -- as well as purely material things. But modality is for the Scholastic in no way grounded in Platonic abstract objects -- including possible worlds considered as abstract objects -- existing in some "third realm" distinct from minds and material things. Neither is it grounded in concrete "possible worlds" of the sort famously posited by David Lewis (1986), which don't really ground possibility at all but eliminate it in favor of what are essentially parallel actual worlds. (Cf. Kripke 1980, p. 45)

Logical and mathematical necessity too, then, are in the Scholastic view not properly thought of in Platonic terms. Like universals, logical and mathematical objects are abstractions, where abstraction presupposes an intellect which does the abstracting (Oderberg 2007, pp. 128-30; Ross 2008, Chapter 1). As with the abstraction of universals, this does not mean (contra Lockean conceptualism) that what is abstracted has no foundation in mind-independent reality. Yet that will seem an insufficient ground for mathematical and logical necessity given that the material world is contingent. If mathematical and logical truths essentially depend on an intellect and yet are necessary truths, then, it is hard to escape the conclusion that they must be grounded in a necessarily existing intellect, viz. the divine intellect. And that is indeed a position that some Scholastic writers have defended (e.g. Oderberg 2007, p. 130). Similarly, pure or logical possibilities, though (since they are not grounded in actually existing things) they can exist only in a mind, cannot plausibly depend on finite minds (since they concern what might have been actual even if no finite mind had existed). Hence they too, Scholastics have argued, must depend on a necessarily existing divine intellect. (Cf. Bittle 1939, Chapter VII; McCormick 1940, pp. 51-55; Renard 1946, pp. 108-12; Koren 1960, pp. 164-67; Ross 2012) But again, pursuing such questions of natural theology is beyond the scope of the present book.

4.1.6 Essentialism in contemporary analytic metaphysics

During the late twentieth century, the development of modal logic and views in the philosophy of language and metaphysics put forward by Saul Kripke (1980) and Hilary Putnam (1975b) led to a renewed interest in essentialism among analytic philosophers. Howev-

238

er, as philosophers sympathetic to the Scholastic tradition have pointed out (Oderberg 2001 and 2007, Chapter 1; Klima 2002), essentialism as contemporary analytic philosophers understand it is very different from the essentialism one finds in Aristotle and in Scholastic writers.

Kripke's version is built around the notion of a *rigid designator*, an expression that refers to the same thing in every possible world in which the thing exists. Proper names and natural kind terms are taken to be rigid designators. Hence "water" and "H_2O," being natural kind terms, would be examples of rigid designators. Since water = H_2O in the actual world and "water" and "H_2O" are rigid designators, then water = H_2O in every possible world. That water = H_2O is thus taken to be a *necessary* truth. Indeed, any identity statement in which the identity sign is flanked by rigid designators is, if true at all, going to be true in every possible world and thus a necessary truth. Such statements, when true, are thus taken to tell us about the essential properties of the things they refer to. Water is thus *essentially* H_2O. On the other hand, if an identity statement in which the identity sign is flanked by rigid designators is false in any possible world, then (since, again, such statements must be true in every possible world if true at all) it is not a necessary truth and so not true at all. Hence it is false in the actual world. If we can determine whether there is at least one possible world in which such a statement is false (where "conceivability" is sometimes taken by adherents of this approach to be a guide to whether such a world is possible), then we have a way of determining whether such identity statements are true in the actual world. This method has been deployed to argue that the mind must not be identical to the brain, since it is claimed that it is at least conceivable, and thus possible, for the mind to exist apart from the brain.

This is of course just a highly simplified sketch, but it gives a sense of the basic approach of this contemporary brand of essentialism and the kind of metaphysical work to which it is put. As the sketch indicates, the notion of possible worlds is crucial to the approach, and a variety of accounts of possible worlds have been developed. As I indicated above, there is also a tendency to identify the essence of a thing with a cluster of properties -- in particular, with the properties a thing has in every possible world. And there is a further tendency to regard the relevant properties in the cluster as those which concern a thing's "internal structure" (Kripke 1980, pp. 120 and 126) or "hidden structure" (Putnam 1975b, p. 241), with physical science providing the stock examples of what counts as such a structure (H_2O in the case of water, molecular motion in the case of heat, etc.).

Naturally the Scholastic metaphysician will welcome the affirmations that things have essences, that these essences are mind-independent rather than merely the products of convention, and that knowing the essence of a thing requires empirical investigation. However, there are aspects of contemporary essentialism that are problematic both in themselves and from a Scholastic point of view. We have already seen, for example, why it is for the Scholastic a serious mistake to think of an essence as a property or cluster of properties.

It is also a mistake to try to determine the essence of a thing by reference to possible worlds. That is not to say that there is never a place for talk about possible worlds. Given that we know the essence of a thing, asking how it might behave in some possible world might be a useful heuristic exercise for some purposes. But as we have seen, in the Scholastic view merely possible worlds exist as objects of thought rather than in a mind-independent way. Hence they can hardly tell us about the essences of things, which *are* real or mind-independent. To appeal to possible worlds in order to determine the essence of a thing gets things the wrong way around.

Appeal to possible worlds could be a useful way to determine the essences of things only if a realist theory of possible worlds were correct, whether this involved treating possible worlds as concrete entities as Lewis does, or as Platonic abstract entities. As we have already seen, the Scholastic metaphysician rejects such entities, but there are other problems besides (Oderberg 2007, pp. 1-6). First of all, such theories are bound to be circular (Ross 1989; Oderberg 2007, pp. pp. 1-2). Their point is to explain modal notions like possibility, necessity, and impossibility in terms of possible worlds, but of course "possible" is itself one of these modal concepts. Hence such theories presuppose precisely what they are supposed to be explaining. And if the possible worlds theorist tries to get around this problem by proposing that it is the worlds themselves, rather than the modal notions, that are somehow what is basic, then he has merely relocated the problem he is supposed to be addressing rather than solved it. The modal properties of things, he tells us, can be explained in terms of the modal properties of possible worlds. But now we need to know why those *worlds* have the modal properties they do. This is hardly an advance, especially since the metaphysical status of possible worlds is less clear and more controversial than that of the things the worlds are invoked in order to explain. (The concept of a "rigid designator" similarly has modal notions built into it, and in general, Putnam's and Kripke's arguments for essentialism rest on nontrivial essentialist assumptions. Cf. Salmon 1981 and Oderberg 2007, pp. 5-6.)

The appeal to possible worlds also gets things the wrong way around in a further respect than the one mentioned above. For it is the essence of water, or of a tree, a dog, or a human being, that determines what will be true of these things in various possible worlds. It is not what is true of them in various possible worlds that determines their essences. As Oderberg writes, the contemporary essentialist who tries to determine the essence of a thing from what is true of it in various possible worlds is "guilty... of confusing the *consequences* of [a thing's] having the essence [it] does with the *constituents* of that essence" and "changes the subject from the possessors of essences to the situations in which those possessors exist" (2007, pp. 3-4).

Kit Fine (1994) argues that while a thing's having a property necessarily or in every possible world might be a necessary condition for its being an essential property, it is not a sufficient condition. To take just one of Fine's examples, if Socrates exists then he necessarily belongs to the singleton set containing him, but it is implausible to hold that belonging to a set is of the *essence* or *nature* of Socrates. As several commentators (Klima 2002; Gorman 2005; Oderberg 2007, pp. 7-12) have pointed out, Fine's objections are not conclusive. Properties like the ones he cites could be ruled out by tightening up the notion of essence to rule out trivial properties; alternatively, it could be argued that there is a *sense* in which belonging to the singleton set containing him is essential to Socrates insofar as it follows from his being an individual thing. However, such moves will require distinguishing characteristics of a thing that are more central to a thing's nature from those that are less central even if they are necessarily true of it, and thereby moving the contemporary essentialist position closer to the Scholastic essentialist's distinction between essence and properties. Fine's objections are well-taken, then, as indicative of the inadequacy of contemporary essentialism if left unmodified.

Finally, while empirical science is certainly crucial to discovering the essences of material substances, it is in the Scholastic view a mistake to *reduce* a material thing's essence to its "internal" or "hidden" microstructure as described by science (Oderberg 2007, pp. 12-18). As we saw in the previous chapter, there is for the Scholastic nothing metaphysically privileged about the microphysical level of description, and there will be substantial forms, and thus true substances, wherever there are irreducible causal powers in the natural world. Furthermore, a substance's micro-level parts exist in it virtually rather than actually. Accordingly, determining the essence of a thing requires attention to macro-level features no less than to the micro-level.

4.2 The real distinction

4.2.1 Arguments for the real distinction

A distinction is commonly drawn in Scholastic metaphysics between the *essence* of a thing (that is to say, *what* the thing is) and the *existence* of the thing (*that* it is). Considered by itself, a contingent thing's essence is taken to be a kind of *potency*, and its existence a kind of *actuality*. For there is nothing in the essence of a tree, for example, that entails that it exists, which is why trees come into being and pass away. *By itself* the essence of a tree specifies a merely potential kind of being. The same is true of the essence of a *Velociraptor* and the essence of a unicorn (if unicorns have essences). That it exists is what makes it the case that a tree is also an actual kind of being, whereas velociraptors and unicorns are merely potential because the first no longer exists and the second never did.

In that which is *pure* actuality, without any passive potency whatsoever (namely God), its essence would not be a kind of potency. Indeed, qua pure actuality its essence would just *be* actuality. Hence

it would not have merely the potency for existence but would necessarily exist. Nor would any distinction we might draw between its essence and its existence be a *real* distinction reflecting any difference
in mind-independent reality, since it would, as it were, just *be* existence. (More on this below.) But what of the distinction Scholastics
draw between essence and existence in contingent things, in things
that are compounds of potency and act?

The claim is *not* that a thing's essence and existence are *separable*; there is no such thing in mind-independent reality as a thing's
essence existing apart from its existence (whatever that would mean)
or a thing's existence existing apart from its essence (whatever that
would mean). (Cf. Renard 1946, p. 52; Koren 1960, p. 135) That raises
the question, though, of what *kind* of distinction -- purely logical, virtual, formal, or real -- there is to be drawn between a contingent
thing's essence and its existence.

As we saw in chapter 1, Scotus and Suarez maintain that in created things a distinction can be real only where it entails separability.
We also saw that, accordingly, they deny that the distinction between
potency and act is a real distinction. In Scotus's view it is merely a
formal distinction, while Suarez regards it as a virtual distinction.
Since essence and existence correspond to potency and act, it is no
surprise that they deny a real distinction here as well. Scotus regards
it too as a formal distinction and Suarez as virtual. But as with the
distinction between act and potency, Aquinas and Thomists following
him, who deny that a real distinction entails separability, insist that
the distinction between essence and existence is a real one.

There are several lines of argument for the real distinction between essence and existence in contingent things. (Cf. Wippel 2000,
Chapter V) One of them is implied by what has just been said. The
distinction between potency and act must, as the Thomist argues (for
reasons set out in chapter 1), be a real distinction. But essence is a
kind of potency and existence is a kind of act. Therefore the distinction between essence and existence is a real distinction. (Cf. Koren
1960, p. 133)

A second argument is from the very contingency of contingent
things. If the existence of a contingent thing was not really distinct
from its essence, then it would have existence just by virtue of its es-

sence. It would exist by its very nature, and would therefore not be contingent at all but necessary. Hence, since it is not necessary but contingent, its existence must be really distinct from its essence. (Cf. Oderberg 2001, p. 39) One objection to this argument is that we need not posit a real distinction between essence and existence in a contingent thing in order to account for its contingency, but can instead point to the facts that it has a cause and has the potentiality for non-existence (Coffey 1970, p. 112). However, this objection simply misses the point. For we need to know *why* a contingent thing's existence would need (or indeed could have) a cause in the first place if its existence were not distinct from its essence, and *why* it has (or indeed could have) a potentiality for non-existence in the first place if its existence were not distinct from its essence. (Cf. Hart 1959, pp. 95-96) If existence were just part of *what it is*, then it would not need something else to cause it, and there would not be anything in it that could give it the potential to go out of existence.

A third argument (which Aquinas presents in Chapter IV of *On Being and Essence*) holds that we can know the essence of a thing without knowing one way or the other whether it exists. Suppose a person had never before heard of lions, velociraptors, or unicorns, and you give him a thorough description of the natures of each. You then tell him that of these three creatures, one exists, one used to exist but is now extinct, and the third never existed; and you ask him to tell you which is which given what he now knows about their essences. He would, of course, be unable to do so. But then the existence of the creatures that exist must be really distinct from their essences, otherwise one *could* know of their existence merely from knowing their essences. (Going in the other direction to the same conclusion, it might also be argued that one could know of a thing *that* it exists without knowing *what* it is. Cf. Oderberg 2001.)

It might be objected that this argument presupposes that we have a *complete* grasp of the essence of a thing, which Aquinas himself does not think we have. For unless we had a complete grasp, how could we know whether or not existence was part of a thing's essence? But the objection fails, for there is a crucial disanalogy between what is uncontroversially a part of a thing's essence, on the one hand, and the existence of the thing on the other. Suppose you judge that a lion is a kind of animal but do not judge that it is a kind of cat. In that case, while you have only *incompletely* conceived of what it is to be a lion, you have not for that reason *misconceived* what it is to be a lion. By contrast, if you not only fail to judge that a lion is a kind of cat but judge that a lion *is not* a kind of cat, then you *have* misconceived what it is to be a lion. Now, if we suppose that you judge that lions don't exist -- perhaps you think they have gone extinct, or that they are creatures of fiction like unicorns -- then while you have judged falsely, you have *not* misconceived *what it is* to be a lion. If the existence of a lion were not distinct from its essence, though, this would not be the case. Judging it to be non-existent would be as much to misconceive *what* it is as judging it to be a non-cat would be. (Cf. Phillips 1950b, p. 197; Oderberg 2007, p. 123)

Another objection would be that to accept the argument in question would entail accepting also the ontological argument for God's existence, which is not only controversial but rejected by Aquinas and Thomists in general. One way this objection has been developed is by way of suggesting that the argument attempts to go from our knowledge of a thing's essence to a judgment about its existential status, just as the ontological argument does. But this is not the case. The ontological argument does try to move from knowledge of God's essence to the conclusion that he exists in reality, but the argument under consideration here insists that from knowledge of a contingent thing's essence we *cannot* know *one way or the other* whether it really exists (Phillips 1950b, p. 198; Koren 1960, p. 136). Alternatively, it might be suggested that by implying that if a thing's essence and existence *were* identical, then we would know from a thing's essence that it exists, the Thomist is essentially committed to the thesis that God's existence can be known from his essence, since they are identical. But that is not the case. All the Thomist is committed to is the thesis that from knowledge of God's essence alone, we can know that *if* God exists *then* he exists necessarily rather than contingently. But to know whether he really does exist we need a further argument. (Cf. Phillips 1950b, p. 198; Oderberg 2007, p. 123) Indeed, the Thomist can turn this objection against the critic. If the existence of a lion, velociraptor, or unicorn were *not* really distinct from its essence, then we should be able to argue, after the fashion of the ontological argument, that lions, velociraptors, and unicorns would exist necessarily rather than contingently, if they exist at all -- which is absurd.

A fourth argument for the real distinction, presented by Aquinas in different versions in various places (including Chapter IV of *On Being and Essence* and *Summa Contra Gentiles* II.52), holds that there could not be more than one thing in which essence and existence are not really distinct. For if essence and existence are not really distinct, then they are identical, and they could be identical only in something whose essence *just is* existence itself. Now for there to be more than one thing that *just is* existence itself, there would have to be something that differentiated these things. In particular, there would have to be distinct parcels of matter that differentiated *this* thing that just is existence itself from *that* thing that just is existence itself; or there would have to be some specific difference that distinguished *this* species of thing that just is existence itself from *that* species of thing that just is existence itself; or there would in some other way have to be something that made it the case that *this* instance of that which just is existence itself differed from *that* instance. But in none of these cases would we really *have* distinct things that were each just existence itself. In fact each would instead be existence *plus* a specific difference, or existence *plus* a parcel of matter, or existence *plus* something that otherwise differentiated one instance from another. (In *Summa Contra Gentiles* II.52, Aquinas offers the analogy of *animality* considered in the abstract. There cannot be more than one thing that *just is* animality in the abstract. If we tried to distinguish more than one such thing by considering e.g. animality as it exists in an ox versus animality as it exists in man, then we would no longer be talking about that which *just is* animality in the abstract, but rather about that which is animality together with the specific nature of an ox, animality together with the specific nature of man, and so forth.) So, there is no sense to be made of there being more than one of something that *just is* existence itself, and thus no way to make sense of there being more than one of something whose essence and existence are not really distinct. Now with contingent things like stones, trees, dogs, people, etc., there *is* (or certainly could be in cases where the class has been reduced to a single member) more than one of each of them. Therefore there is in each of them a real distinction between its essence and its existence.

A possible objection to this argument is that Aquinas has neglected a middle possibility. Why couldn't there be something whose existence was not distinct from its essence, not because its essence *just is* existence itself, but rather because existence is *part of* its essence (Weigel 2008, p. 86; Cf. Kenny 2002, p. 44)? But on reflection this suggestion makes no sense. The essence of human beings, *rational animality*, has *rationality* and *animality* as parts. Suppose *existence* were another part alongside these. Then the existence of the whole human being would depend on this part. But that is no more plausible than saying that the whole human essence, *rational animality*, depends on *animality* alone. Now if someone insisted that the whole essence really does depend on *animality* alone, with *rationality* being entirely derivative, then that would make *animality* itself the true essence and *rationality* a mere property (in the Scholastic sense). Similarly, if someone insisted that the whole human being depended on *existence* considered as a part of the human essence, then this would make *existence* the essence with the rest (*rationality* and *animality*) being mere properties. But then we'd be back with Aquinas's scenario in which for there to be no real distinction between essence and existence would entail that essence *just is* existence itself -- exactly what the objector was trying to avoid. So there really is no middle ground between the case where essence and existence are really distinct and the case where essence just is existence itself. (Cf. Aquinas, *Summa Contra Gentiles* I.22; Weigel 2008, pp. 144-45)

4.2.2 Objections to the real distinction

There are other, more general objections to the doctrine of the real distinction. One possible objection is suggested by some remarks of Alexander Pruss (2006, pp. 209-17, where the context is a discussion, not of the real distinction *per se* but of its role in the Thomistic version of the principle of causality). Pruss writes:

> Consider a puzzle about a given existing thing, say Socrates, on Thomistic principles. Socrates has an essence and an act of existing. When we say that Socrates exists, we are talking about his act, A_1, of existing -- this act of existing is the truthmaker for the claim that Socrates exists. At the same time, the act of existing is itself something that exists -- if it did not, it could not ground Socrates' existing. Socrates' act of existing is not a necessary being, since then Socrates would be a necessary be-

ing. Thus, A_1 itself contingently exists. What is it in virtue of which A_1 itself exists? Well, it does not exist in virtue of A_1's essence, since it is not a necessary being. Thus it exists in virtue of its own act, A_2, of existing. And so on ad infinitum. (p. 209)

Now though Pruss does not do so, one could easily present this as a *reductio ad absurdum* of the doctrine of the real distinction. For if the Thomist purports to explain a substance as a compound of essence and existence, yet has to account for the thing's existence in turn by seeing *it* as compound of essence and existence, and the existence of the existence as itself a further compound of essence and existence *ad infinitum*, then the whole analysis seems bizarre and pointless, explaining nothing.

But as should be obvious from what was said above, Pruss's description misrepresents the Thomistic position. It gives the impression that the Thomist regards a thing's essence and existence as distinct substances, or at least its *existence* as a distinct substance (since Pruss characterizes it as having an essence and existence of its own). And that is precisely what the Thomist denies, since for the Thomist the essence and existence of a thing cannot exist apart from one another. The doctrine of the real distinction can seem to entail that a thing's essence and existence are distinct substances only if we assume, with Scotus and Suarez, that a real distinction entails *separability*; but of course, the Thomist rejects this assumption.

David Twetten (2006) considers an objection he imagines a non-Thomist Aristotelian might raise. For Aristotle a material substance is a composite of form and matter, and Aristotle himself did not posit some further principle, the *existence* of the substance, distinct from these two aspects of its essence. Nor (our imagined Aristotelian might say) is there any need to do so. The only way one could argue for such a further principle is by *assuming* that there is something there in the first place to be distinguished from the form and matter, but such an argument would beg the question against the imagined Aristotelian objector. Hence any Thomist argument for the real distinction must fail.

Twetten thinks this is formidable objection to Aquinas's own arguments for the real distinction, but it seems to me that it is not. For one thing, in Chapter IV of *On Being and Essence*, Aquinas is explicitly concerned to explain how *immaterial* substances, such as angels, can be individuated, and rejects the theory that this can plausibly be accounted for by positing so-called "spiritual matter" (a point emphasized by MacDonald 2002). Only a distinction between the essence and existence of such a substance can account for its differentiation from other such substances. That suffices to show that the notion of a distinction between essence and existence can be independently motivated and then brought to bear on the analysis of material substances as well. Of course, a critic might reject the idea of immaterial substances or of a plurality of such substances (though Aristotle himself, with his plurality of unmoved movers, did not do so). But that is beside the point; what is to the point is that an argument for a distinction between essence and existence in material substances need not beg the question, since the distinction can be defended without appeal to material substances. It is also beside the point that a critic might prefer an appeal to "spiritual matter" to Aquinas's position, because the idea of "spiritual matter" is obviously one that someone might reject whether or not he accepts the Thomist doctrine of the real distinction.

Even apart from the question of immaterial substances, though, the idea of the real distinction can be motivated in a non-question-begging way. Unicorns, if they existed, would be composites of form and matter. Yet they don't exist. Thus the existence of things that do exist must be something additional to their form and matter. Here too, of course, Twetten's imagined critic may raise certain objections, but the point is that whatever else someone might say about such an argument, there is nothing *question-begging* about it. In particular, it doesn't *presuppose* that existing material things have a further principle additional to their form and matter, whether or not the critic agrees that it succeeds in showing that they do.

Furthermore, even if we start, not with immaterial substances or non-existent material substances, but with actual material substances, an argument for the real distinction need not beg the question. Its defender could begin with the point that there is a distinction between essence and existence of at least a *logical* sort to be made, and then go on to argue that the distinction must at the end of the day be a *real* one. In other words, even if the Thomist must begin his argument by making a distinction between essence and existence, it simply doesn't follow that he must argue in a circle, since the *kind* of distinction he starts with need not be the kind he concludes to. Indeed, Twetten himself thinks that Aristotle affirmed at least a "conceptual distinction" between essence and existence, and that appeal to such a distinction can help the Thomist surmount the objection his imagined critic would raise (2006, pp. 84-85). But the Thomist doesn't really need such help, since he already has long had in hand the distinction between a logical and a real distinction.

So, again, it seems to me that Twetten's imagined objection is not as daunting as he supposes. However, Twetten goes on to offer a powerful argument of his own for the real distinction against his imagined Aristotelian critic (2006, pp. 85-91). Twetten develops the argument at some length, but it might be summarized as follows: To avoid acknowledging that there is a real distinction between a thing's essence and its existence, the imagined Aristotelian critic will have to be able to account for a material thing's being actual in terms of its essence -- that is, its matter and form -- alone. But its matter alone cannot be what accounts for it, since matter by itself is pure potency and thus cannot account for actuality. Nor can its form alone be what accounts for it, since on an Aristotelian view form is not actual in the first place apart from matter. Furthermore, form alone cannot account even for a material thing's continued actuality once it comes into being, for if it could do so, it would itself continue in being after the substance of which it is the form was destroyed (which on an Aristotelian view it does not). Nor can the substance comprising form and matter together account for its own actuality, since this really amounts to the form, *qua* what actualizes the matter so as to make a substance, being the explanation of the actuality of the whole -- which, for the reasons just given, cannot be the case. So, there must be something really distinct from a thing's form and matter, and thus really distinct from its essence, that accounts for its actuality. (I independently presented a similar argument in Feser 2011a at p. 258, though what that argument was intended to establish was not the real distinction *per se*, but rather that material substances require a sustaining cause for their continued existence. My own argument was in turn the result of a train of thought inspired by some remarks of Christopher F. J. Martin in his 1997, at pp. 166-7.)

Anthony Kenny (1980, Chapter 2; 2002) has been harshly critical of Aquinas's doctrine of the real distinction, in one place going so far as to judge that "even the most sympathetic treatment of [the doctrine] cannot wholly succeed in acquitting [it] of the charge of sophistry and illusion" (1980, p. 60). Kenny distinguishes between two notions of existence (2002, p. 42). The first is "specific existence," which is expressed by the Fregean existential quantifier. Specific existence, that is to say, is what is captured in statements of the form "There is an x such that..." It has to do with whether or not there is an instance of a certain *species*. Specific existence on this view is thus a second-order predicate of *concepts* -- rather than a first-order predicate of individual objects -- and "There is an x such that x is F" is true of a concept F when F is exemplified. Kenny's second notion of existence is "individual existence," which corresponds to Frege's notion of *Wirklichkeit* and is what is captured in statements like "The Great Pyramid still exists, but the Library of Alexandria does not." Individual existence, that is to say, is just that which the Library of Alexandria lost when it was destroyed, but which the Great Pyramid still has. It has to do with what is true of an *individual* rather than a species.

Now Aquinas says that essence and existence are identical in God but really distinct in everything else. But in Kenny's view this cannot be true on either notion of existence. Suppose we read Aquinas's claim in terms of specific existence. In that case, Kenny argues, either essence and existence are as distinct in God as they are in everything else, or Aquinas's position is simply nonsensical. For what it can intelligibly mean to say that the essence of a thing is distinct from its specific existence is merely something like what is captured in the statement: "We can know what a phoenix is without knowing whether there is an x such that x is a phoenix." But by the same token, we can know what *God* is without knowing whether there is an x such that x is God (Kenny 2002, p. 37). Yet if Aquinas is insisting that essence and specific existence are not distinct in God, then his position is not even intelligible. It amounts to saying something like: "God's essence is there is an x such that..." (2002, pp. 41 and 43-44).

Suppose, then, that what Aquinas has in mind is not specific existence but individual existence. Unlike specific existence, individual existence can intelligibly be predicated of a thing. It makes sense to say of the Great Pyramid that it still exists or of some dog Fido that he still exists. Now what this amounts to, Kenny says, is just for Fido to go on being what he is, namely a dog. If we insist on saying that God's essence and existence are identical, then in Kenny's view this is intelligible if what we mean is just that if God exists then he goes on being what he is, namely God. But in that case essence and existence will be identical not only in God but in Fido and in everything else. In having individual existence, they all go on being what they are (2002, p. 45).

But there are several problems with Kenny's critique, which have been ably exposed by Gyula Klima (2004, 2013a). For one thing, when arguing that the notion of individual existence cannot salvage Aquinas's position, Kenny evidently supposes that a real distinction entails separability. He writes: "Can we say that Fido's essence and Fido's existence are distinct? If a real distinction between A and B means that we can have one without the other, then it seems that the answer must be in the negative" (Kenny 2002, p. 45). But as Klima points out (2013a, p. 33), and for the reasons set out in Chapter 1, a real distinction does *not* entail separability; certainly it begs the question against the Thomist merely to assume otherwise. Hence Fido's being *what* he is -- his essence -- need not be identical to his individual existence, even if we can't have one without the other. And for all Kenny has shown, the arguments for the real distinction we've been considering show that they are not identical.

Kenny begs the question against Aquinas in a much deeper way, however, by simply assuming that any respectable notion of existence must be one acceptable to the Fregean. For Aquinas wouldn't agree with such an assumption in the first place. As Klima writes, "it is ludicrous to claim victory by yelling 'Checkmate!' in a game of poker. But this is precisely what Kenny seems to be doing whenever he is yelling 'You are not a good enough Fregean!' at Aquinas" (2004). Klima goes on to say in the same paper:

[E]ven if the slogan 'existence is not a predicate', taken in the sense that the Fregean second-order concept of the existential quantifier is not a Fregean first-order concept, is trivially true, nevertheless, in that sense it is absolutely irrelevant to anything in medieval philosophy (indeed, to much of the history of philosophy in general), for in that sense it simply establishes a trivial truth concerning a Fregean concept, and says nothing at all about, say, a Thomistic, a Scotistic, or for that matter a Heideggerian concept. On the other hand, if this slogan is taken in the sense in which it is regularly used to castigate medieval (and other) philosophers – that is, in the sense in which it would claim that the equivalents of 'is' or 'exists' as used by these philosophers do not and cannot express a first-level concept – then it is relevant, but trivially false. After all, as our medieval colleagues put it, *verba significant ad placitum* – words signify by convention. Therefore, if by *their* convention, the medievals *did* consistently express a (non-Fregean) first-level concept by means of the relevant Latin words, then it is entirely futile to try to argue that they did not or could not express what they in fact did.

A standard argument for the view that the Fregean notion of specific existence is the only legitimate one is that if existence were a first-level predicate of objects, then (it is claimed) negative existential statements like "Martians do not exist" would be self-contradictory, which they obviously are not. For if we think of this statement as saying that Martians do not have the attribute of existence, this would seem to entail that there are (i.e. there exist) certain creatures, namely Martians, who lack existence. Since that is absurd, the statement "Martians do not exist" cannot be interpreted as denying an attribute of existence to some object or objects. It should rather be interpreted in light of Frege's doctrine of existence as saying something like "It is not the case that there is at least one x such that x is a Martian." That is to say, it says of the concept *being a Martian* that there is nothing to which it applies.

However, as John Knasas has argued (2003, pp. 202-3; Cf. Knasas 2006), regarding existence as a first-level predicate need not have the absurd implication that "Martians do not exist" is self-contradictory. For this would follow only if, when we grasp the concept *Martians*, we necessarily already grasp it as applying to something existing in reality, so that "Martians do not exist" amounts to "The existing Martians do not exist," which of course is self-contradictory. But statements attributing existence or non-existence to a thing, Knasas says, do not function logically in the same way other attributive statements do. In particular, their subjects are grasped in an existence-neutral way. In the case at hand, our mere grasp of the concept *Martians* does not by itself entail either a judgment that they exist or a judgment that they do not, but leaves the question open. "Martians do not exist" thus says, not "The existing Martians do not exist," but rather something like "Martians, which are of themselves existentially neutral, do not in fact exist." In general, for Knasas as for Aquinas, when the mind grasps the essence of a thing it grasps it as something distinct from its existence (or lack thereof), even if that of which the existence is ultimately predicated is the thing itself and not a mere concept.

That we can predicate existence of a thing doesn't entail that it is a *property* or other accident, however. It is *not* a property or accident, for a thing can have properties or other accidents only if it first exists. That treating existence neither in a Fregean way nor as a property or accident might sound odd to some contemporary philosophers only shows, in the Scholastic view, how deeply impoverished is the conceptual machinery they bring to bear on metaphysical questions. Act and potency, form and matter, substance and accident, properties and contingent accidents, essence and existence, etc. -- *all* of these notions are needed if we are to do justice to the structure of reality, and we simply will *not* do justice to it if we insist in a Procrustean fashion on reducing some to the others or on cutting them out altogether. (Cf. Oderberg 2007, pp. 124-5)

There is, in any event, ample reason to doubt that the Fregean notion of existence captures everything that needs to be captured by an analysis of existence. Consider that when we are told that "Cats exist" means "There is at least one x such that x is a cat" or that something falls under the concept *being a cat*, there is still the question of *what makes this the case*, of what it is exactly *in virtue of which* there is something falling under this concept. And the answer to this further question is, as both Knasas and David Braine (2006) have pointed out, what Aquinas is getting at when he argues that the existence of a thing is distinct from its essence (in this case, from the essence of a cat), and must be joined to it, as act to potency, if the thing is to be real.

If contemporary analytic philosophers have difficulty seeing any alternative to the Fregean notion, that says more about them than it does about Aquinas and other Scholastics. To borrow an analogy from Klima (2004), consider the word "bat," which in English can mean either "mouse-like flying mammal," or "wooden implement used in baseball or cricket to hit the ball," or "to blink." Now consider C, a person whose grasp of English is tenuous and who is only familiar with the first of these meanings, who overhears someone uttering the sentence "She didn't bat an eye when he confronted her." C supposes that what the speaker is saying is "She didn't mouse-like flying mammal an eye when he confronted her," and concludes, quite confidently but also quite wrongly, that the speaker is uttering gibberish. This, Klima proposes, is like Rudolf Carnap's confident dismissal of metaphysics on Fregean grounds (Carnap 1959), and also like Kenny's reading of Aquinas in terms of Fregean "specific existence." In each case the critic supposes he has put forward a devastating objection, but in fact has exposed only his own ignorance of the conceptual framework of the person he is criticizing.

Now consider a somewhat more competent English speaker K, who knows the first two meanings of "bat" but not the third, and who also hears someone utter the sentence "She didn't bat an eye when he confronted her." Knowing that to interpret this sentence in the first sense would make gibberish of it and knowing also that "bat" in the second sense can be used in a verbal way, K judges that what the speaker means must be something like "She didn't hit an eye with a baseball bat when he confronted her." This is not gibberish, but it is still so odd that K nevertheless concludes that the speaker must be confused about whatever it is he is trying to describe. This, Klima proposes, is like Kenny's proposed reading of Aquinas in terms of "individual existence."

Just as even K needs to improve his knowledge his English before he can understand, much less criticize, the beliefs of the speaker he has overheard, so too in Klima's view do analytic philosophers need a better understanding of Scholastic logical and semantic doctrines before they can properly understand, much less criticize, Scholastic metaphysical theses. Klima has set out these doctrines in several places (e.g. Klima 1996 and 2013b). Perhaps the key doctrine to keep in mind when approaching the question of the real distinction is Aquinas's theory of *analogy*.

Before addressing that subject, however, it is worthwhile briefly noting what is at stake in the dispute over the real distinction, which might at first glance seem a mere quibble over whether and how to split a certain metaphysical hair. Nothing could be further from the truth. Perhaps the most significant issue that rides on the debate is the cogency of a key argument for the existence of God presented by Aquinas in *On Being and Essence*. For if there is a real distinction between the essence and existence of a thing -- where essence, again, is a kind of potency and existence a kind of act -- then given the principle of causality, the continued existence of such a thing at any moment requires a cause, something which actualizes what would otherwise be merely potential. If this cause is something whose own essence is distinct from its existence, it too will require a sustaining cause. And since what we have here is a series of *essentially ordered* causes, this regress can terminate only in something which can cause the existence of things without itself needing a cause -- something whose essence *just is* existence. A detailed examination of this argument would take us into questions of natural theology that are beyond the scope of the book, but that it shows that the debate over the real distinction is an important one is obvious. (For further discussion of the argument see Feser 2009, pp. 84-88 and Feser 2011a. Cf. Miller 2002 and Vallicella 2002.)

A second reason why the debate over the real distinction is important is that without it, the Thomist claims, we cannot make sense of our ability to know mind-independent reality. (Cf. Phillips 1950b, pp. 201-2; Hart 1959, p. 98; Oderberg 2007, p. 125) It is because each individual thing has an essence distinct from its existence that the intellect can *abstract* that essence and consider it apart from this or that particular existing thing that has it. Now to deny the real distinction between essence and existence is either to collapse essence into existence or to collapse existence into essence. If we collapse the essence of each individual thing into its existence, then there is nothing to abstract and we cannot truly know universals but only be acquainted with this particular existent, that one, and so forth. But for reasons examined above, we cannot coherently deny the reality of universals. If instead we collapse existence into essence, then it is hard to see how we can have knowledge of universals as reflecting anything mind-independent. For existence will just be a feature of the universal essences themselves, rather than something that "ties them down," as it were, to particular concrete existents. That we have knowledge of universal but mind-independent essences, then, is intelligible only if there is in each particular thing we know a distinction between its essence and its existence.

4.3 The analogy of being

The basic idea of the theory of analogy is easy enough to introduce. Everyone is familiar with *univocal* and *equivocal* uses of terms. When I say "Fido is a dog" and "Rover is a dog," I am using the term "dog" univocally, or in the same sense. When I say "There was a bat flying around the attic" and "I swung the bat at it," I am using the using the term "bat" equivocally, or in completely different and unrelated senses. But there is, Thomists argue, an intermediate kind of usage, the *analogical* use of terms. When I say "This wine is still good" and "George is a good man," I am not using the term "good" in exactly the same sense, since the goodness of wine is a very different thing from the goodness of a man, but the two uses are not utterly different and unrelated either. The goodness of the one is *analogous* to that of the other, even if it is not exactly the same thing. Now when we speak of the being or reality of different kinds of things, we are in the Thomist view using the terms in an analogical way. For example, both a substance and its accidents are real or have being, but the being or reality of an accident is not the same as that of a substance. Neither is it totally unrelated, though. Hence they have being or reality not in either univocal or equivocal senses, but in analogous senses.

Things are much more complex than that summary lets on, however, and the theory of analogy is a subject of enormous controversy within Scholastic philosophy. Scotus rejects the Thomistic position, maintaining that our talk of the being or reality of things ought to be understood univocally rather than analogically. Suárez significantly modifies the Thomistic position, and even Thomists disagree among themselves about how to interpret it.

The first complication to take note of is that there are two main types of analogy distinguished by Thomists, the *analogy of attribution* and the *analogy of proportionality*. (Cf. Renard 1946, 92-104; Koren 1960, pp. 31-44; Gardeil 1967, pp. 47-72) A stock illustration of the analogy of attribution would involve sentences like "George is healthy," "This is healthy food," and "George's complexion is healthy." George in this case would be what is called the "primary analogate" and food and George's complexion would be "secondary analogates." What makes the analogy in question here one of attribution is that health exists intrinsically only in George, and it is attributed to the secondary analogates merely by virtue of their relation to the primary analogate -- in the case of food because it is a cause of health in living things like George, and in the case of complexion because it is caused by and a sign of health in living things like George.

The analogy of proportionality is itself divided into two sorts, *proper proportionality* and *improper* or *metaphorical proportionality*. An example of the analogy of proper proportionality would be the predication of life to plants, animals, human beings, and angels. What makes the analogy in question here one of proper proportionality is, first, that life exists *intrinsically* in each of the analogates (in contrast to the analogy of attribution); and secondly, that it exists *formally* in each of them. This latter aspect distinguishes such a case from an analogy of improper or metaphorical proportionality, as when we say (of an animal we see in the zoo) "That is a lion" and (of a certain man) "George is a lion." In this case, what we are predicating of each analogate exists intrinsically in each (which is why this is not an analogy of attribution) but formally only in the animal at the zoo, and merely *figuratively* in the man George. For there is something intrinsically in George (his courage, say) that leads us to call him a lion, but of course the form or nature of being a lion is not literally in him. By contrast, the form or nature of being alive is literally in plants, animals, human beings, and angels, despite their differences.

Now the analogy of improper or metaphorical proportionality is not regarded as important for metaphysics, but the analogy of proper proportionality is, for the traditional Thomist, absolutely crucial to it. For "being" is to be understood as a term applied to substances, to accidents, to things in which essence and existence are distinct, to that in which essence just is existence, and so forth, by an analogy of proper proportionality. Now, the analogy of proper proportionality differs from the univocal use of terms in that the concept expressed is not applied in exactly the same way to each analogate, even if we do not have (as we do in the equivocal use of terms) the expression, in each application of the term, of utterly different concepts. Rather, the concept is applied to all the analogates in an indistinct and indeterminate way on the basis of a real likeness or similarity they bear to one another.

Of course, a univocal term can be applied to very different things, but there is a crucial difference in the case of an analogical term like "being." A univocal term like "animal" is applied to things as diverse as fish, birds, reptiles, etc. because these are all *species* (in the traditional logical sense, not the modern biological sense) of animal. "Animal" is applied in just the same way to all of them, to name a *genus* under which they fall, and what distinguishes each from the other is captured by its *specific difference*. But "being," the Thomist argues, does *not* name a genus, so that substance, accident, etc. are not to be understood as different *species* of being. Man falls under the genus animal and has the specific difference of rationality; gold falls under the genus metal and has the specific difference of having atomic number 79; and so forth. We can grasp *rationality* without grasping *animality*, and we can grasp *having atomic number 79* without grasping *being a metal*. In that sense each of these specific differences is *extrinsic* to the genus under which the thing it specifies falls. By contrast, we *cannot* grasp what it is to be a substance or an accident without grasping them as having being. In that sense they are *not* extrinsic to being. There is nothing that *can* serve as a specific difference to mark out something as a species within being considered as a purported genus, because the only thing extrinsic to being is non-being or nothing, and non-being or nothing cannot differentiate anything, precisely *because* it is nothing. (Cf. Koren 1960, pp. 19-31; Gardeil 1967, pp. 44-47; Oderberg 2007, pp. 105-108)

So, though *being* in its relation to substance, accident, etc. superficially resembles the relationship between genus and species, that is not in fact how they are related, and thus "being" cannot be predicated of things in a univocal way. Again, though, neither is it predicated of them equivocally. It is rather predicated of things on the basis of a "proportional similarity" between them. The notion of a proportional similarity can be illustrated by the analogical use of a term like "seeing," as when one says "I see the tree in front of me" and "I see that the Pythagorean theorem is true." These are obviously not univocal uses, since the way one sees with one's intellect is radically different from the way one sees with one's eyes. But they are not completely unrelated, as the meanings of equivocal terms are. For the eyes are to a tree as the intellect is to the Pythagorean theorem. It is the *similarity* of the relations between the eyes and the tree on the one hand and the intellect and the Pythagorean theorem on the other that grounds the application of the same concept "seeing," applied in an indistinct or indeterminate way, to each of them. And when we more distinctly or determinately conceptualize the "seeing" involved in seeing the tree (which involves light from a material object striking the eyes) and the "seeing" involved in seeing the theorem (which involves understanding the logical relationships between concepts), they are not conceived of as species of the same genus, as things described univocally are.

We apply "being" and related terms to different things in the same manner. The existence of a man is to his essence as the existence of an angel is to *his* essence, as the existence of God is to *his* essence. The existence of each is related to its essence in a different way: In the case of God, his existence is *identical* to his essence; in the case of an angel, existence actualizes an essence to which it is *not* identical, where what is actualized is the essence of something essentially immaterial; in the case of a man, existence actualizes the essence of something with (in the Scholastic view) *both* material and immaterial operations; and so forth. Because the relations are not absolutely identical the predication is not univocal; but because there is nevertheless a *similarity* between the relations, the predications are not equivocal. They are predications of a sort intermediate between equivocal and univocal predications -- in particular, predications by an analogy of proper proportionality.

This does not exclude our predicating being of things also by an analogy of attribution. If an argument for God's existence like the one of Aquinas's *On Being and Essence* is accepted, then God is the primary analogate in such a predication insofar as his essence just is existence, whereas all other things are secondary analogates insofar as they are beings only by virtue of having been caused to exist by God. In the case of the analogy of proper proportionality as well, God could be said to be the "primary analogate" once we reason to his existence as the source of the being of other things. However, it does not follow that one has to *know* of God's existence, or to conceive of a first analogate of any sort, in order to be able to predicate being of things by an analogy of proper proportionality. (Cf. Renard 1946, pp. 99-101; Gardeil 1967, pp. 61-64)

The analogy of proper proportionality is in any event, at least according to the traditional view among Thomists, fundamental to a proper understanding of being. To be sure, the view is controversial. Suárez substitutes for it a notion of the "analogy of intrinsic attribution," according to which what is predicated of a secondary analogate is predicated of it by virtue of something intrinsic to it, and not merely by virtue of an extrinsic relation to the primary analogate -- a position which many Thomists regard as collapsing into a univocal predication of being (Renard 1946, pp. 103-4; De Raeymaeker 1954, pp. 49-51; Anderson 1969, Chapter IX). Scotus explicitly insists on treating being as a univocal rather than analogical concept, despite agreeing with the Thomist that being is not a genus -- though for the Thomist there is no stable way to combine these theses (Phillips 1950b, pp. 171-2; Gardeil 1967, pp. 64-65). Even Thomists disagree about the relative importance of the analogy of proper proportionality versus the analogy of attribution. Especially controversial among Thomists in recent decades has been the question of whether Cajetan's (1953) historically influential views about analogy (which are reflected in the summary offered above) are in fact correct either as an interpretation of Aquinas's position or in their own right. Much ink has been spilt both by those critical of Cajetan (Burrell 1973; Klubertanz 1960; Lyttkens 1952; McInerny 1996; Montagnes 2004) and those broadly sympathetic to him (Anderson 1969; Garrigou-Lagrange 1950; Hochschild 2010; Long 2011; Maritain 1995; Phelan 1941). And there are certainly complexities in the analogical use of language that go well beyond those captured by the distinctions just surveyed. (Cf. Ross 1981 and 1998.)

For present purposes it will suffice to note that on the traditional Thomist view, whatever the details, the doctrine of the analogy of being is inevitable given the real distinction between potency and act, which is itself necessary to avoid the extremes of Parmenides and Heraclitus. (Cf. Renard 1946, p. 91; Phillips 1950b, pp. 170-1; Gardeil 1967, p. 47; Anderson 1969, pp. 304-10; Long 2011, pp. 1-37) For *being-in-potency* is not *being-in-act*, but precisely because it is not nothing either, it is still really a kind of *being*. And since it is (the Thomist argues) really distinct from act, it can be being in only an analogous rather than a univocal or equivocal sense. More explicitly, the reasoning can be represented as follows:

1. Act is real, i.e. it has being.

2. Potency is real, i.e. it has being.

3. Potency is really distinct from act.

4. If potency had being in the same, univocal sense in which act does, then it wouldn't be really distinct from act.

5. If potency had being only in an equivocal sense then it wouldn't have being at all.

6. The only sense remaining is an analogous sense.

7. So potency has being in a sense that is analogous to that in which act has it.

Now, Eleatic views -- like those of Parmenides and Zeno themselves, or Spinoza, or Minkowski and the contemporary four-dimensionalist metaphysicians he inspired, or the David Lewis-style modal realist -- explicitly or implicitly deny premise 2 of this argument. The problem with such views, the Scholastic argues, is that they thereby explicitly or implicitly deny the reality of change, yet cannot do so coherently. Hence while their denial of 2 enables them to treat being univocally rather than analogously, it does so at an unacceptable cost. Heraclitean views explicitly or implicitly deny premise 1. Such views at least implicitly regard all talk of being as equivocal, denying as they do any stable or common natures of things that language might capture. The Scholastic takes their position also to be incoherent. Scotists and Suarezians instead deny premise 3 -- as, implicitly and in their different ways, do contemporary writers like Armstrong who would reduce "dispositional" properties to "categorical" ones (thereby collapsing potency into act) and pan-dispositionalists (who essentially collapse act into potency). The Thomist argues that to deny 3 is implicitly to deny either 2 or 1 as well, and thereby implicitly to fall into either an Eleatic or Heraclitean position.

Now premise 4 seems clearly true upon reflection. If potency and act had being or reality in *exactly the same* sense, then (given that being is not a genus, with act and potency as species) what could that mean if not that potency is really a kind of act or that act is really a kind of potency? (It is no accident that those who deny the real distinction between act and potency also tend to be those who explicitly or implicitly regard being as a univocal concept.) Premise 5 also seems clearly true upon reflection. For what could it mean to have "being" only in a sense that is *totally unrelated* to the sense in which act has it unless it is just to be utterly unreal? Premise 6 too is clearly true insofar as the univocal use of terms, the equivocal use, and the analogous use as the middle ground between them, exhaust the possibilities for the literal use of terms.

Now, as we have seen over the course of this book, when applied to various specific metaphysical issues the theory of act and potency yields distinctive accounts of causal powers, substances and their accidents, essence and existence, etc. Hence a causal power is a kind of potency, matter is a kind of potency and form that which actualizes it, a substance is in a sense in potency relative to its accidents, essence is a kind of potency relative to existence, and so forth. That being is predicated of act and potency in an analogous sense thus entails that it is also predicated of form and matter, of a substance and powers and other accidents, of the essence of a thing and its existence, etc., in an analogous sense.

So, if we take seriously the theory of act and potency, as well as the theories of causation, substance, essence, and other metaphysical notions which follow from it, then we cannot fail to take seriously also the doctrine of the analogy of being. And as we have seen, contemporary analytic metaphysicians have at least to a significant extent rediscovered Scholastic insights on the issues named. As with the other Scholastic ideas they have *not* yet rediscovered, the theory of analogy commends itself to them, and promises to shed light on the rest. Indeed, it is an especially fitting object for their reconsideration, given both the logico-linguistic concerns that have always lain at the heart of the analytic tradition, and the revival of metaphysics that it has seen in recent years.

Bibliography

Adams, Marilyn McCord. 1987. *William Ockham*, Volume II (Notre Dame, IN: University of Notre Dame Press).

Anderson, James F. 1969. *The Bond of Being: An Essay on Analogy and Existence* (New York: Greenwood Press).

Anscombe, G. E. M. 1981a. *From Parmenides to Wittgenstein* (Minneapolis: University of Minnesota Press).

Anscombe, G. E. M. 1981b. "'Whatever has a Beginning of Existence must have A Cause': Hume's Argument Exposed." In Anscombe 1981a.

Anscombe, G. E. M. 1981c. *Metaphysics and the Philosophy of Mind* (Minneapolis: University of Minnesota Press).

Anscombe, G. E. M. 1981d. "Times, Beginnings, and Causes." In Anscombe 1981c.

Antonietti, A., A. Corradini, and E.J. Lowe, eds. 2008. *Psycho-Physical Dualism Today: An Interdisciplinary Approach* (Lanham, MD: Lexington Books/Rowman and Littlefield).

Ariew, André. 2002. "Platonic and Aristotelian Roots of Teleological Arguments." In Ariew, Cummins, and Perlman 2002.

Ariew, André. 2007. "Teleology." In Hull and Ruse 2007.

Ariew, André, Robert Cummins, and Mark Perlman, eds. 2002. *Functions: New Essays in the Philosophy of Psychology and Biology* (Oxford: Oxford University Press).

Aristotle. 1996. *Physics.* Translated by Robin Waterfield (Oxford: Oxford University Press).

Aristotle. 2004. *The Metaphysics.* Translated by Hugh Lawson-Tancred (London: Penguin Books).

Armstrong, D. M. 1983. *What is a Law of Nature?* (Cambridge: Cambridge University Press).

Armstrong, D. M. 1989. *Universals: An Opinionated Introduction* (Boulder: Westview Press).

Armstrong, D. M. 1996a. "Dispositions as Categorical States." In Armstrong, Martin, and Place 1996.

Armstrong, D. M. 1996b. "Reply to Martin." In Armstrong, Martin, and Place 1996.

Armstrong, D. M. 2005. "Four Disputes About Properties." *Synthese* 144: 309-20.

Armstrong, D. M., C. B. Martin, and U. T. Place. 1996. *Dispositions: A Debate*, ed. Tim Crane (London: Routledge).

Aune, Bruce. 1985. *Metaphysics: The Elements* (Minneapolis: University of Minnesota Press).

Barrett, Jeffrey. 1999. *The Quantum Mechanics of Minds and Worlds* (Oxford: Oxford University Press).

Bedau, Mark A. and Paul Humphreys, eds. 2008. *Emergence: Contemporary Readings in Philosophy and Science* (Cambridge, MA: The MIT Press).

Beebee, Helen, Christopher Hitchcock, and Peter Menzies, eds. 2009. *The Oxford Handbook of Causation* (Oxford: Oxford University Press).

Bennett, M. R. and P. M. S. Hacker. 2003. *Philosophical Foundations of Neuroscience* (Oxford: Blackwell).

Bhaskar, Roy. 2008. *A Realist Theory of Science* (London: Routledge).

Bird, Alexander. 2007. *Nature's Metaphysics: Laws and Properties* (Oxford: Clarendon Press).

Bird, Alexander. 2013. "Limitations of Power." In Groff and Greco 2013.

Bittle, Celestine N. 1936. *Reality and the Mind: Epistemology* (Milwaukee: Bruce Publishing Company).

Bittle, Celestine N. 1939. *The Domain of Being: Ontology* (Milwaukee: Bruce Publishing Company).

Bittle, Celestine N. 1941. *From Aether to Cosmos: Cosmology* (Milwaukee: Bruce Publishing Company).

Bittle, Celestine N. 1950. *The Science of Correct Thinking: Logic*, Revised (Milwaukee: Bruce Publishing Company).

Boulter, Stephen. 2013. "The Aporetic Method and the Defense of Immodest Metaphysics." In Feser 2013c.

Braine, David. 2006. "Aquinas, God, and Being." In Paterson and Pugh 2006.

Brower, Jeffrey E. 2012. "Matter, Form, and Individuation." In Davies and Stump 2012.

Brown, Christopher M. 2005. *Aquinas and the Ship of Theseus* (London: Continuum).

Brown, Patterson. 1969. "Infinite Causal Regression." In Kenny 1969.

Bunge, Mario. 2009. *Causality and Modern Science*, Fourth revised edition (New Brunswick: Transaction Publishers).

Burrell, David. 1973. *Analogy and Philosophical Language* (New Haven: Yale University Press).

Cajetan, Thomas De Vio Cardinal. 1953. *The Analogy of Names and the Concept of Being*, translated by Edward A. Bushinski and Henry J. Koren (Pittsburgh: Duquesne University Press).

Callender, Craig, ed. 2002. *Time, Reality, and Experience* (Cambridge: Cambridge University Press).

Carlson, John W. 2012. *Words of Wisdom: A Philosophical Dictionary for the Perennial Tradition* (Notre Dame, IN: University of Notre Dame Press).

Carnap, Rudolf. 1959. "The Elimination of Metaphysics through Logical Analysis of Language." In A. J. Ayer, ed., *Logical Positivism* (New York: The Free Press).

Cartwright, Nancy. 1989. *Nature's Capacities and their Measurement* (Oxford: Clarendon Press).

Cartwright, Nancy. 1992. "Aristotelian Natures and the Modern Experimental Method." In John Earman, ed., *Inference, Explanation, and Other Frustrations: Essays in the Philosophy of Science* (Berkeley and Los Angeles: University of California Press).

Cartwright, Nancy. 1993. "In Defence of 'This Worldly' Causality: Comments on van Fraassen's *Laws and Symmetry*" *Philosophy and Phenomenological Research* 53: 423-9.

Cartwright, Nancy. 1999. *The Dappled World: A Study of the Boundaries of Science* (Cambridge: Cambridge University Press).

Cartwright, Nancy. 2005. "No God; No Laws." In S. Moriggi and E. Sindoni, eds., *Dio, la Natura e la Legge: God and the Laws of Nature* (Milan: Angelicum-Mondo X).

Cartwright, Nancy. 2008. "Reply to Stathis Psillos." In Hartmann, Hoefer, and Bovens, eds., 2008.

Cartwright, Nancy and John Pemberton. 2013. "Aristotelian Powers: Without Them, What Would Modern Science Do?" In Groff and Greco 2013.

Chakravartty, Anjan. 2007. *A Metaphysics for Scientific Realism* (Cambridge: Cambridge University Press).

Chakravartty, Anjan. 2013. "Dispositions for Scientific Realism." In Groff and Greco 2013.

Chalmers, David. 1996. *The Conscious Mind* (Oxford: Oxford University Press).

Churchland, Paul M. 2013. *Matter and Consciousness*, Third edition (Cambridge, MA: The MIT Press).

Clarke, W. Norris. 1994. "The Limitation of Act by Potency in St. Thomas: Aristotelian-ism or Neoplatonism?" In W. N. Clarke, *Explorations in Metaphysics: Being - God - Person* (Notre Dame: University of Notre Dame Press).

Clarke, W. Norris. 2001. *The One and the Many: A Contemporary Thomistic Metaphysics* (Notre Dame, IN: University of Notre Dame Press).

Clatterbaugh, Kenneth. 1999. *The Causation Debate in Modern Philosophy 1637 - 1739* (London: Routledge).

Coffey, P. 1958a. *Epistemology or The Theory of Knowledge, Volume I* (Gloucester, MA: Peter Smith).

Coffey, P. 1958b. *Epistemology or The Theory of Knowledge, Volume II* (Gloucester, MA: Peter Smith).

Coffey, P. 1970. *Ontology or The Theory of Being: An Introduction to General Metaphysics* (Gloucester, MA: Peter Smith).

Collins, John, Ned Hall, and L. A. Paul, eds. 2004a. *Causation and Counterfactuals* (Cambridge, MA: The MIT Press).

Collins, John, Ned Hall, and L. A. Paul. 2004b. "Counterfactuals and Causation: History, Problems, and Prospects." In Collins, Hall, and Paul 2004a.

Connell, Richard J. 1988. *Substance and Modern Science* (Houston: Center for Thomistic Studies).

Copleston, Frederick. 1993. *A History of Philosophy*, Volume III (New York: Doubleday).

Cottingham, John. 1986. *Descartes* (Oxford: Basil Blackwell).

Craig, William Lane. 1993a. "The Finitude of the Past and the Existence of God." In Craig and Smith 1993.

268

Craig, William Lane. 1993b. "The Caused Beginning of the Universe." In Craig and Smith 1993.

Craig, William Lane, ed. 2002a. *Philosophy of Religion: A Reader and Guide* (New Brunswick, NJ: Rutgers University Press).

Craig, William Lane. 2002b. "The *Kalam* Cosmological Argument." In Craig 2002a.

Craig, William Lane and J. P. Moreland, eds. 2009. *The Blackwell Companion to Natural Theology* (Oxford: Wiley-Blackwell).

Craig, William Lane and Quentin Smith. 1993. *Theism, Atheism, and Big Bang Cosmology* (Oxford: Clarendon Press).

Crane, Tim. 2003. *The Mechanical Mind*, Second edition (London: Routledge).

Crisp, Thomas M., Matthew Davidson, and David Vanderlaan, eds. 2006. *Knowledge and Reality: Essays in Honor of Alvin Plantinga* (Dordrecht: Springer).

Cross, Richard. 1999. *Duns Scotus* (Oxford: Oxford University Press).

Cross, Richard. 2005. *Duns Scotus on God* (Aldershot: Ashgate).

Cullen, Christopher M. 2006. *Bonaventure* (Oxford: Oxford University Press).

Damschen, Gregor, Robert Schnepf, and Karsten R. Stüber, eds. 2009. *Debating Dispositions* (Berlin: Walter de Gruyter).

Davidson, Donald. 1980. "Mental Events." In Donald Davidson, *Essays on Actions and Events* (Oxford: Oxford University Press).

Davies, Brian, ed. 2002. *Thomas Aquinas: Contemporary Philosophical Perspectives* (Oxford: Oxford University Press).

Davies, Brian. 2004. *An Introduction to the Philosophy of Religion*, Third edition (Oxford: Oxford University Press).

Davies, Brian and Eleonore Stump, eds. 2012. *The Oxford Handbook of Aquinas* (Oxford: Oxford University Press).

Davies, Paul. 1999. *The Fifth Miracle: The Search for the Origin and Meaning of Life* (New York: Simon and Schuster).

De Raeymaeker, Louis. 1954. *The Philosophy of Being: A Synthesis of Metaphysics* (St. Louis: B. Herder Book Co.).

Descartes, Rene. 1985. *The Philosophical Writings of Descartes*, Volume 2. Translated by J. Cottingham, R. Stoothoff, and D. Murdoch (Cambridge: Cambridge University Press).

269

Des Chene, Dennis. 1996. *Physiologia: Natural Philosophy in Late Aristotelian and Cartesian Thought* (Ithaca: Cornell University Press).

Donceel, J. F. 1961. *Philosophical Psychology*, Second edition (New York: Sheed and Ward).

Dretkse, Fred. 1977. "Laws of Nature." *Philosophy of Science* 44: 248-68.

Ducasse, C. J. 1965. "Causation: Perceivable? Or Only Inferred?" *Philosophy and Phenomenological Research* 26: 173-9.

Dupré, John. 1993. *The Disorder of Things: Metaphysical Foundations of the Disunity of Science* (Cambridge, MA: Harvard University Press).

Eddington, Sir Arthur. 1963. *The Nature of the Physical World* (Ann Arbor: The University of Michigan Press).

Effler, Roy R. 1962. *John Duns Scotus and the Principle "Omne Quod Movetur Ab Alio Movetur"* (St. Bonaventure, NY: The Franciscan Institute).

Elder, Crawford L. 2004. *Real Natures and Familiar Objects* (Cambridge, MA: The MIT Press).

Elder, Crawford L. 2011. *Familiar Objects and their Shadows* (Cambridge: Cambridge University Press).

Ellis, Brian. 2001. *Scientific Essentialism* (Cambridge: Cambridge University Press).

Ellis, Brian. 2002. *The Philosophy of Nature: A Guide to the New Essentialism* (Chesham: Acumen).

Ellis, Brian. 2009. *The Metaphysics of Scientific Realism* (Montreal and Kingston: McGill-Queen's University Press).

Ellis, Brian and Caroline Lierse. 1994. "Dispositional Essentialism." *Australasian Journal of Philosophy* 72: 27-45.

Feser, Edward. 1998. "Can phenomenal qualities exist unperceived?" *Journal of Consciousness Studies* 5: 405-14.

Feser, Edward. 2006a. *Philosophy of Mind* (Oxford: Oneworld Publications).

Feser, Edward. 2006b. "Hayek the cognitive scientist and philosopher of mind." In Edward Feser, ed., *The Cambridge Companion to Hayek* (Cambridge: Cambridge University Press).

Feser, Edward. 2007. *Locke* (Oxford: Oneworld Publications).

Feser, Edward. 2008. *The Last Superstition: A Refutation of the New Atheism* (South Bend: St. Augustine's Press).

Feser, Edward. 2009. *Aquinas* (Oxford: Oneworld Publications).

Feser, Edward. 2010a. "Teleology: A Shopper's Guide." *Philosophia Christi* 12: 142-59.

Feser, Edward. 2010b. "Classical Natural Law Theory, Property Rights, and Taxation" *Social Philosophy and Policy* 27: 21-52.

Feser, Edward. 2011a. "Existential Inertia and the Five Ways." *American Catholic Philosophical Quarterly* 85: 237-67.

Feser, Edward. 2011b. "Hayek, Popper, and the Causal Theory of the Mind." In Marsh 2011.

Feser, Edward. 2012. "The Medieval Principle of Motion and the Modern Principle of Inertia." *Proceedings of the Society for Medieval Logic and Metaphysics* 10: 4-16.

Feser, Edward. 2013a. "Kripke, Ross, and the Immaterial Aspects of Thought." *American Catholic Philosophical Quarterly* 87: 1-32.

Feser, Edward. 2013b. "Between Aristotle and William Paley: Aquinas's Fifth Way." *Nova et Vetera* 11: 707-49.

Feser, Edward, ed. 2013c. *Aristotle on Method and Metaphysics* (Basingstoke: Palgrave Macmillan).

Feser, Edward. 2013d. "Motion in Aristotle, Newton, and Einstein." In Feser 2013c.

Feser, Edward. 2013e. "Being, the Good, and the Guise of the Good." In Novotný and Novák 2013.

Feser, Edward. 2013f. "The New Atheists and the Cosmological Argument." *Midwest Studies in Philosophy* 37: 154-77.

Feser, Edward. 2013g. "The Role of Nature in Sexual Ethics." *The National Catholic Bioethics Quarterly* 13: 69-76.

Fine, Kit. 1994. "Essence and Modality." In J. E. Tomberlin, ed., *Philosophical Perspectives 8: Logic and Language* (Atascadero, CA: Ridgeview Publishing Company).

Fine, Kit. 1999. "Things and their Parts." *Midwest Studies in Philosophy* 23: 61-74.

Fine, Kit. 2010. "Towards a Theory of Part." *Journal of Philosophy* 107: 559-89.

Fodor, Jerry. 1974. "Special Sciences." *Synthese* 28:77-115.

Foot, Philippa. 2001. *Natural Goodness* (Oxford: Clarendon Press).

Freddoso, Alfred J. 1988. "Medieval Aristotelianism and the Case against Secondary Causation in Nature." In Morris 1988.

Freddoso, Alfred J. 1991. "God's General Concurrence with Secondary Causes: Why Conservation is Not Enough." *Philosophical Perspectives* 5: 553-585.

Freddoso, Alfred J. 1994. "God's General Concurrence with Secondary Causes: Pitfalls and Prospects." *American Catholic Philosophical Quarterly* 67: 131-156.

Freddoso, Alfred J. 2002. "Suarez on Metaphysical Inquiry, Efficient Causality, and Divine Action." In Suarez 2002.

Freddoso, Alfred J. 2012. "Oh My Soul, There's Animals and Animals: Some Thomistic Reflections on Contemporary Philosophy of Mind." Unpublished draft available at: http://www3.nd.edu/~afreddos/papers/Oh%20My%20Soul.pdf Accessed November 24, 2013.

Gale, Richard M., ed. 2002. *The Blackwell Guide to Metaphysics* (Oxford: Blackwell).

Garber, Daniel. 1992. *Descartes' Metaphysical Physics* (Chicago: University of Chicago Press).

Gardeil, H. D. 1967. *Introduction to the Philosophy of St. Thomas Aquinas IV: Metaphysics* (St. Louis: B. Herder Book Co.).

Garrigou-Lagrange, Reginald. 1939. *God: His Existence and His Nature*, Volume I (St. Louis: B. Herder Book Co.).

Garrigou-Lagrange, Reginald. 1950. *Reality: A Synthesis of Thomistic Thought* (St. Louis: B. Herder Book Co.).

Geach, P. T. 1980. *Reference and Generality*, Third edition (Ithaca: Cornell University Press).

Geisler, N. 1997. *Creating God in the Image of Man?* (Minneapolis: Bethany House Publishers).

Gerson, Lloyd P. 1987. "Two criticisms of the principle of sufficient reason." *International Journal for Philosophy of Religion* 21: 129-42.

Gill, Mary-Louise and James Lennox. 1994. *Self-Motion from Aristotle to Newton* (Princeton: Princeton University Press).

Gilson, Etienne. 1952a. *Being and Some Philosophers*, Second edition (Toronto: Pontifical Institute of Mediaeval Studies).

Gilson, Etienne. 1952b. "Les Principes et les Causes." *Revue Thomiste* LII: 39-63.

272

Gilson, Etienne. 1999. *The Unity of Philosophical Experience.* (San Francisco: Ignatius Press).

González, Ana Marta, ed. 2008. *Contemporary Perspectives on Natural Law* (Aldershot: Ashgate).

Gordon, David. 1984. "Anscombe on Coming into Existence and Causation." *Analysis* 44: 52-54.

Gorman, Michael. 2005. "The Essential and the Accidental." *Ratio* 18: 276-89.

Gracia, Jorge J. E. 1982. *Francis Suarez on Individuation: Metaphysical Disputation V: Individual Unity and Its Principle* (Milwaukee, WI: Marquette University Press).

Groarke, Louis. 2009. *An Aristotelian Account of Induction* (Montreal and Kingston: McGill-Queen's University Press).

Groff, Ruth, ed. 2008. *Revitalizing Causality* (London: Routledge).

Groff, Ruth and John Greco (eds.). 2013. *Powers and Capacities in Philosophy: The New Aristotelianism* (London: Routledge).

Grove, Stanley F. 2008. *Quantum Theory and Aquinas's Doctrine on Matter.* PhD thesis, Catholic University of America.

Gurr, John E. 1956. "Some Historical Origins of Rationalism in Catholic Philosophy Manuals." *Proceedings of the American Catholic Philosophical Association* XXX: 170-80.

Gurr, John Edwin. 1959. *The Principle of Sufficient Reason in Some Scholastic Systems 1750 - 1900* (Milwaukee: Marquette University Press).

Haldane, John. 1999. "A Return to Form in the Philosophy of Mind." In Oderberg 1999.

Haldane, John J. 2002a. "A Thomist Metaphysics." In Gale 2002.

Haldane, John J, ed. 2002b. *Mind, Metaphysics, and Value in the Thomistic and Analytical Traditions* (Notre Dame, IN: University of Notre Dame Press).

Handfield, Toby, ed. 2009. *Dispositions and Causes* (Oxford: Clarendon Press).

Harper, Thomas. 1940. *The Metaphysics of the School.* In three volumes (New York: Peter Smith).

Harré, R. and E. H. Madden. 1975. *Causal Powers* (Oxford: Basil Blackwell).

Harré, Rom. 2013. "Powerful Particulars Revisited." In Groff and Greco 2013.

Hart, Charles A. 1959. *Thomistic Metaphysics: An Inquiry into the Act of Existing* (Englewood Cliffs, NJ: Prentice-Hall).

Hartmann, Stephan, Carl Hoefer, and Luc Bovens, eds. 2008. *Nancy Cartwright's Philosophy of Science* (London: Routledge).

Hattab, Helen. 2012. "Suárez's Last Stand for Substantial Form." In Hill and Lagerlund 2012.

Hawthorne, John. 2006. *Metaphysical Essays* (Oxford: Oxford University Press).

Hawthorne, John and Daniel Nolan. 2006. "What Would Teleological Causation Be?" In Hawthorne 2006.

Healey, Richard. 2002. "Can Physics Coherently Deny the Reality of Time?" In Callender 2002.

Heil, John. 2003. *From an Ontological Point of View* (Oxford: Clarendon Press).

Heil, John. 2012. *The Universe As We Find It* (Oxford: Clarendon Press).

Heisenberg, Werner. 2007. *Physics and Philosophy* (New York: HarperCollins).

Hill, Benjamin and Henrik Lagerlund, eds. 2012. *The Philosophy of Francisco Suárez* (Oxford: Oxford University Press).

Hochschild, Joshua P. 2010. *The Semantics of Analogy: Rereading Cajetan's* De Nominum Analogia (Notre Dame, IN: University of Notre Dame Press).

Hoenen, Peter. 1955. *The Philosophical Nature of Physical Bodies* (West Baden Springs, IN: West Baden College).

Hoffman, Joshua and Gary S. Rosenkrantz. 1994. *Substance Among Other Categories* (Cambridge: Cambridge University Press).

Hoffman, Joshua and Gary S. Rosenkrantz. 1997. *Substance: Its Nature and Existence* (London: Routledge).

Hoffman, Paul. 2009. "Does Efficient Causation Presuppose Final Causation? Aquinas vs. Early Modern Mechanism." In Newlands and Jorgensen 2009.

Huemer, Michael and Ben Kovitz. 2003. "Causation as Simultaneous and Continuous." *The Philosophical Quarterly* 53: 556-65.

Huenemann, Charlie. 2008. *Understanding Rationalism* (Stocksfield: Acumen).

Hull, David L. and Michael Ruse, eds. 2007. *The Cambridge Companion to the Philosophy of Biology* (New York: Cambridge University Press).

274

Humphreys, Paul. 2008. "How Properties Emerge." In Bedau and Humphreys 2008.

Ingham, Mary Beth and Mechthild Dreyer. 2004. *The Philosophical Vision of John Duns Scotus* (Washington, D. C.: Catholic University of America Press).

Jackson, Frank. 1982. "Epiphenomenal Qualia." *Philosophical Quarterly* 32: 127-36.

Jackson, Frank. 1998. *From Metaphysics to Ethics: A Defence of Conceptual Analysis* (Oxford: Clarendon Press).

Jaworski, William. 2011. *Philosophy of Mind: A Comprehensive Introduction* (Oxford: Wiley-Blackwell).

John Duns Scotus. 1987. *Philosophical Writings*. Translated by Allan Wolter (Indianapolis: Hackett Publishing Company).

Johnson, Monte Ransome. 2005. *Aristotle on Teleology* (Oxford: Oxford University Press).

Johnston, Mark. 2006. "Hylomorphism." *Journal of Philosophy* 103: 652-98.

Jubien, Michael. 1997. *Contemporary Metaphysics* (Oxford: Blackwell).

Kekes, John. 1980. *The Nature of Philosophy* (Oxford: Basil Blackwell).

Kenny, Anthony, ed. 1969. *Aquinas: A Collection of Critical Essays* (New York: Doubleday).

Kenny, Anthony. 1980. *Aquinas* (Oxford: Oxford University Press).

Kenny, Anthony. 1989. *The Metaphysics of Mind* (Oxford: Oxford University Press).

Kenny, Anthony. 1993. *Aquinas on Mind* (London: Routledge).

Kenny, Anthony. 2002. *Aquinas on Being* (Oxford: Clarendon Press).

Kim, Jaegwon. 1998. *Mind in a Physical World* (Cambridge, MA: The MIT Press).

Kim, J., E. Sosa, and G. Rosenkrantz, eds. 2009. *A Companion to Metaphysics*, Second edition (Oxford: Wiley-Blackwell).

King, Peter. 1994. "Duns Scotus on the Reality of Self-Change." In Gill and Lennox 1994.

King, Peter. 2003. "Scotus on Metaphysics." In Williams 2003.

Kistler, Max and Bruno Gnassounou, eds. 2007. *Dispositions and Causal Powers* (Aldershot: Ashgate).

Klima, Gyula. 1996. "The Semantic Principles Underlying Saint Thomas Aquinas's Metaphysics of Being." *Medieval Philosophy and Theology* 5: 87-141.

Klima, Gyula. 2002. "Contemporary 'Essentialism' vs. Aristotelian Essentialism." In Haldane 2002.

Klima, Gyula. 2004. "On Kenny on Aquinas on Being." *International Philosophical Quarterly* 44: 567-80.

Klima, Gyula. 2012. "Whatever Happened to Efficient Causes?" *Proceedings of the Society for Medieval Logic and Metaphysics* 10: 22-30.

Klima, Gyula. 2013a. "Aquinas vs. Buridan on Essence and Existence." In Charles Bolyard and Rondo Keele, eds., *Later Medieval Metaphysics: Ontology, Language, and Logic* (New York: Fordham University Press).

Klima, Gyula. 2013b. "Being, Unity, and Identity in the Fregean and Aristotelian Traditions." In Feser 2013c.

Klocker, Harry R. 1968. *God and the Empiricists* (Milwaukee: Bruce Publishing Company).

Klubertanz, George P. 1953. *The Philosophy of Human Nature* (New York: Appleton-Century-Crofts).

Klubertanz, George P. 1960. *St. Thomas Aquinas on Analogy* (Chicago: Loyola University Press).

Klubertanz, George P. 1963. *Introduction to the Philosophy of Being*, Second edition (New York: Appleton-Century-Crofts).

Knasas, John F. X. 2003. *Being and Some Twentieth-Century Thomists* (New York: Fordham University Press).

Knasas, John F. X. 2006. "Haldane's Analytic Thomism and Aquinas's *Actus Essendi*." In Paterson and Pugh 2006.

Koons, Robert C. 2000. *Realism Regained: An Exact Theory of Causation, Teleology, and the Mind* (Oxford: Oxford University Press).

Koren, Henry J. 1955. *An Introduction to the Philosophy of Animate Nature* (St. Louis: B. Herder Book Co.)

Koren, Henry J. 1960. *An Introduction to the Science of Metaphysics* (St. Louis: B. Herder Book Co.).

Koren, Henry J. 1962. *An Introduction to the Philosophy of Nature* (Pittsburgh: Duquesne University Press).

Koren, Henry J., ed. 1965. *Readings in the Philosophy of Nature* (Westminster, MD: The Newman Press).

Koslicki, Kathrin. 2008. *The Structure of Objects* (Oxford: Oxford University Press).

Krauss, Lawrence M. 2012. *A Universe from Nothing* (New York: Free Press).

Kripke, Saul. 1980. *Naming and Necessity* (Cambridge: Harvard University Press).

Ladyman, James and Don Ross with David Spurrett and John Collier. 2007. *Every Thing Must Go: Metaphysics Naturalized* (Oxford: Oxford University Press).

Lamont, John. 2007. "Fall and Rise of Aristotelian Metaphysics in the Philosophy of Science." *Science and Education* 18: 861-84.

Lewis, David. 1973. "Causation," *Journal of Philosophy* 70: 556-67.

Lewis, David. 1986. *On the Plurality of Worlds* (Oxford: Blackwell).

Lewis, David. 1997. "Finkish dispositions." *Philosophical Quarterly* 47: 143-58.

Long, Steven A. 2011. *Analogia Entis: On the Analogy of Being, Metaphysics, and the Act of Faith* (Notre Dame, IN: University of Notre Dame Press).

Loux, Michael J. 2002. *Metaphysics: A Contemporary Introduction*, Second edition (London: Routledge).

Lowe, E. J. 1999a. *The Possibility of Metaphysics: Substance, Identity, and Time* (Oxford: Clarendon Press).

Lowe, E. J. 1999b. "Form without Matter." In Oderberg 1999.

Lowe, E. J. 2002. *A Survey of Metaphysics* (Oxford: Oxford University Press).

Lowe, E. J. 2006. *The Four-Category Ontology* (Oxford: Clarendon Press).

Lyttkens, Humpus. 1952. *The Analogy between God and the World* (Uppsala: Almqvist and Wiksells).

MacDonald, Scott. 2002. "The *Esse/Essentia* Argument in Aquinas's *De ente et essentia*." In Davies 2002.

Mackie, J. L. 1982. *The Miracle of Theism* (Oxford: Clarendon Press).

Madden, James D. 2013. *Mind, Matter, and Nature: A Thomistic Proposal for the Philosophy of Mind* (Washington, D.C.: Catholic University of America Press).

Marenbon, John. 2009. "The Medievals." In Beebee, Hitchcock, and Menzies 2009.

Maritain, Jacques. 1939. *A Preface to Metaphysics* (New York: Sheed and Ward).

Maritain, Jacques. 1995. *The Degrees of Knowledge* (Notre Dame, IN: University of Notre Dame Press).

Marmodoro, Anna, ed. 2010. *The Metaphysics of Powers* (London: Routledge).

Marsh, Leslie, ed. 2011. *Hayek in Mind: Hayek's Philosophical Psychology* (Bingley: Emerald Group Publishing).

Martin, C. B. 1996a. "Properties and Dispositions." In Armstrong, Martin, and Place 1996.

Martin, C. B. 1996b. "Final Replies to Place and Armstrong." In Armstrong, Martin, and Place 1996.

Martin, C. B. 2008. *The Mind in Nature* (Oxford: Clarendon Press).

Martin, C. F. J. 1997. *Thomas Aquinas: God and Explanations* (Edinburgh: Edinburgh University Press).

McCormick, John F. 1940. *Scholastic Metaphysics, Part I: Being, Its Division and Causes* (Chicago: Loyola University Press).

McInerny, D. Q. 2004. *Metaphysics* (Elmhurst, PA: Priestly Fraternity of St. Peter).

McInerny, D. Q. 2007. *Epistemology* (Elmhurst, PA: Priestly Fraternity of St. Peter).

McInerny, Ralph. 1996. *Aquinas and Analogy* (Washington, D.C.: Catholic University of America Press).

McMullin, Ernan, ed. 1963. *The Concept of Matter in Greek and Medieval Philosophy* (Notre Dame, IN: University of Notre Dame Press).

Mellor, D. H. 1974. "In Defense of Dispositions." *The Philosophical Review* 83: 157-81.

Merricks, Trenton. 2001. *Objects and Persons* (Oxford: Oxford University Press).

Mertz, D. W. 1996. *Moderate Realism and Its Logic* (New Haven: Yale University Press).

Miller, Barry. 1982. "Necessarily Terminating Causal Series and the Contingency Argument." *Mind* XCI: 201-15.

Miller, Barry, 1992. *From Existence to God: A Contemporary Philosophical Argument* (London: Routledge).

Miller, Barry. 2002. *The Fullness of Being: A New Paradigm for Existence* (Notre Dame, IN: University of Notre Dame Press).

Molnar, George. 2003. *Powers: A Study in Metaphysics* (Oxford: Oxford University Press).

Montagnes, Bernard. 2004. *The Doctrine of the Analogy of Being according to Thomas Aquinas*, translated by E. M. Macierowski (Milwaukee: Marquette University Press).

Moreland, J. P. 2001. *Universals* (Montreal and Kingston: McGill-Queen's University Press).

Morris, Thomas V., ed. 1988. *Divine and Human Action: Essays in the Metaphysics of Theism* (Ithaca, NY: Cornell University Press).

Mumford, Stephen. 1998. *Dispositions* (Oxford: Oxford University Press).

Mumford, Stephen. 2007. *David Armstrong* (Montreal and Kingston: McGill-Queen's University Press).

Mumford, Stephen. 2009. "Causal Powers and Capacities." In Beebee, Hitchcock, and Menzies 2009.

Mumford, Stephen. 2013. "The Power of Power." In Groff and Greco 2013.

Mumford, Stephen and Rani Lill Anjum. 2011. *Getting Causes from Powers* (Oxford: Oxford University Press).

Nagel, Thomas. 1979. "What is it like to be a bat?" In *Mortal Questions* (Cambridge: Cambridge University Press).

Nagel, Thomas. 1997. *The Last Word* (Oxford: Oxford University Press).

Nagel, Thomas. 2012. *Mind and Cosmos* (Oxford: Oxford University Press).

Newlands, Samuel and Larry M. Jorgensen, eds. 2009. *Metaphysics and the Good: Themes from the Philosophy of Robert Merrihew Adams* (Oxford: Oxford University Press).

Nolan, Daniel. 2005. *David Lewis* (Montreal and Kingston: McGill-Queen's University Press).

Noone, Timothy B. 2003. "Universals and Individuation." In Williams 2003.

Novák, Lukáš, Daniel D. Novotný, Prokop Sousedik, and David Svoboda, eds. 2012. *Metaphysics: Aristotelian, Scholastic, Analytic* (Frankfurt: Ontos Verlag).

Novotný, Daniel D. and Lukáš Novák, eds. 2013. *Neo-Aristotelian Perspectives in Metaphysics* (London: Routledge).

Nozick, Robert. 2001. *Invariances: The Structure of the Objective World* (Cambridge, MA: Harvard University Press).

O'Callaghan, John P. 2003. *Thomist Realism and the Linguistic Turn* (Notre Dame, IN: University of Notre Dame Press).

Oderberg, David S. 1993. *The Metaphysics of Identity over Time* (London: Macmillan).

Oderberg, David S., ed. 1999. *Form and Matter: Themes in Contemporary Metaphysics* (Oxford: Blackwell).

Oderberg, David S. 2001. "How to Win Essence Back from Essentialists." *Philosophical Writings* 18: 27-45.

Oderberg, David S. 2002. "Hylomorphism and Individuation." In Haldane 2002b.

Oderberg, David S. 2004. "Temporal Parts and the Possibility of Change." *Philosophy and Phenomenological Research* 69: 686-708.

Oderberg, David S. 2005. "Hylemorphic Dualism." In E.F. Paul, F.D. Miller, and J. Paul, eds., *Personal Identity* (Cambridge: Cambridge University Press).

Oderberg, David S. 2006. "Instantaneous Change without Instants." In Paterson and Pugh 2006.

Oderberg, David S. 2007. *Real Essentialism* (London: Routledge).

Oderberg, David S. 2008a. "Teleology: Inorganic and Organic." In González 2008.

Oderberg, David S. 2008b. "Concepts, Dualism, and the Human Intellect." In Antonietti, Corradini, and Lowe 2008.

Oderberg, David S. 2009a. "The Non-Identity of the Categorical and the Dispositional." *Analysis* 69: 677-84.

Oderberg, David S. 2009b. "Persistence." In Kim, Sosa, and Rosenkrantz 2009.

Oderberg, David S. 2011a. "Essence and Properties." *Erkenntnis* 75: 85-111.

Oderberg, David S. 2011b. "The World is not an Asymmetric Graph." *Analysis* 71: 3-10.

Oderberg, David S. 2012a. "No Potency without Actuality: The Case of Graph Theory." In Tahko 2012.

Oderberg, David S. 2012b. "Graph Structuralism and its Discontents: Rejoinder to Shackel." *Analysis* 72: 94-8.

Oderberg, David S. 2012c. "Hume, the Occult, and the Substance of the School." *Metaphysica* 13: 155-74.

Oderberg, David S. 2012d. "Survivalism, Corruptionism, and Mereology." *European Journal for Philosophy of Religion* 4: 1-26.

Oderberg, David S. 2013a. "Synthetic Life and the Bruteness of Immanent Causation." In Feser 2013c.

Oderberg, David S. 2013b. "Is Form Structure?" In Novotný and Novák 2013.

Oderberg, David S., ed. 2013c. *Classifying Reality* (Oxford: Wiley-Blackwell).

Osler, Margaret J. 1996. "From Immanent Natures to Nature as Artifice: The Reinterpretation of Final Causes in Seventeenth-Century Natural Philosophy," *The Monist* 79: 388-407.

Ott, Walter. 2009. *Causation and Laws of Nature in Early Modern Philosophy* (Oxford: Oxford University Press).

Owens, Joseph. 1955. "The Causal Proposition -- Principle or Conclusion?" *The Modern Schoolman* XXXII: 159-71, 257-70, 323-39.

Owens, Joseph. 1963. *An Elementary Christian Metaphysics* (Milwaukee: Bruce Publishing Company).

Pasnau, Robert and Christopher Shields. 2004. *The Philosophy of Aquinas* (Boulder: Westview Press).

Paterson C. and M.S. Pugh, eds. 2006. *Analytical Thomism: Traditions in Dialogue* (Aldershot: Ashgate).

Paul, L. A. 2009. "Counterfactual Theories." In Beebee, Hitchcock, and Menzies 2009.

Peterson, John. 1999. *Introduction to Scholastic Realism* (New York: Peter Lang).

Peterson, John. 2008. *Aquinas: A New Introduction* (New York: University Press of America).

Phelan, Gerald B. 1941. *Saint Thomas and Analogy* (Milwaukee: Marquette University Press).

Phillips, R. P. 1950a. *Modern Thomistic Philosophy, Volume I: The Philosophy of Nature* (Westminster, MD: The Newman Press).

Phillips, R. P. 1950b. *Modern Thomistic Philosophy, Volume II: Metaphysics* (Westminster, MD: The Newman Press).

Place, U. T. 1996. "Dispositions as Intentional States." In Armstrong, Martin, and Place 1996.

Plantinga, Alvin. 1974. *The Nature of Necessity* (Oxford: Clarendon Press).

Popper, Karl R. 1962. *The Open Society and Its Enemies, Volume 2* (New York and Evanston: Harper and Row).

Popper, Karl R. 1968. *Conjectures and Refutations: The Growth of Scientific Knowledge* (New York: Harper and Row).

Popper, Karl R. 1979. *Objective Knowledge: An Evolutionary Approach*, Revised edition (Oxford: Clarendon Press).

Popper, Karl. 1992. *Unended Quest: An Intellectual Autobiography* (London: Routledge).

Price, Huw and Richard Corry, eds. 2007. *Causation, Physics, and the Constitution of Reality: Russell's Republic Revisited* (Oxford: Clarendon Press).

Pruss, Alexander R. 2006. *The Principle of Sufficient Reason: A Reassessment* (Cambridge: Cambridge University Press).

Pruss, Alexander R. 2009. "The Leibnizian Cosmological Argument." In Craig and Moreland 2009.

Psillos, Stathis. 2002. *Causation and Explanation* (Montreal and Kingston: McGill-Queen's University Press).

Psillos, Stathis. 2008. "Cartwright's Realist Toil: From Entities to Capacities." In Hartmann, Hoefer, and Bovens, eds., 2008.

Psillos, Stathis. 2009. "Regularity Theories." In Beebee, Hitchcock, and Menzies 2009.

Putnam, Hilary. 1975a. "What is mathematical truth?" In Hilary Putnam, *Mathematics, Matter, and Method: Philosophical Papers, Volume 1* (Cambridge: Cambridge University Press).

Putnam, Hilary. 1975b. "The Meaning of 'Meaning.'" In Hilary Putnam, *Mind, Language, and Reality: Philosophical Papers, Volume 2* (Cambridge: Cambridge University Press).

Quine, W. V. 1960. *Word and Object* (Cambridge, MA: The MIT Press).

Quine, W. V. 1969. "Natural Kinds." In *Ontological Relativity and Other Essays* (New York: Columbia University Press).

Quine, W. V. 1980a. *From a Logical Point of View*, Second edition, Revised (Cambridge, MA: Harvard University Press).

Quine, W. V. 1980b. "Two Dogmas of Empiricism." In Quine 1980a.

Quine, W. V. 1980c. "Reference and Modality." In Quine 1980a.

Quinn, Philip L. and Charles Taliaferro, ed., *A Companion to Philosophy of Religion* (Oxford: Blackwell).

Rea, Michael C. 2002. *World Without Design: The Ontological Consequences of Naturalism* (Oxford: Clarendon Press).

Rea, Michael C. 2011. "Hylomorphism Reconditioned." *Philosophical Perspectives* 25: 341-58.

Read, Rupert and Kenneth A. Richman, eds. 2007. *The New Hume Debate*, Revised edition (London: Routledge).

Reichenbach, Bruce R. 1972. *The Cosmological Argument: A Reassessment* (Springfield, IL: Charles C. Thomas).

Renard, H. 1946. *The Philosophy of Being* (Milwaukee: Bruce Publishing Company).

Rickaby, John S. 1901. *General Metaphysics*, Third edition (London: Longmans, Green, and Co.).

Rizzi, Anthony. 2004. *The Science Before Science* (Baton Rouge, LA: IAP Press).

Robinson, Howard. 1982. *Matter and Sense* (Cambridge: Cambridge University Press).

Rosenberg, Alex. 2011. *The Atheist's Guide to Reality* (New York: W. W. Norton and Company).

Ross, James F. 1969. *Philosophical Theology* (Indianapolis: Bobbs-Merrill).

Ross, J. F. 1981. *Portraying Analogy* (Cambridge: Cambridge University Press).

Ross, James F. 1989. "The Crash of Modal Metaphysics." *Review of Metaphysics* 43: 251-79.

Ross, James F. 1992. "Immaterial Aspects of Thought." *The Journal of Philosophy* 89: 136-50.

Ross, James. 1998. "Religious Language." In Brian Davies, ed., *Philosophy of Religion: A Guide to the Subject* (Washington, D.C.: Georgetown University Press).

Ross, James. 2008. *Thought and World: The Hidden Necessities* (Notre Dame, IN: University of Notre Dame Press).

Ross, James. 2012. "Merely Metaphysical Possibility." In Gregory T. Doolan, ed., *The Science of Being as Being* (Washington, D.C.: Catholic University of America Press).

Rota, Michael. 2004. "Substance and Artifact in Thomas Aquinas." *History of Philosophy Quarterly* 21: 241-59.

Rota, Michael. 2012. "Comments on Feser's 'The Medieval Principle of Motion and the Modern Principle of Inertia.'" *Proceedings of the Society for Medieval Logic and Metaphysics* 10: 17-19.

Rowe, William L. 1997. "Cosmological Arguments." In Quinn and Taliaferro 1997.

Rowe, William L. 1998. *The Cosmological Argument* (New York: Fordham University Press).

Royce, James E. 1961. *Man and His Nature* (New York: McGraw-Hill Book Company).

Runggaldier, Edmund. 2012. "Potentiality in Scholasticism (*potentiae*) and the Contemporary Debate on 'Powers.'" In Lukáš Novák, Daniel D. Novotný, Prokop Sousedík, and David Svoboda, eds., *Metaphysics: Aristotelian, Scholastic, Analytic* (Frankfurt: Ontos Verlag).

Russell, Bertrand. 1954. *The Analysis of Matter* (New York: Dover Publications).

Russell, Bertrand. 1985. *My Philosophical Development* (London: Unwin Paperbacks).

Russell, Bertrand. 1988. *The Problems of Philosophy* (Buffalo: Prometheus Books).

Russell, Bertrand. 2003. "On the Notion of Cause." In Bertrand Russell, *Russell on Metaphysics*, ed. Stephen Mumford (London: Routledge).

Russell, Bertrand and F. C. Copleston. 1964. "A Debate on the Existence of God." In John Hick, ed., *The Existence of God* (New York: Macmillan).

Ryle, Gilbert. 1949. *The Concept of Mind* (London: Hutchinson).

Salmon, Nathan U. 1981. *Reference and Essence* (Princeton, NJ: Princeton University Press).

Schaffer, Jonathan. 2007. "The Metaphysics of Causation." *Stanford Encyclopedia of Philosophy.* URL: http://plato.stanford.edu/entries/causation-metaphysics/ Accessed September 22, 2013.

Schrödinger, Erwin. 1956. "On the Peculiarity of the Scientific World-View." In *What is Life? and Other Scientific Essays* (New York: Doubleday).

Schrödinger, Erwin. 1992. "Mind and Matter." In *What is Life?* with *Mind and Matter* and *Autobiographical Sketches* (Cambridge: Cambridge University Press).

Schwartz, Daniel, ed. 2012. *Interpreting Suárez: Critical Essays* (Cambridge: Cambridge University Press).

Sellars, Wilfrid. 1956. "Empiricism and the Philosophy of Mind." In H. Feigl and M. Scriven, eds., *Minnesota Studies in the Philosophy of Science*, Volume I (Minneapolis: University of Minnesota Press).

Sellars, Wilfrid. 1963. *Science, Perception, and Reality* (London: Routledge).

Shields, Christopher. 2007. *Aristotle* (London: Routledge).

Sidelle, Alan. 1989. *Necessity, Essence, and Individuation: A Defense of Conventionalism* (Ithaca, NY: Cornell University Press).

Sider, Theodore. 2001. *Four-Dimensionalism: An Ontology of Persistence and Time* (Oxford: Clarendon Press).

Smart, J. J. C. and J. J. Haldane. 2003. *Atheism and Theism*, Second edition (Oxford: Blackwell).

Smith, G. and L. Kendzierski. 1961. *The Philosophy of Being* (New York: Macmillan).

Smith, Vincent Edward. 1950. *Philosophical Physics* (New York: Harper and Brothers).

Smith, Wolfgang. 2005. *The Quantum Enigma* (Hillsdale, NY: Sophia Perennis).

Stebbing, L. Susan. 1958. *Philosophy and the Physicists* (New York: Dover).

Strawson, Galen. 2008. "The Identity of the Categorical and the Dispositional." *Analysis* 68: 271-82.

Strawson, P. F. 1959. *Individuals: An Essay in Descriptive Metaphysics* (London: Methuen).

Stump, Eleonore. 2003. *Aquinas* (London: Routledge).

Stump, Eleonore. 2006. "Substance and Artifact in Aquinas's Metaphysics." In Crisp, Davidson, and Vanderlaan 2006.

Stump, Eleonore. 2013. "Emergence, Causal Powers, and Aristotelianism in Metaphysics." In Groff and Greco 2013.

Suárez, Francisco. 1994. *On Efficient Causality: Metaphysical Disputations 17 - 19*. Translated by Alfred J. Freddoso (New Haven: Yale University Press).

Suárez, Francisco. 2002. *On Creation, Conservation, and Concurrence: Metaphysical Disputations 20 - 22*. Translation and introduction by Alfred J. Freddoso (South Bend, IN: St. Augustine's Press).

Suárez, Francisco. 2004. *The Metaphysical Demonstration of the Existence of God: Metaphysical Disputations 28 - 29*. Translated by John P. Doyle (South Bend, IN: St. Augustine's Press).

Sweeney, Leo, William J. Carroll, and John J. Furlong. 1996. *Authentic Metaphysics in an Age of Unreality*, Second edition (New York: Peter Lang).

Swinburne, Richard. 1979. *The Existence of God* (Oxford: Clarendon Press).

Tahko, Tuomas E, ed. 2012. *Contemporary Aristotelian Metaphysics* (Cambridge: Cambridge University Press).

Thomas Aquinas. 1948. *Summa Theologica.* Translated by the Fathers of the English Dominican Province (New York: Benziger Bros.).

Thomas Aquinas. 1965a. *Selected Writings of St. Thomas Aquinas.* Translated by Robert P. Goodwin (Upper Saddle River, NJ: Prentice-Hall).

Thomas Aquinas. 1965b. "On Being and Essence." In Aquinas 1965a.

Thomas Aquinas. 1965c. "The Principles of Nature." In Aquinas 1965a.

Thomas Aquinas. 1975. *Summa Contra Gentiles.* Translated by Anton C. Pegis, James F. Anderson. Vernon J. Bourke, and Charles J. O'Neil (Notre Dame: University of Notre Dame Press).

Thomas Aquinas. 1994. *Commentary on Aristotle's De Anima.* Translated by Kenelm Foster, O.P. and Silvester Humphries, O.P. (Notre Dame, IN: Dumb Ox Books).

Thomas Aquinas. 1995. *Commentary on Aristotle's* Metaphysics. Translated by John P. Rowan (Notre Dame, IN: Dumb Ox Books).

Thomas Aquinas. 1999. *Commentary on Aristotle's* Physics. Translated by Richard J. Blackwell, Richard J. Spath, and W. Edmund Thirlkel (Notre Dame, IN: Dumb Ox Books).

Thomasson, Amie L. 2007. *Ordinary Objects* (Oxford: Oxford University Press).

Thompson, Michael. 1995. "The Representation of Life." In Rosalind Hursthouse, Gavin Lawrence, and Warren Quinn, eds., *Virtues and Reasons: Philippa Foot and Moral Theory* (Oxford: Clarendon Press).

Tooley, Michael. 1977. "The Nature of Laws." *Canadian Journal of Philosophy* 74: 667-98.

Twetten, David B. 2006. "Really distinguishing essence from *esse.*" *Proceedings of the Society for Medieval Logic and Metaphysics* 6: 57-94.

Unger, Peter. 2006. *All the Power in the World* (Oxford: Oxford University Press).

Urban, Wilbur. 1900. *The History of the Principle of Sufficient Reason: Its Metaphysical and Logical Formulations* (Princeton, NJ: Princeton University Press).

Vallicella, William F. 2002. *A Paradigm Theory of Existence: Onto-Theology Vindicated* (Dordrecht: Kluwer Academic Publishers).

Van Brakel, J. 2000. *Philosophy of Chemistry* (Leuven: Leuven University Press).

Van Inwagen, Peter. 1983. *An Essay on Free Will* (Oxford: Oxford University Press).

Van Inwagen, Peter. 1990. *Material Beings* (Ithaca, NY: Cornell University Press).

Van Steenberghen, Fernand. 1949. *Epistemology* (New York: Joseph F. Wagner, Inc.).

Van Steenberghen, Fernand. 1952. *Ontology* (New York: Joseph F. Wagner, Inc.).

Wallace, W. A. 1956. "Newtonian Antinomies Against the *Prima Via,*" *The Thomist* 19: 151-92.

Wallace, William A. 1996. *The Modeling of Nature* (Washington, D.C.: Catholic University of America Press).

Wallace, William A. 1997. "Thomism and the Quantum Enigma." *The Thomist* 61: 455-68.

Walsh, W. H. 1963. *Metaphysics* (New York: Harcourt, Brace, and World, Inc.).

Weigel, Peter. 2008. *Aquinas on Simplicity* (New York: Peter Lang).

Weinberg, Julius R. 1964. *A Short History of Medieval Philosophy* (Princeton, NJ: Princeton University Press).

Weisheipl, James A. 1985. *Nature and Motion in the Middle Ages*, ed. William E. Carroll (Washington, D. C.: Catholic University of America Press).

White, Thomas Joseph. 2009. *Wisdom in the Face of Modernity: A Study in Thomistic Natural Theology* (Ave Maria, FL: Sapientia Press of Ave Maria University).

Wilhelmsen, Frederick D. 1956. *Man's Knowledge of Reality: An Introduction to Thomistic Epistemology* (Englewood Cliffs, NJ: Prentice-Hall).

William of Ockham. 1990. *Philosophical Writings.* Translated by Philotheus Boehner, revised by Stephen F. Brown (Indianapolis: Hackett Publishing Company).

William of Ockham. 1991. *Quodlibetal Questions, Volumes 1 and 2: Quadlibets 1 - 7.* Translated by Alfred J. Freddoso and Francis E. Kelley (New Haven: Yale University Press).

Williams, Thomas, ed. 2003. *The Cambridge Companion to Duns Scotus* (Cambridge: Cambridge University Press).

Wippel, John F. 2000. *The Metaphysical Thought of Thomas Aquinas* (Washington, D.C.: Catholic University of America Press).

Wittgenstein, Ludwig. 1968. *Philosophical Investigations*, Third edition. Translated by G.E.M. Anscombe (New York: Macmillan).

Wolter, Allan. 1963. "The Ockhamist Critique." In McMullin 1963.

Wolter, Allan. 1986. *Duns Scotus on the Will and Morality* (Washington, D.C.: Catholic University of America Press).

Wood, Rega. 1990. "Ockham on Essentially-Ordered Causes: Logic Misapplied." In Wilhelm Vossenkuhl and Rolf Schönberger, eds., *Die Gegenwart Ockhams* (Weinheim).

Woolhouse, R. S. 1983. *Locke* (Minneapolis: University of Minnesota Press).

Wuellner, Bernard. 1956a. *Dictionary of Scholastic Philosophy* (Milwaukee: Bruce Publishing Company).

Wuellner, Bernard. 1956b. *Summary of Scholastic Principles* (Chicago: Loyola University Press).

Index

Ancient and medieval authors are indexed according to their given names.